PUTTING THEORY TO WORK

Developments in Psychoanalysis Series

Series Editors: Peter Fonagy, Mary Target, and Liz Allison

Other titles in the series:

PUTTING THEORY TO WORK

How are Theories Actually Used in Practice?

Edited by

Jorge Canestri

Routledge
Taylor & Francis Group

LONDON AND NEW YORK

First published 2012 by Karnac Books Ltd.

Published 2018 by Routledge
2 Park Square, Milton Park, Abingdon, Oxon OX14 4RN
711 Third Avenue, New York, NY 10017, USA

Routledge is an imprint of the Taylor & Francis Group, an informa business

British Library Cataloguing in Publication Data

A C.I.P. for this book is available from the British Library

ISBN 9781855755871 (pbk)

Edited, designed and produced by The Studio Publishing Services Ltd
www.publishingservicesuk.co.uk
e-mail: studio@publishingservicesuk.co.uk

CONTENTS

ACKNOWLEDGEMENTS

The editor and authors of this book would like to thank the European Psychoanalytical Federation for the support they gave to this project.

ABOUT THE EDITOR AND CONTRIBUTORS

Werner Bohleber, Dr phil, psychoanalyst in private practice in Frankfurt. Training and supervising analyst, former President of the German Psychoanalytical Association (DPV). Member of the Board of Representatives of the International Psychoanalytical Association (IPA) (2003–2007). Co-Chair for Europe of the IPA Research Advisory Board (2000–2008). Member of the EPF Working Party on Theoretical Issues. Editor of the German psychoanalytic journal *Psyche*. Author of several books and numerous articles. His latest book is *Destructiveness, Intersubjectivity, and Trauma. The Identity Crisis of Modern Psychoanalysis.* London, Karnac, 2010.

Lilia Bordone de Semeniuk, MD Buenos Aires University. Training and supervising analyst at the Buenos Aires Psychoanalytical Association (Apdeba). She teaches theory of psychoanalytical technique at the Institute of Psychoanalysis of the Buenos Aires Psychoanalytical Association. Director of the Training Committee of her Society. Founding member of the Working Party on Implicit Theories in the Latin American Psychoanalytic Federation (FEPAL). Recent papers presented at IPA Congresses include: 2005. Río de Janeiro: "Consecuencias del trauma del campo de concentración"; 2009.

Chicago: "Invariancia y transformación estructural. Los tiempos subjetivos". During several workshop in 2008, 2009, 2010, and 2011 she presented papers on the arguments of implicit theories and the theories in the mind of the analyst in clinical work.

Dieter Bürgin, Prof. Dr med. Born in Basel 1939. He studied medicine in Basel and Paris (1957–1963) and trained in Adult Psychiatry and Child and Adolescent Psychiatry. From 1965–1973 he received training in Psychoanalysis in Basel, Zürich, and Freiburg i.Br. and obtained Full Membership of the Swiss Psychoanalytic Society and the IPA in 1973. Further training included postgraduate psychoanalytic training in Child and Adolescent Psychoanalysis: at the Hampstead Clinic, London, at the British Institute of Psychoanalysis, at the Tavistock Clinic, and at the Brent Centre (M. and E. Laufer), London (1973–1974). From 1975 to 2004 he was Head of the Child and Adolescent Department at the University of Basel, and Chairman of the University Clinic for Child and Adolescent Psychiatry. He qualified as training analyst of the Swiss Psychoanalytic Society in 1978. Since 1984 he has been Full Professor for Child and Adolescent Psychiatry at the University of Basel, and during 1996–1997 was Dean of the Medical Faculty at the same University. From 1996–2000 he was Vice President of the Swiss Psychoanalytic Society and in 2001 became Member of the Swiss Academy of Medical Sciences. Since 2001 he has been a Member of the Research Committee of the IPA. From 2004 to 2006 he was President of the Swiss Psychoanalytic Society and since 2005 has been in private psychoanalytic practice. Between 2008–2012 he was Editor General of the EPF Executive.

Jorge Canestri, MD, is psychiatrist and training and supervising analyst of the Italian Psychoanalytical Association (AIPsi) and the Argentine Psychoanalytic Association (APA), is a former president of the Italian Psychoanalytical Association (2007–2009), professor of Health Psychology until 2008 at Rome 3 University and invited professor at the Université Paris X, Nanterre. He has been one of the Mary S. Sigourney Award recipients in 2004 and chair of the 42nd Congress of the International Psychoanalytic Association (IPA) in Nice (2001); IPA global representative for Europe from 2005 to 2007 and representative for Europe to the IPA Executive Committee from 2007 to 2009. He is currently chair of the Working Party on Theoretical Issues of the

European Psychoanalytical Federation; European editor of the International Journal of Psycho-Analysis; member of the Advisory Board of Philoctete, New York, USA, and chair of the IPA's International New Groups Committee. Canestri has published numerous psychoanalytical papers in books and reviews. He is co-author, with J. Amati-Mehler and S. Argentieri, of *The Babel of the Unconscious. Mother Tongue and Foreign Languages in the Psychoanalytic Dimension* (Int. Universities Press, 1993); and editor, with M. Leuzinger-Bohleber and A. U. Dreher, of *Pluralism and Unity? Methods of Research in Psychoanalysis* (International Psychoanalysis Library, 2003); of *Psychoanalysis: From Practice to Theory* (Wiley, 2006); with G. Ambrosio and S. Argentieri, of *Language, Symbolisation, and Psychosis* (Karnac, 2007); with L. Glocer Fiorini, of *The Experience of Time. Psychoanalytic Perspectives* (Karnac, 2009); with M. Leuzinger-Bohleber and M. Target, of *Frühe Entwicklung und ihre Störungen. Klinische, konzeptuelle und empirische psychoanalytische Forschung*; and editor (with Marianne Leuzinger-Bohleber and Mary Target) of *Early Development and its Disturbances* (Karnac, 2010). Furthermore, he is director of the webpage: *Psychoanalysis and logical mathematical thought*.

Beatriz de León de Bernardi is an Uruguayan psychologist and psychoanalyst. She is Full Member and training analyst of the Uruguayan Psychoanalytic Association (APU). Past President of the APU and has formerly been Director of the Scientific Committee and Editor of the *Uruguayan Journal of Psychoanalysis*. She has published papers and books in different languages on psychoanalytic topics, mainly about the patient–analyst interaction and the analyst contribution to the analytic process, the countertransference and about the work of Madeleine and Willy Baranger and Heinrich Racker. She has received the Award of the Latin-American Psychoanalytical Federation (FEPAL) on 1992 and the Training Today Award on 2009.

Paul Denis, MD, Full Member and supervising analyst, Paris Psychoanalytic Society, former Director of *Revue Française de psychanalyse*.

Peter Fonagy, PhD, FBA, is Freud Memorial Professor of Psychoanalysis and Head of the Research Department of Clinical, Educational and Health Psychology at University College London;

Chief Executive of the Anna Freud Centre, London. He is Director, UCLPartners Mental Health Programme and is National Clinical Lead on the Improved Access to Psychological Therapies for Children and Young People. He is Consultant to the Child and Family Program at the Menninger Department of Psychiatry and Behavioral Sciences at the Baylor College of Medicine. He holds a visiting professorships at the Child Study Centre, Yale University and at McLean's Hospital, Harvard University. He is on the editorial board of 25 journals and currently chairs the Research Board of the International Psycho-analytic Association. He is a clinical psychologist and a training and supervising analyst in the British Psycho-Analytical Society in child and adult analysis.

Professor Charles Hanly is a psychoanalyst in private practice, a training analyst at the Toronto Institute of Psychoanalysis and a Professor Emeritus at the University of Toronto. After undergraduate studies at the University of Toronto, he studied at Oxford University on a Woodrow Wilson Fellowship before taking his PhD at the University of Toronto. He completed his psychoanalytic training and became a member of the Canadian Psychoanalytic Society in 1974. He has been highly active in the International Psychoanalytical Association (IPA), having a leadership role in enabling the independent groups in the US to become Component Societies of the IPA, in fostering the redevelopment of psychoanalysis in Eastern Europe, and in the formation of International New Groups. He served numerous times on the Executive Council and the Board of Representatives, and, since 2009, he has been the association's President. Prof. Hanly is the author of four books, and more than seventy clinical and scientific papers, in the field of psychoanalysis.

Dorothy E. Holmes, PhD is a practicing psychoanalyst in Bluffton, SC. She is Professor Emeritus at The George Washington University, Washington, DC, where until June, 2011, she was Director of the Professional Doctor of Psychology Program and its Director of Clinical Training. She also is teaching, training and supervising analyst Emeritus of the Baltimore-Washington Institute for Psychoanalysis. Her areas of scholarly publications include multicultural competence, the impact of race, gender, and social class on ego functioning and the treatment process, and the impact of the superego on ego functioning.

Her numerous career awards include a Lifetime Career Achievement Award from Division 39 of the American Psychological Association.

Samuel Zysman, MD. After practising as a paediatrician, he moved into child psychiatry and made psychoanalytical training at the Argentine Psychoanalytica Association. Currently training analyst and Professor at the Buenos Aires Psychoanalytical Association. He has written many papers on psychoanalytic technique, child analysis, ethics and psychoanalysis, literature and psychoanalysis, etc. His current focus is on the psychoanalytic study of actions, cognitive processes, and the meta-psychological status of scientific theories.

Peter Fonagy, Mary Target & Liz Allison

After the first hundred years of its history, psychoanalysis has matured into a serious, independent intellectual tradition, which has notably retained its capacity to challenge established truths in most areas of our culture. Above all, psychoanalytic ideas have given rise to an approach to the treatment of mental disorders and character problems, psychodynamic psychotherapy, which has become a thriving tradition in most countries, at least in the Western world. With an ever-expanding evidence base, based on randomised controlled trials as well as investigations of brain function, psychodynamic psychotherapy can aspire to legitimacy in the world of science, yet retains a unique perspective on human subjectivity which continues to justify its place in the world of humanities and all spheres where human culture is systematically studied.

The biological psychiatrist of today is called to task by psychoanalysis, as much as was the specialist in nervous diseases of Freud's time, in turn of the century Vienna. Today's cultural commentators, whether for or against psychoanalytic ideas, are obliged to pay attention to considerations of unconscious motivation, defences, the formative impact of early childhood experience, and the myriad other discoveries which psychoanalysts brought to twentieth century culture.

Twenty-first century thought implicitly incorporates much of what was discovered by psychoanalysis in the last century. Critics who try to pick holes in or even demolish the psychoanalytic edifice are often doing this from ramparts constructed on psychoanalytic foundations. A good example of this would be the recent attacks by some cognitive behaviour therapists upon psychodynamic approaches. Vehement as these are, they have to give credit to psychoanalysis for its contribution to cognitive therapeutic theory and technique. These authors point to the advances they have made in relation to classical ideas, but rarely acknowledge that the psychodynamic approach has also advanced. An unfortunate feature of such debates is that often attacks on psychoanalysis are addressed to where the discipline was fifty or even seventy-five years ago.

Both the epistemology and the conceptual and clinical claims of psychoanalysis are often passionately disputed. We see this as a sign that psychoanalysis may be unique in its capacity to challenge and provoke. Why should this be? Psychoanalysis is unrivalled in the depth of its questioning of human motivation, and whether its answers are right or wrong, the epistemology of psychoanalysis allows it to confront the most difficult problems of human experience. When else is the motivation of both victim and perpetrator of sexual abuse going to be simultaneously considered? What other discipline will take the subjectivity of a newborn, or in fact, an *in utero* infant as a serious topic for study? The discipline, which has found meaning in dreams, continues to search for understanding in relation to acts of the greatest humanity and inhumanity. It remains committed to attempting to understand the most subtle aspects of the intersubjective interplay that can occur between two individuals, one struggling to overcome the barriers that another has elected to create in the path of their own progress through the world. Paradoxically, our new understanding of the physical basis of our existence—our genes, nervous systems, and endocrine functioning—rather than finally displacing psychoanalysis, has created a pressing need for a complementary discipline which considers the memories, desires, and meanings which are beginning to be recognised as influencing human adaptation even at the biological level. How else, other than through the study of subjective experience, will we understand the expression of the individual's biological destiny, within the social environment?

It is not surprising, then, that psychoanalysis continues to attract some of the liveliest intellects in our culture. These individuals are by no means all psychoanalytic clinicians, or psychotherapists. They are distinguished scholars in an almost bewildering range of disciplines, from the study of mental disorders with their biological determinants to the disciplines of literature, art, philosophy, and history. There will always be a need to explicate the meaning of experience. Psycho-analysis, with its commitment to understanding subjectivity, is in a leading position to fulfil this intellectual destiny. We are not surprised at the upsurge of interest in psychoanalytic studies in universities in many countries, which is driven by the limitations of understanding that modern science, including modern social science, all too often provides. The courageous accounts of psychoanalysts meet a funda-mental human need for discovering the meaning behind actions, and meets this need head on. While some may consider psychoanalytic accounts speculative, we must not forget that in relation to many descriptions of action, feeling, and cognition the explorations of psychoanalysis based in the consulting room have proved to be profound and readily generalisable. No one now doubts the reality of childhood sexuality, no one believes the conscious mind, in any sense, represents the boundaries of subjectivity. Non-conscious conflict, defence, the mental structures that encode the quality of early rela-tionships into later interpersonal functioning, and the motivation to become attached and to look after others, represent early psycho-analytic discoveries that have become an inalienable part of twenty-first century culture. The books in this series will aim to address the same intellectual curiosity that has made these educational projects so successful.

The theme of our series is a focus on advances in psychoanalysis and hence our series title *Developments in Psychoanalysis*. In our view while psychoanalysis has a glorious and rich history, it also has an exciting future, with dramatic changes and shifts as our understand-ing of the mind is informed by scientific, philosophical, and literary enquiry. Our commitment is to no specific orientation, to no particu-lar professional group, but to the intellectual challenge to explore questions of meaning and interpretation systematically, and in a scholarly way. Nevertheless, we would be glad if this series particu-larly spoke to the psychotherapeutic community, to those individuals who use their own minds and humanity to help others in distress.

In this volume, Jorge Canestri and his colleagues capture some of the untapped richness of psychoanalytic thinking. They engage in mining the unconscious theories, which explain to us how psychoanalysts understand their patients implicitly. The idea that psychoanalysts have more to say about the nature of the mind than has been published in books on psychoanalysis is important and innovative. It fits the theme of this series in searching for what is actual, functional, and observable in psychoanalytic theory and practice. Paradoxically, as Canestri and his colleagues show, what we see when we observe the psychoanalyst at work are their unconscious ideas about their patients as well as their conscious constructions, even their attitudes to their conscious theories are often beyond their awareness.

This is a unique book which we are delighted to see in our series. It is fully consistent with our wish to communicate some of the intellectual excitement that we feel about the past, present, and future of psychoanalytic ideas, and which we enjoy seeing in our students each year. We hope that our work with the authors and editors in the series will help to make these ideas accessible to an even larger group of students, scholars, and practitioners worldwide.

Peter Fonagy, Mary Target, and Liz Allison
University College London

INTRODUCTION

Jorge Canestri

Four years ago we published the book *Psychoanalysis From Practice to Theory*. In it, we tried to give an account of our reflections and our research on the meaning, the use, and status of the implicit theories of analysts in their clinical work. This project of systematic qualitative research was started in 2000 by the Working Party on Theoretical Issues (WPTI) of the European Psychoanalytical Federation. The development of the project owes a great deal to the collaboration of all the colleagues who participated in the presentation of clinical material as well as in the subsequent analyses and discussions. There were many of them and from all regions: Europe, North America, and Latin America. Shortly after this had produced its first results, we began to receive requests to organise other groups in the Americas. Little by little they have become independent and have acquired their own characteristics. The main working nucleus of the Working Party on Theoretical Issues has remained the same, composed of Werner Bohleber, Jorge Canestri (Chair), Paul Denis and Peter Fonagy. After a lengthy experience analysing clinical material by using the specific instrument that we had designed called *The map of private (implicit, preconscious) theories in clinical practice*, the Working Party has begun to apply the acquired knowledge and the ideas that have been developed to some specific areas in the analytical field, for example, the theoretical and clinical aspects of trauma. It is our intention to give an account of this work in the near future.

We have asked ourselves why a project of this kind has had so much success, as shown by the interest it has created and by the formation of similar groups within the psychoanalytical societies and groups of colleagues belonging to different societies. We think it is interesting to identify some of the reasons that may have contributed to this fact, not necessarily in order to emphasise the hypothetical merits of the Working Party on Theoretical Issues, but because this could help to identify some of the particular characteristics of our practice as well as some of its problems.

In the first place, we have inverted the canonical order of *from theory to practice* and have substituted instead *from practice to theory*— as in the title of our book. In order to make the inversion, it was necessary to construct a programme that would explore our clinical work from *the inside*, while at the same time elaborating a specific methodology. We have tried to provide some points of reference to this process in reverse. We began by acknowledging the fact that many efforts have been made to analyse the phenomenon of "theoretical pluralism" of contemporary psychoanalysis, the internal coherence and consistence of the different theories and the level of congruence between them. We believe that there has not been as much diligence in confronting the *reality* of our clinical practice, that is, what it *really is*, and not what we say it is or what we would like it to be.

We have also inverted another habitual tendency that regularly proposes alternatives to the understanding that the analyst has acquired of his patient; alternatives that usually lead to a supervision of the colleague, either explicit or masked.

Reversing this tendency means shifting the focus of our attention from the patient to the analyst. It no longer implies analysing the patient's mental processes, but the inferential processes of the analyst. What use does the analyst make of the theories he has incorporated, how has he adopted and adapted them in and to his internal world, which are his implicit theories, his presuppositions, and his prejudices? Which are the preconscious, and above all the unconscious, influences that condition, guide, and characterise his comprehension and his interpretations?

Although we cannot claim absolute originality, because various authors have already explored these matters, we can perhaps be proud of the systematic nature of our research, the characteristics of its methodology, and the creation of an appropriate instrument for our analyses. We think this may have helped promote the diffusion of the programme throughout the world.

We have also tried to specify the epistemological foundations of the project. In doing so we discussed and rejected the suitability of a scientific model that may be appropriate for those disciplines that use calculus and propose repeatable verification experiments, but it is not appropriate for the specificity of psychoanalysis. Equally inadequate is the classical distinction that neo-empirical logic makes between the context of discovery and the context of justification, introduced by Hans Reichenbach. The context of justification concerns the validation of the hypothesis: how we know whether it is true or false, and what evidence we have to corroborate it. If the context of discovery implies the production of hypotheses, theories and concepts—a production in which various psychological and social factors concur—then its dissociation from the context of justification and its exclusion from the study of how a discipline is made up, would appear to be particularly incongruent, even more so if the discipline is psychoanalysis. Clinical experience is the ideal place in which the analyst constructs, together with the patient, those intermediate theoretical segments (hypotheses of conjunction between the observable and theory) that allow for the creation of a shared narrative that is, moreover, specific to a given situation. Therefore, systematically investigating and analysing with an appropriate instrument all that occurs in the relation between practice and theory from the viewpoint of the creation of new theoretical segments in clinical work seems essential to us. This is the heuristic role of clinical experience in psychoanalysis.

Not even in this case can we claim originality, since many epistemologists presently consider that the sharp distinction between the context of discovery and the context of justification is neither legitimate nor useful. The heuristic characterisation, the heuristic course of theory, for example, the theory-we-reached-in-a-certain-manner, is more congruent with our clinical–theoretical experience. It is, therefore, a matter of considering the theory together with its heuristics. The modality with which a theory was constructed thus becomes decisive for the evaluation of its scientific merits, contrary to the distinction proposed by Reichenbach, and the empirical support itself becomes dependent on heuristics.

We will elaborate and develop these concepts further in the Conclusions since, besides representing the epistemological foundation of our project, they could enable us to make some progress in today's discussions on theoretical pluralism.

In this book, that ideally represents the continuation of the one mentioned above, we intend to concentrate on the use that we make of theories in clinical work by specifically analysing some clinical material. Three chapters of the book are entirely devoted to this aim. We have to thank all those colleagues who presented their cases for their valuable collaboration and for giving us permission to publish them. Three other chapters are theoretical: the first one presents the general problem of the use of both public and private theories in clinical practice; the second is an epistemological and psychoanalytical reflection on theories in psychoanalysis; the third chapter offers an alternative and/or complementary interpretation of private or implicit theories from the point of view of the object relations theory.

One chapter integrates theory and clinical work in analysis regarding the use of implicit theories in supervision, and therefore in the training of the analyst. The Conclusions deal with the task of summarising the results of ten years of experience.

The reader of this book will notice that we often use three terms to identify the type of theory we are referring to: implicit, private, and preconscious. In this case they are to be considered as synonyms. Implicit stands for "judgment or concept or fact that, without being formally and expressly enunciated, is however contained, by inference, in another judgment, or concept, or fact". Every theoretical segment or partial model that the analyst constructs in his clinical work remains, by definition, private until, as Sandler notes, it finds the right conditions to emerge in a "plausible and psychoanalytically socially acceptable way" (Sandler, 1983, p. 38). Bion (1992) proposes facilitating a transformation in the analyst "that enables [internal, unconscious processes] to be communicated to another . . ." This has been and still is precisely the meaning of the project we have developed: to identify the implicit and private theories of the analyst at work, and make them public if they should prove to have a certain consistency and be of use in clinical work.

In his pioneering work on this topic, it is again Sandler who uses the concept of preconscious (or descriptive conscious) in order to describe this type of theory. Clearly, Sandler has the Freudian "topographical" concept in mind since in the same year he writes, together with Anne-Marie Sandler, an equally well known work: "The 'second censorship', the 'three box model' and some technical implications, in which the authors attempt to integrate the "topographical" with the "structural" theory. Some valid objections could be raised concerning the pertinence of using the term "preconscious" to speak about these theoretic segments (see Dreher, 2000, for example); however, we have decided to keep this denomination, together with those of implicit theories and private theories, because we think it has its usefulness. One evident use is that of emphasising how the preconscious, besides being descriptively unconscious, contains material that sinks its roots in the unconscious. This is particularly important in regard to the theoretical segments that the analyst constructs in his clinical work, to the extent that, as Bion mentions, they are undoubtedly in relationship with unconscious processes in a dynamic and no longer descriptive sense.

In Chapter One (W. Bohleber) the author analyses in great detail and with attentive reference to the bibliography and the history of the topic of implicit theories, the particular relationship that exists in our discipline between theory and praxis, inasmuch as he considers that it differs from the type of relationship that exists in other scientific disciplines. The analyst does not approach his clinical experience armed with an "official" theory to apply; but he has to construct "temporal models, 'in the situation' that can evolve dynamically and that also possess a certain heuristic value" (Canestri, 2006). The analyst also has to consider the fact that he places pre-conceptions before his listening and, as the author says, "this also applies to the theories and concepts that, in advance, shape the analyst's preliminary and thereby pre- or unconscious mode of perception and experience". In agreement with what has just been said, Bohleber, quoting Schülein (2003), thinks that the activity of the subject who does research forms a constitutive part of the theory.

The author completes the picture with a study of the functions of theory in constituting the identity of the analyst; he quotes Grossman (1995) who believes that theory becomes a function of object relations, and Hamilton (1996) who analyses the analysts' attachment relationship with theories.

The wish to learn a theory and a technique goes hand-in-hand with that of belonging to a school of thought and to a psychoanalytical community of other colleagues.

Bohleber quotes various authors who, from different points of view, agree with each other on what the function of theory should be when listening to the patient: the theory "enables the analyst to modulate strong affective influencing factors", "protect against the pressure resulting from the development of transference and countertransference", is a necessary element for "triangulating" the space within the analyst-patient relationship, etc. Theory is remembered and re-created in clinical practice in strict reference to our patient and in that specific situation.

In this operation the analyst brings into play a wide variety of elements, some deriving from the official theories, although characterised by the specific modalities with which they were learned and then elaborated. Others belong to the private theories of the analyst, and others are "invented" for the occasion with more or less fortune. Their life may be short—they are needed for that specific moment and then they disappear; or they may survive if they are highly ranked enough to allow them to then become public.

A long paragraph of this chapter is devoted to the concept of theory as metaphor, or to its "transitional" function. Bohleber says that: "Such a metaphor-driven understanding of the development of concepts supports and underlines Sandler's notion that concepts in psychoanalysis are elastic, as well as his conception of private theories, which in the analyst pave the way for a further development of public analytical theoretical concepts." Following this, the author specifically develops the issue of the formation and function of private theories, and immediately afterwards he proposes a detailed examination of a vector model of implicit (pre-conscious) theoretical thinking and an illustration of each vector. As mentioned above, this model is the one that we constructed along the same lines as an instrument that has helped provide an accurate analysis of clinical material, as well as being the result of our research.

In Chapter Two: "Do analysts do what they say they do?" Peter Fonagy shows how to use this instrument, that is, the vector model, as he comments on and analyses some interesting clinical material provided by Dorothy Holmes (APsaA) during a panel coordinated by Irene Cairo (APsaA) in which Peter Fonagy and I presented our current research on implicit theories in clinical practice. The title of the chapter is the one that the coordinator had chosen for the panel.

Fonagy illustrates his (and our) task very clearly when stating that, "My task here is not to listen to the patient and hear, or pretend to hear, experiences that the analyst indicated no awareness of. In this presentation I am illustrating something rather different, illustrating the act of listening to the analyst, showing understanding of the analytic understanding. I am trying to uncover the analyst's hidden (implicit or preconscious) assumptions that help explain *her* understanding of the patient's material". This attitude is the one on which we have always based our work, trying to avoid any type of "supervision" of the working of the analyst, any "super-understanding" of the patient, in order to concentrate, as in this example, on the implicit assumptions that lead *this analyst* to the understanding of *this patient*.

From a theoretical and methodological point of view our postulation is that the analyst at work, if he carries out his task well, constructs what I have called "temporal models in situation", that is, models that are applied to a specific situation and that ideally must have a heuristic potential.

In this book we have tried to provide various examples of how to analyse the material that colleagues from different regions have supplied to us in function of our project: *to understand the analytic understanding*.

In Chapter Three: "Theoretical and clinical reflections on public and private theories", Charles Hanly presents a scholarly, precise, and convincing examination of the theme of implicit theories from an epistemological and clinical point of view.

He begins by examining the ideas of Collinwood and Hegel concerning the fact that contemporary historians "implicitly express but do not state the latent assumptions of their own epoch when they write the histories of earlier epochs". Something similar is manifested in the clinical practice of analysts; in which can be found the unacknowledged private theories that are not recognised and articulated explicitly in their publications. The author provides various examples of this duality and formulates two important questions relative to our research, which I will quote: "What if there is an inescapable tangle of implicit, unacknowledged, and unexamined assumptions . . . in psychoanalytic explanations?", and "What if the analyst who 'discovers' implicit theorising in the work of a colleague is him/herself inevitably deploying, without being aware of doing so, his/her own unconscious implicit theorising?"

Hanly identifies two opposing epistemological positions which attempt to answer these questions: the first seems to be a post-modern version of an ancient subjective idealism, while the other adheres to scientific realism. The author promotes critical realism, which recognises that this subjectivity could produce cognitive entanglements, but also that when they occur they can be overcome.

" 'Critical' " in " 'critical realism' ", says Hanly, "refers to a capacity for self-criticism informed by the psychoanalytic understanding of the subjective sources of observational and conceptual error, strengthened by analysis, sustained and improved by self-analysis or by further analysis".

There follows a detailed, in depth and convincing analysis and an interesting dialogue with the works of Bohleber and Fonagy. Hanly particularly mentions Fonagy's comment in the previous chapter on Dorothy Holmes' excellent case.

In the sequence of these first three chapters the reader will find a concrete example of what we have been trying to study during these past years.

Hanly concludes by pointing out how, from the research undertaken and from the clinical and theoretical experience, one can understand the complexity of the task of theory-building in psychoanalysis.

In Chapter Four, Samuel Zysman develops "The case of Albert" which is commented by Paul Denis. He explains that his external collaboration with the project of the EPF Working Party on Theoretical Issues began following an invitation of the WPTI at the IPA Congress in New Orleans (2004), and then subsequently continued. The clinical material discussed here was presented at the IPA Congress in Rio de Janeiro (2005).

Zysman begins with a reflection on the actual fact of presenting material. Two intertwined phenomena appear frequently: "One of them is the tendency to substitute a fully detailed transcription with 'illustrative' vignettes or with a sort of personal description made by the analyst where some selected pieces of true session material are included", the second one is "the existence in us all of a strong tendency to mistake the examination of clinical material in search of unconscious (implicit) theories with a clinical supervision".

These two phenomena have been very seriously taken into consideration in our research: the material to be analysed always had to be "a fully detailed transcription" of sessions, and their commentator, who worked with a group of colleagues who met especially for the purpose, was instructed to avoid the spontaneous tendency to supervise the colleague who presented the material.

Zysman, besides continuing his relationship with the WPTI (as can be seen, he has two works in this book and one in the previous book) has also organised first in Argentina and then in Latin America for FEPAL (Federation of Psychoanalytic Societies of Latin America), a research structure similar to the one in Europe. As we have explained above, this has also happened in North America.

The author presents his patient and describes two sessions in full detail. As Paul Denis says in his comment on the case, it is possible to follow the analyst's inferential logic—with all the limitations imposed by having to isolate a segment of the process—inasmuch as the analyst has reproduced as faithfully as possible what happened between himself and his patient.

The comment by Denis is just as precise in that it provides the reader with a perspective on the explicit as well as the implicit theoretical and technical trajectories.

Chapter Five consists of a clinical case which Lilia Bordone de Semeniuk presented in a panel organised by the WPTI at the IPA Congress in Chicago (2009): "The case of Floppy: case history and session". The presentation was accompanied by three discussions by colleagues coming from different regions and different psychoanalytical schools. This, together with the high quality of the clinical case, makes for particularly interesting reading.

Werner Bohleber introduces the panel saying: "In this work we want to arrive at a deeper understanding of how the analyst uses psychoanalytic theory in his clinical work. We want to offer greater theoretical illumination to the cognitive–affective space of the preconscious in which the public and the private implicit theories and their content and motives are established."

Peter Fonagy, who was the Chair of the panel, begins by saying that: "The big and refreshing difference between standard psychoanalytic commentary on case reports and our efforts to map implicit theories in clinical practice is that the focus in the former case is on the patient, at what the patient is '*really* trying to communicate', whereas in unearthing implicit theories the concern is with the analyst's preconscious and unconscious mind (Canestri, 2006; Canestri, Fonagy, Bohleber, & Dennis, 2006)."

Together with Peter Fonagy, the other two colleagues who comment on the case—Beatriz de León de Bernardi and Dieter Bürgin—create an interesting dialogue with each other through which the reader will be able to enter without difficulty into the dynamics of the implicit and explicit theoretical choices of the analyst and of the colleagues discussing the case.

Chapter Six is "Supervision in psychoanalytical training: the analysis and the use of implicit theories in psychoanalytical practice".

The objective of this chapter is to propose a comprehensive reflection on the concept of supervision and on its function in psychoanalytical training. Particular attention is given to the use of the analyst's implicit theories in clinical practice and an example of a supervision has been analysed using the "Map"—the conceptual instrument that is the result of the qualitative research carried out within the WPTI of the European Psychoanalytical Federation.

The history of the concept is studied, following its progress and its transformations, and critically analysing its links to theory. The author states that supervision can be seen as a field of variable dimensions, that the configuration of the field ensues from the vertex of observation chosen by the supervisor, and it derives directly from the theory that informs the supervision and from its pre-established goals. Supervision could be the preferred place to deepen, investigate, and work on translating theory into practice and practice into theory.

A thorough analysis of the implicit theories that the analyst uses in his clinical work, facilitated by the use of "The map of implicit (private, preconscious) theories in clinical practice", proves to be of great assistance in supervision. As well as having a relevant function in helping to discover "if we do what we think we do", a careful study of the implicit theories also trains the analysts to link working hypotheses (interpretations) to theory and to compare their respective theories and clinical methods.

Chapter Seven by Samuel Zysman is "Theories as objects: a psychoanalytic inquiry into minds and theories".

In *Psychoanalysis: From Practice to Theory* (Canestri, 2006), in a paper entitled "Infantile sexual theories and cognitive development", Zysman had presented and developed some ideas on cognitive development from the point of view of psychoanalysis. The Freudian conceptualisation on infantile sexual theories was the basis from which all the subsequent forms of theorisation of the individual derived.

In this present work Zysman takes a step forward and describes a permanent "theorising activity" with probably innate roots. On this occasion he says that:

> The idea that I wish to introduce (which may also be called a theory) is to consider them [theories] as "objects", both internal and external, employing this term with the meaning and scope it has in the theory of object relations. Such particular "objects" would consist in the theoretical statements they are made of, and they would establish relations among them and with other similar "objects". In turn, and in such condition, they could be included regularly in metapsychological statements, which is precisely what we need to account for their vicissitudes as contents of our minds".

The author is aware of the fact that it may perhaps be difficult for some of us to conceive theories as objects, considering that we are usually used to thinking of theories *on* objects and not *as* objects. A series of questions could be raised. In order to facilitate exposition and discussion Zysman groups them into: mostly clinical, mostly epistemological, and mostly metapsychological.

I am sure that the reader will be stimulated by his hypotheses and the way he considers the theme of implicit theories.

In the last chapter, Chapter Eight, "Conclusions", Jorge Canestri attempts to draw some conclusions from this research that has already been going on for ten years and that continues in its task of analysing the implicit theories on specific psychoanalytical issues. The aim of this final chapter is to analyse what this research has taught us so far, to have a look at the problems that may face us ahead, and to consolidate certain epistemological decisions that today could perhaps be described with more precision.

We think that readers will be interested in our book and in the prospects for the future that derive from it.

In order to facilitate the reading of the discussions, we here include as an appendix the instrument we created in our research (see Canestri, 2006) and that we used for the analysis of the clinical material.

References

Bion, W. R. (1992). *Cogitations*. London: Karnac.
Canestri, J. (Ed.) (2006). *Psychoanalysis: From Practice to Theory*. London: Wiley.

Dreher, A. U. (2000). *Foundations for Conceptual Research in Psychoanalysis*. London and New York: Karnac.

Sandler, J. (1983). Reflections on some relations between psychoanalytic concepts and psychoanalytic practice. *International Journal of Psycho-analysis, 64*: 35–46.

Schülein, J. A. (2003). On the logic of psychoanalytic theory. *International Journal of Psycho-Analysis, 84*: 315–330.

CHAPTER ONE

The use of public and of private implicit theories in the clinical situation

Werner Bohleber

Introduction

In order to understand the role played by theory in psychoanalysis, its development, and specific formation, it is necessary to become aware of the particularities of the relationship between theory and praxis that distinguishes psychoanalysis from other scientific fields.

The naïve observer might assume that we have stored psychoanalytic theory in our memory, either according to particular schools or more comprehensively, and during analytical sessions we simply retrieve the proper concepts and part-theories that fit with the material as it unfolds, thereby allowing a fuller psychoanalytic understanding. But even the hermeneutic circle points out that we encounter what another person says with certain preconceptions, leading us to expand or change what we hear in the process of understanding. This also applies to the theories and concepts that, in advance, shape the analyst's preliminary and thereby pre- or unconscious mode of perception and experience. We are all familiar with clinical discussions among colleagues in which the same material can be understood using different concepts. This indicates that analysts enter into an active and personal engagement with certain theories that extend far beyond the mere application of the theory as an element of a body of knowledge. The activity of the investigating subject is constitutive of theory, which in turn remains tied to the subject (Schülein, 1999).

In trying to arrive at a deeper understanding of how the analyst uses psychoanalytic theory in his practical clinical work, we discover a number of important aspects that I will now outline.

Theories and identity of the psychoanalyst

In their public form, theories are a system of thought, that in principle anyone can learn and apply. If we become familiar with theories in the course of our psychoanalytic training and adapt them to our own thinking, then this does not take place in a vacuum; rather, it occurs as part of an inner relationship to and within an intellectual confrontation with psychoanalytical authorities. The striving to learn and apply consensually validated technical principles and procedures is accompanied by the wish to belong to a psychoanalytical group or school of thought. Spezzano (1998) speaks of a "clinical triangle" in which we always find ourselves. The analyst not only stands in relation to the patient, but also to the virtual community of psychoanalytical practitioners with whom he seeks an inner consensus when applying theoretical concepts and technical principles. A narcissistic satisfaction results from sharing therapeutic ideals and concepts with others to whom one feels connected. In this way, as Grossmann has observed (1995), theories become inner representatives of the group and its authority. Here theory becomes a function of object relations. Hamilton (1996) speaks of an attachment relationship that analysts enter into with specific theories and with charismatic analysts, providing them with a feeling of security. This is most likely to occur in treatment situations, which are shaped by persistent insecurity and emotional pressure.

Theories and the process of clinical insight

Various analysts have emphasised the protective or buffer function of theory in the analytical process of insight and understanding, which enables the analyst to modulate strong affective influencing factors and to remain calm and attentive when they arise (Almond, 2003; Smith, 2003a,b). Caper (1997) believes that as a good internal object, psychoanalysis and its theory protect against the pressure resulting from the development of transference and countertransference, as well as against compliance with or conformity to the patient's narcissistic resistance. According to Britton (1998), theory is the element in the triangular space of analyst and patient that ensures the analyst's ability to think.

Reder (2002) works from the assumption that in the clinical process of gaining insight, we understand and express our selves, our own mental states, and those of the other in the language of a developed and sophisticated version of common-sense psychology. In it the analyst also conveys his insights in dialogue with the analysand. When we activate the theoretical knowledge within ourselves, our perception is divided between that which we actually experience in the analytic encounter and that which theory requires us to look for. Theory is a construction of a very special kind, not formulated in the language of clinical experience. In order to bring both into contact, we have to transform theoretical knowledge by making our common-sense psychological knowledge congruent with theoretical knowledge and thereby assimilate it. Thus, the concept of Oedipus complex or repression provides a structure with which we can arrive at a different understanding and conceptualisation of certain life experiences. This assimilation is a personal act, which inspires the analyst in his reflections on himself and his analytical work and helps him to increasingly acquire clinical-psychoanalytical competence. Yet such a theoretically enlightened common-sense psychological knowledge is always in danger of again being watered down by general ideological elements. In order to retain the integrity of our psychoanalytic knowledge, it is necessary to employ theoretical work that deconstructs common-sense knowledge. Reder thereby ascribes theory with a security function for analytical knowledge. Later, in my discussion of the function of private theories, I will examine to what degree it is possible to make such a more or less strict deconstructive division between common-sense psychological and psychoanalytical theoretical knowledge.

Parsons (1992) has shown how in our daily work with patients we do not simply retrieve theoretical ideas and concepts from memory; instead, the process of discovery occurs in such a way that we have to, as it were, rediscover the theory based on the clinical material, even though for the most part we have already internalised it. But which theories do we rediscover? These are elements of theory that appear to fit with the clinical material at the moment, but may also be dismissed later on. This process of searching and adjusting proceeds repeatedly in a circular motion. Within this cycle, concepts are rediscovered and refined; in addition, an individual integration of various theory elements takes place simultaneously in the analyst's preconscious. One reason for this is that in the analyst's mind theories are available in a much less elaborate and finished form than they are in their public version. In this way the analyst can integrate various concepts from different authors and schools of thought he prefers into a theoretical framework that bears a highly personal stamp, and is aligned with both his scientific and pre-scientific convictions. This is how the analyst adopts und metabolises conceptions and technical treatment principles that correspond to his personality and have proved themselves most effective in working with his patients (Pulver, 1993; Spezzano, 1998).

So far we have been considering published concepts and theories. But now we are encountering an amalgam of public theory elements in the analyst's preconscious which can assume various personal forms. Added to this mix are the analyst's personal convictions and private theories; their influence is largely responsible for adopted public theories becoming individually adapted theories.

Leuzinger-Bohleber (Leuzinger-Bohleber & Fischmann, 2006) describes the analyst's process of clinical insight not as a personally coloured amalgam of elements of public theories, in which his private theories are also included, but rather as a circular and primarily preconsciously operating process of discovery stemming from metaphors and mini-models specific to the situation, and increasingly involving higher levels of abstraction of concepts and theoretical models in addition to private theories. This process is generally not just run through once, but repeatedly, in order to arrive at an ever-more adequate understanding of the clinical material.

Metaphors and the metaphorical function of theories

Reed (2003) distinguishes between two functions of psychoanalytic theories. On the one hand, they describe mental processes in an objective and universally applicable form. On the other, theories also help the clinician to concretely conceptualise that which is inside the patient that he has not yet understood, but has sensed and perceived intuitively; they can thereby bring it out, capture it in words, and make it communicable. Reed terms this a "transitional function" of theory, which is comparable to the function of metaphor.[1] What the analyst can at first only grasp intuitively and only vaguely verbalise he seeks to connect with concepts and theoretical elements, in order to give it a more precise form and meaning. When theories are used as metaphors, this gives them an individual shape, which can deviate from their official version. On the other hand, metaphors are also embedded in theories, which, in turn, can influence the perception and conceptualisation of mental activity both pre- and unconsciously. Metaphors function by way of their visual and symbolic attraction to the mental processes and can therefore be far more formative for insight than abstract ideas and conceptions. Reed (2003) has examined spatial metaphors that are contained within various theoretical conceptions of the psyche. The classical model sees the psyche as a space extending in depth which contains significant content that is to be uncovered. It is a closed intrapsychic space for the most part, extending between the mental agencies with a deeply embedded unconscious. The analyst is an observer and archaeologist, who listens and uncovers hidden meanings. Even when the patient perceives him with transference fantasies, he remains separate. In the Kleinian model we find a metaphorical space in which the processes of projective identification unfold. This space extends horizontally and parts of the self cross into the other as an object, just as parts of the other are assimilated into the self. Although it is conceived as a whole, the self is imagined as dispersed and split. Self and object are therefore no longer perceived in terms of theory as being completely separated. Through the exchange of projected and then re-introjected parts of the self a better mental integration becomes possible. Winnicott's model of potential space was the starting point for a third form of analytical spatial conceptions. Here the metaphorical space belongs neither to the patient nor to the analyst, but is instead the creation of their profound communication and belongs to each of them together. Ogden (1997) calls it a space of the "analytic third". The patient as well as the analyst therefore go through transformations and that which has yet to be understood can acquire symbolic representation. Not only do these metaphorically driven conceptions of the psyche determine the analyst's sense of the therapeutic relationship and, in particular, his understanding of transference and countertransference processes, they also situate the ensemble of the other concepts he is apt to apply.

Metaphors are often chosen in order to find analogies that make the mental capable of any form of description. We know that Freud frequently used metaphors in this way and did so masterfully.[2] Metaphors can provide analogies that make a complex matter perceivable in a relatively precise manner and concrete enough to describe, but they also possess a semantic space that contains an excess of other potential meanings. These are not initially subsumed by the formation of the concept, and later, as the theory develops, they retroactively unfold to create an expanded meaning for the concept. As an example I would like to mention here the mirror metaphor that Freud introduced in order to describe the attitude of the analyst toward his patient. The analyst, he writes, "should be opaque to his patients and, like a mirror, should show them nothing but what is shown to him" (1912e, p. 118). In keeping with the empirical scientific ideal of his time, with this metaphor Freud gives expression to the imperative of obtaining the most undistorted and objective knowledge possible of the patient's psychic reality. It was subsequently subjected to a far-reaching critique and today is considered largely outmoded in its original form. This metaphorical formation of an analogy for the analytic process of insight also retarded the development of an adequate concept of countertransference. The mirror metaphor is a guiding metaphor in the Western world for the process of discovery and has two main trajectories of meaning. While for Freud the dominant meaning was that of a passive mirror meant to supply as undistorted a reflection as possible, a meaning has subsequently unfolded, primarily in the work of Winnicott and Green, of a living mirror that actively adjusts to its objects. This was prefigured as early as Lacan (1949) when he describes the function of the real mirror image for the emergence of a unified (if illusory) image of the self and for the capacity of humans to reflect. According to Winnicott (1971), the child discovers his self in that which he sees reflected of himself in the face of the mother. For Winnicott psychotherapy metaphorically has the function of the face which reflects that which is visible so that the patient can find his own self (1971, p. 135). In Green's work (1975) the reflective function of the mirror as a metaphor comes to the fore. The passage of the self through an other as a mirror can develop into an inner mirror of the self and thereby into the capacity for self-reflection. For Green the work of the mirror itself is an element of the metaphor that has been neglected until now. For him the mirror is the absent third, the father, who in the reflecting expression of the mother is also always present.[3]

With this example of the unfolding of a metaphor in the formation of analytical theories, I wanted to point out how multifaceted the meaning space of metaphorical concepts can be and how this can subsequently contribute to the development of analytic concepts. The meaning of many concepts in psychoanalysis is therefore not only defined by abstract descriptions, but they also often have a metaphorical semantic field, which can also point the way toward the path of a further development. Such a metaphor-driven understanding of the development of concepts supports and underlines Sandler's notion that concepts in psychoanalysis are elastic, as well as his conception of private theories, which in the analyst pave the way for a further development of public analytical theoretical concepts. I will take this up in a moment, but I would first like to mention a related idea.

Psychoanalysis as connotative theory formation

Schülein (1999; 2003) has made the epistemological qualification that psychoanalysis is a connotative theory. In contrast to the nomological reality of the natural sciences, which produce denotative theories, he conceives of the field of inquiry of psychology as an autopoetic reality, which organises and guides itself. Connotative theorising extrapolates configurations of reality from the stream of external events and brings them into meaningful contexts as concepts. Various configurations can be grasped and understood in numerous theoretical conceptualisations. Connotative concepts are therefore by definition open, ambiguous, and capable of expansion. Many matters are also only to be grasped by way of metaphors. Connotative theories remain tied to practice. Because in their application they are always constituted anew, personal competence determines the degree to which connotations can be meaningfully and productively generated and applied. It follows that the acceptance of connotative theories is dependent upon their reproductive process, giving them much more of a social stamp than denotative theories (Schülein, 1999, p. 402).

The formation and function of private theories

While Schülein conducted an epistemological study of the logic of psychoanalysis, in the 1980s Sandler developed a conception of private theories, which he distilled from the examination of the actual concrete use of theories by analysts in clinical practice. For him there are also no exact definitions of psychoanalytic concepts with unambiguous meanings. In order to understand them, one has to be familiar with their application. With increasing clinical experience, every analyst constructs an array of theoretical segments that are directly related to his clinical work. They have the character of part-theories, of schemata and models, and represent an amalgam of public theory elements and one's own clinical experience, as well as personal life experience, individual values, and private philosophies or ideologies. We use many of these implicit theories and concepts without ever having consciously articulated them. In a descriptive sense they are unconscious. They are held in reserve in the preconscious to be retrieved when necessary. As long as they remain unconscious, they can coexist without difficulty, even if they contradict one another. The implicit private part-theories formed during clinical work by individual analysts are often more suitable and useful than public theories. According to Sandler, this is due to the process of forming individual clinical experience, whereby the meaning of concepts and part-theories become stretched and begin to deviate from public theories to varying degrees. Some especially creative analysts are successful in consciously reflecting on these stretched and divergent meanings of concepts and formulating them for the body of psychoanalytic knowledge. It is primarily concepts at a mid-level of clinical generalisation whose meaning-space has further developed fluidly and synergistically in this way: transference, object relationships, conflict, drive/motive, defence, sense of safety, etc.

Sandler examined this stretching of concepts first by way of the term transference (1983), and later in an examination conducted at the Sigmund-Freud-Institut together with Institute colleagues on the use of the concept of trauma (Sandler, Dreher, & Drews, 1987, 1991). I will concentrate here on transference. For Freud transference was a specific form of memory in which the past is not remembered, but experienced and repeated in the relationship with the analyst. The linkage of the concept of transference to the repetition of the past and to memory processes long remained the official definition. With time, however, the concept's meaning was stretched. Freeman Sharpe described in the 1930s how the unstructured nature of the analytical situation activated fantasies in the patient about the analyst that did not necessarily represent a repetition of the past (Sharpe, 1930). In order to conceptually capture the patient's special relationship to the analyst, one turned to the concept of transference. This shows how readily this concept in implicit private theoretical use could be equated with the analytical relationship. With Anna Freud's (1936) description of a whole class of object-related defences, and Melanie Klein's (1946) work on projective identification, object-related processes became the centre of theoretical reflection on the concept of transference, and the analysis of the here-and-now of the analytical interaction took precedence over the reconstruction of one's infant past. The inclusion of a variety of object-related activities that did not have to be a repetition of the relationship to significant objects in the past was the actual extension and stretching of the concept. This understanding has largely established itself today, most strongly in Kleinian analysis.

Dreher (2000) has more strictly systematised private implicit theories, as Sandler has conceived of them. She makes a distinction between the following:

- commonly shared implicit theories of the psychoanalytic milieu in which the analyst was trained
- individual ideas of the analyst, which arise during his clinical activity and represent a mixture of explicit theories and his own, in part provisional thoughts and assumptions, that can most certainly contain creative elements for a future transformation of concepts
- unconscious ideas representing motives and value judgments rooted in the analyst's personality and life experience.

For Sandler, the specific connection between praxis and theory, in conjunction with the coexistence of public and private implicit theories, is also the reason why psychoanalysis will never be a complete and comprehensive theory, but rather a body of ideas and concepts that are flexibly, and by no means seamlessly, interrelated. For Sandler, the function of private theories, namely that of making flexible the theories acknowledged up to now, of stretching them and making them elastic,

is also the explanation for why there has been an organic and continuous advancement of psychoanalytic theory; it is likewise the guarantee
that this will continue to be the case.

A somewhat broader consideration, however, makes apparent that
the further development of concepts was by no means always as
continuous and organic as Sandler assumes. In his investigations he
primarily examined the Anglo-American cultural and language area.
Analytical groups from other intellectual and cultural traditions have
often extended the meaning-space of concepts quite differently and
completely independently based on their own culturally specific
preconceptions.

In addition, the continuous stretching of the meaning-space of
concepts did not automatically lead to ever increasing integration of
clinical phenomena; instead, some clinical insights were also lost and
eliminated from the conceptual meaning-space. Let us continue with
the example of transference. For Freud the meaning and specific
content of the concept of transference was still closely connected to the
repetition and reconstruction of the past, but the further development
broke the close link between these concepts and autobiographical
memory, as well as the reconstruction of the past, receded to the
margins or completely disappeared from theoretical formulations of
the concept of transference (Bohleber, 2007).

Stein (2005) has examined how ties of loyalty not only bolster clinical thinking, but also hinder it, concealing lacunae in clinical theory
or retarding the extension of concepts that clinically seemed readily
applicable, yet remained in analysts' implicit–private realm for far too
long. Stein points to the tension that exists between private and public
theories. The larger it is, the greater the analyst's fear of criticism
when he puts his theories up for discussion; as a consequence, some
creative theoretical notions are never fully formulated. It also seems
plausible to assume that analysts' private theories are especially prone
to take root in the gaps and on the weak points of the public body of
psychoanalytic theoretical knowledge.

Recently Peter Fonagy (2003) has issued a vehement critique of the
entire relationship between theory and praxis in psychoanalysis in
which he draws a completely different conclusion as Sandler about
the stretching of concepts. In his view stretching has led to a lose definition of concepts that has misled analysts to construct a defensive
attitude against the operationalisation of concepts and to instead

prefer ambiguity. The consequence, he finds, has been a multiplication of theories and a neglect of the criterion of parsimony that would have made it possible to eliminate rival theories. Instead, a polymorphous use of theories has developed along with a body of theory that exceeds the abilities of the individual to summarise it, let alone to integrate it. Apart from two or three core psychoanalytic theories Fonagy does not want any of the other theories that he finds over-specified to be considered scientific in a strict sense. He relegates them to something like a pre-scientific theoretical space, when he attributes them as acts of imagination with a high heuristic value for gaining insight into the individual psyche and the subtle aspects of the infinitely complex system of human subjectivity. In doing so, Fonagy finds himself in the realm of the hermeneutic, that is, a type of scientific–theoretical systemisation that uses different premises to conceptualise the relationship of theory to praxis as a post-empiricist science, as represented by Fonagy.

My thoughts thus far have primarily focused on the creative, stimulating function of the analyst's private implicit theories that in many cases have brought about valuable expansions to the psychoanalytic body of theory. Private theories are not always a creative resource, however, as they may also have a highly idiosyncratic significance. This increases the danger that personal convictions can take the forefront that are no longer scientifically valid and communicable. In addition, we often encounter an inflated idealisation of certain theories or concepts. The personal convictions expressed in private theories shape the meanings the analyst assigns to the clinical material and also determine his emotional response to it. In doing so, private theories can serve as an important indicator of the analyst's countertransference (Purcell, 2004). This must be analysed instead of being further theoretically elaborated.

A vector model of implicit (preconscious) theoretical thinking

The Working Party on Theoretical Issues of the European Psychoanalytical Federation (EPF)[4] has assumed the task of more closely examining analysts' private theories. The aim was to offer greater theoretical illumination to the cognitive–affective space of the preconscious in which these theories, and their content and motives, are established. In order to work out a model for this, a specific methodologically systematic approach was not chosen; instead, psychoanalytical means were used to explore the preconscious psychological space of theory. In clinical work with the patient a great deal of what takes place is routine for the experienced analyst. When asked, he at first has difficulties explaining his mode of operation, focusing of perception, conceptual considerations, and formulations of interventions. They must first be subjected to an introspective inquiry in order to become accessible. Hence, at work here are theory elements, models, and individual beliefs on which the analyst orients himself, along with mindsets and convictions operating largely implicitly or preconsciously. In the emerging heuristic model the members of the Working Party began by conceptually grouping the various theoretical and motivational elements, the structures of knowledge, and their topographical classification. They ordered them along vectors, which seek to illuminate the theoretical space along various trajectories. The vectors are not independent of each other and various elements ordered along one vector can also be situated along another. In terms of a model, these vectors interact dynamically and determine clinical judgment formation and the analyst's therapeutic intervention according to their validity.

I would now like to introduce an outline of this mapping of private/implicit theories. For a more detailed presentation I will have to refer you to the map developed by the Working Party (Canestri, Bohleber, Denis, & Fonagy, 2006).

We define psychoanalytic theory, as used by the individual clinician, as an amalgam of three elements:

- Thinking based on public theories.
- Private theoretical thinking.
- The implicit use of explicit theories, meaning the way in which public theories are used differently from how they were intended.

These private implicit theories can be conscious or preconscious. Especially when they remain in the preconscious, they can be formed together with unconscious influences.

By tracing six vectors we have attempted to dissect this amalgam into its component parts. In the following I can only offer a brief and relatively rough outline of the six.[5]

Topographical vector

This vector is made up of the psychic levels upon which theoretical thinking takes place. The *conscious level* contains, for example, revisions of theories that came about through influences other than the original geographical–cultural factors, though they are not designated as such. Hence, the same official theories of a British Kleinian analyst can differ from those of a North- or South-American Kleinian analyst. Or, to take a further example, on the conscious level we find fully formed private theories that are not publicly acknowledged. Examples include the analyst's own personal "hobby horses".

Preconscious theories include subjective theory elements drawn from one's own sense of self. Analysts are also shaped by a common-sense psychology, in which the implicit value systems of the respective culture are at work without the analyst being aware of it. Psychoanalytic theories can be used eclectically, without this being consciously reflected upon. Certain fundamental epistemological assumptions that one has can also have a preconscious influence on theoretical convictions. Thus, we often find, for example, that an analyst who epistemologically adheres to a narrative coherence theory of truth simultaneously holds to an intersubjective conception of the analytical relationship (Hamilton, 1993). This level would also include metaphors that imply certain theoretical conceptions. To return to the spatial metaphors for the psyche, "deep" is associated with authenticity and the surface with superficiality.

Unconscious influences can be found in the repression of concepts or in the countertransference, where certain theories are favoured. In this regard a theory can also be used as a defence to protect against fears. An example would be a theory that cannot find an application because it would bring erotic transference into focus, which triggers too many fears. A theory can likewise be used to protect the narcissism of the analyst or serve as the object of aggressive impulses toward the patient.

Conceptual vector

This vector generally consists of the various formations of a worldview or ideology. The position ascribed to libidinal desires and the meaning given to external reality is just as subject to the influence of a worldview as is one's attitude towards, for example, marriage and divorce. An analyst might, for instance, have a more tragic–stoic or a more romantic point of view. Such worldviews and ideological convictions are much more influential in our choice of certain theories than we might think.

This vector is also concerned with concepts borrowed from other psychoanalytical schools of thought; this does not have to apply to just one concept, however, but can relate to several stemming from various theoretical approaches. The result can be an implicit and heterogeneous eclecticism, but also a largely coherent amalgamation of the theory developed in individual clinical experience.

This vector also includes general clinical attitudes and positions: if, for example, certain concepts are favoured, or if dreams are given preference over other material. A further example is the significance granted to the past as opposed to the here and now.

In addition, this also includes the implicit theories about analytical processes of transformation and the envisioned aims of the analytical treatment. I would now like to present a few examples in greater detail.

To begin, a few examples of implicit theories about what *transformation* makes possible:

- Making the unconscious conscious is itself therapeutic.
- When I make it clear to a patient how unconscious mechanisms work, he will feel better.
- Bringing the patient into contact with feelings he tries to split off is helpful to him.
- The patient should be able to temper his superego and forgive himself.
- The patient should be able to present himself to the analyst openly and without defence.

Implicit conceptions about which *analytical strategies* are most likely to bring about a transformation include the following:

- The patient should concentrate more on his inner world than external reality.
- Multiple self-representations are to be developed with the aim of helping the patient to be increasingly able to assume an observing stance toward himself.

Implicitly operating target goals of what should be achieved with the patient influence the way in which he is treated. These include:

- The patient should be able to make genuine relationships.
- The patient should be able to lead a genuine dialogue with himself. The aim is to develop an authentic self.
- The patient should be able to tolerate the autonomy of an other.

"Action" vector

This vector consists of the way the analyst acts in regard to the patient. This includes the role ascribed to free floating attention in listening, for example, as well as strategies and background assumptions about how interventions are verbally formulated and how one interacts with the patient in practice. In listening theories usually have less influence in the choice of a "selected fact" and the formulation of an intervention based upon it. In the concrete choice of words the influence of private theories is substantial. An example: whether an interpretation of the patient is formulated in the singular or directed interactively in the form of "we". In one's behaviour toward the patient, various cultural standards play a role, as do implicit behavioural strategies derived from the theory of treatment.

Vector of "object relations of knowledge"

This vector applies to the analyst's relationship to his theories and concepts. They have the character of "inner objects" to which an object relationship is established. At work here are unconscious aspects of the relationship to those whom we assume to have conceived of, or adhere to, certain ideas or theories. This includes the affiliations resulting from the system of psychoanalytic training as well as a pluralistic openness or a dogmatic orientation on a theoretical tradition in the institute were one was trained. The transgenerational dynamic is an important element on this vector, when, for example, the rejection or idealisation of the ideas of prior generations of psychoanalysts is involved. Likewise, the attachment relationship to theories is included here.

Vector of "coherence vs. contradiction"

This vector is comprised of the way in which the analyst deals with contradictions theoretically and the implicit assumptions underlying it. It asks the following questions:

- Can the ambiguity in the analytical situation be seen as a progressive moment or does clarity have to predominate?
- Are metaphors or polymorphous concepts used that tolerate, not eliminate contradictions?
- Can creative solutions be found by placing value on polysemie and the elasticity of concepts?

Developmental vector

This vector traces the position the analyst takes in regard to developmental theory in evaluating his patient. It is concerned with the following:

- If and how certain developmental stages are weighted, for instance Oedipal *vs.* pre-Oedipal.
- If one thinks in terms of positions or along a linear, genetically temporal axis.
- Which model conceptions of developmental fixation or maturity are implicitly at work.
- The theoretical significance ascribed to dependency, etc. An implicit theory might, for instance, state something along the lines of "The patient must first become a child again in order to become independent afterwards".

My presentation of the model here will have to remain incomplete, but I hope that despite its abstraction, the illustrations I chose as examples helped to make its main contents clear. The model will have to prove itself in the analysis of analytical session protocols. The aim of such an analysis is not to demonstrate a different or seemingly better understanding of the analytical session, but instead to use the analyst's reactions and interventions to hypothesise about the way in which he was thinking theoretically and which implicit theories he applied either consciously or unconsciously. Such an approach might at first seem unusual because in the discussion of cases we are simply not used to this. In clinical workshops using this method, however, it quickly became apparent that after a phase of adjusting one's approach and shifting the focus of attention, the perception and retrograde study of implicitly operating theories in the analyst's deliberations and interventions led to new approaches to clinical procedure and to a new awareness of the value of theory in everyday practice.

Conclusion

Referencing public theories in psychoanalysis is not sufficient for the task of breaking down the analyst's analytical practice, epistemological approach, and practice-oriented knowledge. As the problem of translating theory into praxis demonstrates, we are not only reliant upon our own subjectivity in the clinical perception of the complex interaction with the patient, that is, of transference and countertransference; rather, this also shapes the clinical–theoretical knowledge with which we work and with which we understand and ascribe meaning to the patient's associations and behaviour. On one hand, theory has a function for the analyst's identity formation, in addition to its attachment or security function, which comes to bear primarily in phases of insecurity and massive emotional turbulence in the interaction with the patient. On the other hand, theory also acquires a central hermeneutic function. Insight in the clinical situation occurs against the backdrop of theoretical application-driven knowledge that can be obtained, but also dismissed again in order to give priority to other, more applicable theory elements with which the clinical material can be better broken down and understood. This process of discovery has the structure of a hermeneutic circle that can be traversed by various theory segments in generating new meaning. We thereby place the patient's statements in a theoretically determined "contextual horizon" (Boesky, 2005), that we can change and that can be expanded in practice. This problem of translating theory into practice calls for a "subjective adaptation of the theory", which then turns into a "therapist-specific (personal) theory" (Thomä & Kächele, 1987). Thomä and Kächele relate this subjective adaptation solely to official theories, above all those of causal and change knowledge. This adaptation is intensified even further by the implicit use of official theories and, even more so, their extensive intermingling with the analyst's private –implicit theories. This applies not only to analysts who work pluralistically, but to all analysts who are convinced that they consistently work according to a theory tied to a particular school of thought. Because many of these private theories are preconscious, and shape therapeutic practice accordingly, the act of rationally elucidating therapeutic practice becomes more difficult and complex. This leads to two questions posed by Irene Cairo as chair of a panel on private theories in the winter meeting of the American Psychoanalytic Association in 2004: "Do analysts do what they say they do?" or, more pointedly, "Do we know what we are doing?" (Silvan, 2005). This line of inquiry is concerned with the correspondence or discrepancy that exists between the conception of the theory we believe to be at the root of our practice, on the one hand, and our actual practice on the other. This question can only be addressed by a subsequent analysis of session material, and even there, only within limits. Using the vector model presented earlier, the analyst's theoretical space, as actualised by the session, can be illuminated along the vectors provided. The various vectors or categories listed above are so multifaceted and complex that only some of the hidden yet determining theoretically informed assumptions, convictions, and frames of reference can be elicited, though they continually influence the application of explicit theories or directly determine our therapeutic practice. This does not mean that our understanding of the patient, our interpretations, and therapeutic practice as a whole cannot be coherent, goal-oriented, and effective. The implicit enrichment and amalgamation of explicit and private theories provide therapeutic practice with an individual colouration and thereby an authenticity, which we know has a therapeutic effect. However, implicit theories can also be so idiosyncratic that they hinder the understanding of the other or even make it impossible.

This peculiarity of psychoanalytic practice, with its use of theories that bear the stamp of the implicit and personal, should not provide grounds for approaching them with scholarly suspicion. Rather, these facts impart its concepts with an elasticity and a fluid field of meaning, which makes it possible for creative analysts to devise an initially implicit expansion or reformulation of a concept, the practical testing and confirmation of which can then lead to the formulation of an explicit and public concept, or to a corresponding partial theory.

Now one final point: if we take private theories into consideration, then we can also arrive at a better understanding of the course of discussions and controversies between analysts with different theoretical and technical positions. All too often these debates are determined by defence strategies in order to defend one's own theories, by the inability to give open-minded consideration to the arguments of other participants, and to accept these arguments in a probative identification. These controversial debates also activate the private, preconscious, and unconscious theory elements of the participants, which are shaped by the personal parameters discussed above. Making these debates productive would necessitate analytical reflection on one's own implicitly operating theories, which could thereby be made explicit.[6]

Notes

1. In a metaphor an idea or image from one realm is conveyed into another, thereby connecting heterogeneous contexts. Looking at these realms together is tied to similarities, whereby the meaning from one area is carried over into another. By way of this structure metaphorical thinking can serve as a catalyst in making visible that which has yet to be conceptualised (Haverkamp, 1983). We use metaphors for the construction of reality and our experience of the world. Seen in this way, metaphors perform a paradigmatic function within thinking and strongly influence perception. On the significance of metaphors for psychoanalysis see Arlow (1979), Buchholz (1998), and Wurmser (1983).
2. "What is psychical is something so unique and peculiar to itself that no one comparison can reflect its nature. The work of psycho-analysis suggests analogies with chemical analysis, but it does so just as much with the intervention of a surgeon or the manipulations of an orthopaedist or the influence of an educator" (Freud, 1919a, p. 161).
3. I cannot go into the findings here of modern infant and child research, which have demonstrated in another way the great significance of mirroring processes for development. These have in turn been made productive for revised theoretical conceptions of the psychotherapeutic process ("mentalisation-based treatment", Allen & Fonagy 2006; Bateman & Fonagy 2004; Fonagy, Gergely, Jurist, & Target, 2002). This is discussed in greater detail in Bohleber (2010).
4. The members of the Working Party are Werner Bohleber, Jorge Canestri (chair), Paul Denis, and Peter Fonagy.
5. I would like to point out here that these vectors are heuristic in nature and should not be reified by ascribing them with an external existence independent of the model.
6. Bernardi used a specific example to conduct an outstanding analysis of such controversies and the reason for their failure, as well as the conditions necessary for their success (2002).

References

Allen, J., & Fonagy, P. (Eds.) (2006). *Handbook of Mentalization-Based Treatment*. Chichester: Wiley.

Almond, R. (2003). The holding function of theory. *Journal of the American Psychoanalytical Association, 51*: 131–153.

Arlow, J. (1979). Metaphor and the psychoanalytic situation. *Psychoanalytic Quarterly, 48*: 363–385.

Bateman, A., & Fonagy, P. (2004). *Psychotherapy for Borderline Personality Disorder. Mentalization-Based Treatment*. Oxford: Oxford University Press.

Bernardi, R. (2002). The need for true controversies in psychoanalysis: the debates on Melanie Klein and Jacques Lacan in the Rio de la Plata. *International Journal of Psycho-Analysis, 83*: 851–873.

Boesky, D. (2005). Psychoanalytic controversies contextualized. *Journal of the American Psychoanalytical Association, 53*: 835–863.

Bohleber, W. (2007). Remembrance, trauma and collective memory. The battle for memory in psychoanalysis. *International Journal of Psycho-Analysis, 88*: 329–352.

Bohleber, W. (2010). *Destructiveness,Intersubjectivity, and Trauma. The Identity Crisis of Modern Psychoanalysis*. London: Karnac.

Britton, R. (1998). *Belief and Imagiantion. Explorations in Psychoanalysis*. London: Routledge.

Buchholz, M. (1998). Die Metapher im psychoanalytischen Dialog. *Psyche-Zeitschrift fur Psychoanalyse und Ihre Anwendunden, 52*: 545–571.

Canestri, J., Bohleber, W., Denis, P., & Fonagy, P. (2006). The map of private (implicit, preconscious) theories in clinical practice. In: Canestri, J. (Ed.): *Psychoanalysis: from Practice to Theory* (pp. 29–43). London: Wiley.

Caper, R. (1997). A mind of one's own. *International Journal of Psycho-Analysis, 78*: 265–278.

Dreher, A. U. (2000). *Foundations for Conceptual Research in Psychoanalysis*. London and New York: Karnac.

Fonagy, P. (2003). Complexities in the relationship of psychoanalytic theory to technique. *Psychoanalytic Quarterly, 72*: 13–48.

Fonagy, P., Gergely, G., Jurist, E., & Target, M. (2002). *Affect Regulation, Mentalization, and the Development of the Self*. New York: Other Press.

Freud, A. (1936). *The Ego and the Mechanisms of Defence*. London: Hogarth.

Freud, S. (1912e). Recommendations to physicians practising psychoanalysis. *S.E., 12*: 109–120. London: Hogarth.

Freud, S. (1919a). *Advances in Psycho-Analytic Therapy. S.E., 17*: 159–168. London: Hogarth.

Green, A. (1975). The analyst, symbolization and absence in the analytic setting (on changes in analytic practice and analytic experience). *International Journal of Psycho-Analysis, 56*: 1–22.

Grossman, W. (1995). Psychological vicissitudes of theory in clinical work. *International Journal of Psycho-Analysis, 76*: 885–899.

Hamilton, V. (1993). Truth and reality in psychoanalytic discourse. *International Journal of Psycho-Analysis, 74*: 63–79.

Hamilton, V. (1996). *The Analyst's Preconscious.* Hillsdale, NJ: Analytic Press.

Haverkamp, A. (1983). *Theorie der Metapher.* Darmstadt: Wiss. Buchgesellschaft 2. Aufl. 1996.

Klein, M. (1946). Notes on some schizoid mechanisms. In: *Diess: Envy and gratitude and other works 1946–1963* (pp. 1–24). London: Hogarth, 1975.

Lacan, J. (1949). Das Spiegelstadium als Bildner der Ichfunktion. In: *Ders: Schriften I,* (pp. 61–70). Olten: Walter, 1973.

Leuzinger-Bohleber, M., & Fischmann, T. (2006). What is conceptual research in psychoanalysis? *International Journal of Psycho-Analysis, 87*: 1355–1386.

Ogden, T. (1997). Reverie and metaphor. Some thoughts on how I work as a psychoanalyst. *International Journal of Psycho-Analysis, 78*: 719–732.

Parsons, M. (1992). The refinding of theory in clinical practice. *International Journal of Psycho-Analysis, 73*: 103–116.

Pulver, S. (1993). The eclectic analyst, or the many roads to insight and change. *Journal of the American Psychoanalytical Association, 41*: 339–357.

Purcell, S. D. (2004). The analyst's theory: A third source of counter-transference. *International Journal of Psycho-Analysis, 85*: 635–652.

Reder, J. (2002). From knowledge to competence. Reflections on theoretical work. *International Journal of Psycho-Analysis, 83*: 799–809.

Reed, G. (2003). Spatial metaphors of the mind. *Psychoanalytic Quarterly, 72*: 97–129.

Sandler, J. (1983). Reflections on some relations between psychoanalytic concepts and psychoanalytic practice. *International Journal of Psycho-Analysis, 64*: 35–46.

Sandler, J., Dreher, A. U., & Drews, S. (1987). *Psychisches Trauma: Ein Konzept im Theorie-Praxis-Zusammenhang.* Frankfurt a.M.: Sigmund-Freud-Instituts.

Sandler, J., Dreher, A. U., & Drews, S. (1991). An approach to conceptual research in psychoanalysis illustrated by a consideration of psychic trauma. *International Review of Psychoanalysis, 18*: 133–142.

Schülein, J. A. (1999). *Die Logik der Psychoanalyse. Eine erkenntnistheoretische Studie.* Gießen: Psychosozial-Verlag.

Schülein, J. A. (2003). On the logic of psychoanalytic theory. *International Journal of Psycho-Analysis, 84*: 315–330.

Sharpe, E. F. (1930). *Collected Papers on Psycho-Analysis.* London: Hogarth, 1950.

Silvan, M. (2005). Panel report "Do we do what we think we do?" Implicit theory in the analyst's mind. *Journal of the American Psychoanalytical Association*, 53: 945–956.

Smith, H. (2003a). Theory and practice: intimate partnership or false connection? *Psychoanalytic Quarterly*, 72: 1–12.

Smith, H. (2003b). Can we integrate the diverse theories and practices of psychoanalysis? *Journal of the American Psychoanalytical Association*, 51(Supplement): 127–144.

Spezzano, C. (1998). The triangle of clinical judgement. *Journal of the American Psychoanalytical Association*, 46: 365–388.

Stein, Y. (2005). *The Psychoanalysis of Science. The Role of Metaphor, Paraprax, Lacunae and Myth*. Brighton: Sussex Academic.

Thomä, H., & Kächele, H. (1987). *Psychoanalytic practice. Vol. 1 Principles*. Berlin: Springer. [Reprint (1994), NJ: Jason Aronson.]

Winnicott, D. W. (1971). *Playing and Reality*. London: Tavistock.

Wurmser, L. (1983). Plädoyer für die Verwendung von Metaphern in der psychoanalytischen Theoriebildung. *Psyche-Zeitschrift für Psychoanalyse und Ihre Anwendunden*, 37: 673–700.

CHAPTER TWO

Do analysts do what they say they do? Clinical material

Dorothy E. Holmes

The three sessions of psychoanalytic case material presented below are from the four times a week (Monday to Thursday) analysis of a late forty-year-old female medical doctor in a field unrelated to mental health. She has been married for twenty-four years and is the mother of two young adult, unmarried daughters recently graduated from college, and a son who is a college-bound high school senior. The patient has been in analysis for two and a quarter years. Before analysis, she had had long-term individual, group, and marital therapy with another clinician who referred her to me. She wanted psychoanalysis because she felt she had reached a plateau in the earlier therapies and had not been able to achieve freedom from recurring feelings of emptiness, self-recrimination, and lack of vitality. In consultation with me she described a drab marriage with profound mutual isolation and suspicion, sparse sex, and hundreds of thousands of dollars of debt stemming from her husband's low level of productivity in his health professional practice and bad business practices. Jointly incorporated, my patient is legally co-responsible for the debt and feels emotionally responsible for it as well.

The patient's history includes parental divorce when she was seven, a hostile relationship with her mother until her mother's death ten years ago, a father lost to her from the age of thirteen until she was in college and just as they were getting reacquainted, he died suddenly. In describing her relationship with her mother, she reported that she vowed to never depend on her mother after her parents' divorce. The vow stemmed from feeling humiliated when she was returned to her mother after briefly being in her father's custody, given that she had chosen to be with him and it did not work out. She pined for her father and maintained minimal contact with him until he moved across country when she was in her early teens. The patient described being raped twice, once at about eight years old by an older neighbourhood boy, and in her mid-teens when she was "date raped". She also reported putting herself in other childhood and teenage situations where she could have been sexually or otherwise exploited again, but was not, such as hitching rides from strangers. She has four siblings, one younger, and all of whom thrive in their professional lives; one, an older sister, is divorced. The others seem to be in good marriages. The patient thrives professionally, has numerous good friends, is in good physical health and is athletic, albeit she tends to be moderately overweight. She is good looking, wears beautiful, custom-made jewellery, but otherwise goes unadorned. She has warm, caring relationships with her children, but tends to get overinvolved with them.

Dr Jones' manner of presentation in analysis tends to be cautious and ponderous at times, and her mood sombre. By her own words, she rarely notices "flowers blooming or the sun shining; I just don't see them". On occasion she displays wry humour which she can enjoy. She comes across as highly intelligent and as high functioning, even with her obvious relational disturbances.

The patient's early transference reaction to me was dominated by her resistance to being dependent on me. This pattern was illustrated by keeping her beeper and telephone on and regularly interrupting sessions to respond. When she herself seemed to grow weary of this approach, she was able to work with me to begin to understand her resistance. We came to understand it as a way of managing her dread of being on the receiving end of inadequate care-giving by others, including me, and the anxiety-making sense of emptiness and absence she associates with relying on anyone else. In addition she continues to work to understand her need to keep a competitive advantage over me, to provide better than I do. In this way she would void her need of me and avoid emotional contact with me as one who, like her mother, would be harsh and condescending, and as such, would add to her sense of herself as bad and unworthy. She realised she had no inner picture of a warm, giving mother who could help her feel that she is a good and lively person. In addition, she has gained some understanding that by setting me aside, she tries to gratify the fantasy of regaining her father and becoming his favourite.

What do I say I do?

I think of this patient as having a strong ego in general. Often, she makes good analytic use of defence analysis, in which a defence is demonstrated to her such that she recognises its arousal in relation to an emerging threatening awareness. The good use she often makes of such an approach is that she further associates in an increasingly complex and revealing way. However, there are times when she is stymied by dread of being "dropped", (i.e., left/abandoned), and consequently being left feeling hollow, empty, and bereft. She does not fragment at these times and does not need supportive interventions, but also cannot do standard defence analysis in that even if she continues to associate, the associations are not rich or evocative; they seem obsessively over-detailed, repetitive, and uninformative. At those times, I use a variety of interpretive approaches (sometimes in displacement): I sometimes emphasise that she fears me as one who will abandon her or drop her. At other times, I speak to her of a barely recognisable longing for me to provide safety for her to be in touch with her true thoughts and feelings. At other times, I interpret the complex ways in which she tries to control or cure that which she loathes or longs for in herself by attending to it in others. I also interpret how and why she and the other (most often her husband) use one another for discharge or containment of painful feelings and self-perceptions and for targets of blame when faced ultimately with sickening frustration and emptiness. I believe these approaches help restore her higher level functioning with which she is then able to do more effective defence analysis. I believe the process material samples some but not all of the approaches mentioned.

Do I do what I say I do?

Three sessions

Session 1: Monday, November 24, 2003

In the sessions preceding this one, the patient had reported with pride that in a complex office management situation in her office, she had not immediately stepped in, but rather had allowed staff to handle it as much as possible. However, in a slip of the tongue, at first she confused the sequence of events, and erroneously presented that she had stepped in too quickly. Thus, her "old" tendency unconsciously gained representation even as she shared about her pride in what she actually had done. At the end of the session immediately preceding this one, I reminded the patient that next week we would meet Monday to Wednesday, given it was Thanksgiving. She asked with refreshing spontaneity, "So, do we meet on Friday?" I noted that the question was said with freshness and spontaneity and wondered if we could consider it when we would not have to rush our consideration of it. She agreed after a brief consideration of her fear of being without a session, lest she feel too alone with painful worry about her current situation.

> *Patient*: I have to put an end to never-ending turmoil. I found out yesterday there's even more financial trouble at the office. Bob (husband) is in even more trouble financially. One of the creditors (for a debt of $400,000 for which my patient is co-responsible) is calling the note due; he has an attorney helping him. (Long silence)
>
> *Analyst*: You refer to the increased trouble as being "at the office", as "Bob's" and that he is being helped by an attorney. In so doing, you give us another chance to understand how you try to manage pain associated with needing help for yourself by keeping the troubles at a distance from you.
>
> *P*: My hands are tied. I can't ask the lawyer for help because he's doing it pro bono. I know I need help, too. He didn't tell me again this time until the eleventh hour because he sees himself as protecting himself from me (reference to husband's accusation that she has weakened him over the years and turned him into an ineffectual person). I feel a strong urge to continue here by defending why I think Bob needs to take responsibility at this point, not me. If he could only initiate some action, like exploring use of retirement funds to help defray debt, then he'd see how much time it takes to address these issues properly, and he'll see that he has some

responsibility. I think I'll propose to him that he take such action though he doesn't listen to me, and I can't change him. (Patient continues in this vein ruminatively for ten minutes.)

A: You hope against hope that you can find a way to revive him as a proper care-taker of himself and you.

Session 2: Tuesday, November 25

P: I still use so much denial and fantasy about Bob. Until you said what you did at the end yesterday, what I really do with him was so far from my conscious mind. Unless I learn to do something else, I have to use denial. Otherwise, I wouldn't be able to sleep at night. Right now I am aware of how much danger I'm in. I did confront him last night about why he waited so long to tell me about this latest development. (Patient began to yawn repeatedly and seemed to be falling asleep.)

A: Denial trying to gather you up in its grip now and have you fall asleep.

P: (Patient chuckled, and said:) I'll think about that, too. When I asked Bob, he said what I knew he would, that he was afraid of my response, that is, that I would just tear him down like I have over the past twenty years. I did get angry, but I told him that by not telling me until the last minute that he was not giving me a fair opportunity to respond with a cooler head. He said he had given me some information earlier about having negotiated a lower monthly payment and I had said, "good". I don't remember that, but I believe him, and it made me realise even more how I'm willing to deny the ongoing reality and bury my head with the slightest suggestion of even a minor change. The lower payment sounded good, but in reality, he hasn't made them. Still, it doesn't excuse him from having not informed me all along that he wasn't keeping up with the rene-gotiated payments. I finally realised I had to confront him because I don't want to end up in court. This is all so very telling. Once again I'm faced with a situation with him that I find incredible—that I don't fully under-stand or want to accept. I tried to review with him that he had given me earlier information and I'd said "good", and that my saying "good" was a way of showing confidence in him, and that he didn't need to be afraid of me. He responded by launching into an attack on me for having made him into a fearful person. He even said that he wasn't responsible for his practice debt, but that I was, and that he wasn't responsible for fixing what I broke. I can't believe that he believes that, but I have to because that's the way he acts. Still, it's hard for me to move on because I still have this fantasy that he is a replacement for my lost father whom I lost three times. Deep down, I feel I have to do anything to make sure it doesn't happen again. To go that far is incredible.

A: You try to handle despairing feelings by disbelieving what's immediately in front of you.

P: Well, the more I witness . . .

A: To say "witness" is a way to remove yourself from your immediate distress and awareness of your painful reality, perhaps to protect the fantasy of recovering your lost dad.

P: I ask myself why do I try so hard to understand him? Is that part of my denial, thinking that he can't believe those things he says about me?

A: There are additional ways to understand it, including that the two of you play out with each other important fantasies of what each is to deliver to the other. When what is wanted isn't forthcoming, rage, rebuke, and blaming come with the disillusionment you feel. In order to try to avoid these reactions which you find abhorrent, you tend to recycle into fantasies of even more desperate fixes.

P: At one point a while back, he said he'd get his retribution. Even as angry as I was last night, I don't know why I'm not totally prepared to move on.

A: I think your husband's explanation may appeal to something in a deep recess of your mind that says if something horrific happens, it *is* someone else's fault. Deep down you believe what he in effect says about himself, "I'm broken but I didn't break myself and so I don't have to fix what's broken". In your day-to-day reality, it is inconvenient and uncomfortable to be the targeted one whose fault it is. At the same time, in that place inside of yourself where you feel responsible for having lost your father and having been an unworthy daughter for your mother, you feel broken, and you want desperately not to be responsible and not to be broken, and you like your husband's message. Those parts of your own mind excuse the pain and inconvenience of being the targeted one, because the whole scenario involves disavowing blame and responsibility as a way of avoiding very painful rebukes and reproaches. You link yourself to his rebuking voice, even as you play out trying to do its bidding by trying to fix everything. Thus, you stay in place right where you are.

Session 3: Wednesday, November 26

P: It scares me, the thought that I benefit from acting in the ways we discussed yesterday.

A: I think we'd be helped to know what you mean by "benefit"?

P: I think it's not in reality. I'm being crushed by what I do, but even in fantasy, or to preserve a fantasy, what I'm doing isn't working. This is very difficult for me; I'm sad; I'm angry, but it's not as awful as I once imagined . . . Last night I was with my kids. I tried to join their joy. We were able to give to each other, though at times, I threatened to withdraw. When I left here yesterday, I called our lawyer myself and instructed him to try to negotiate a lower lump sum payment (*vs.* lower monthly payments that had not been made). The call involved me facing certain realities: my husband's idea that he's going to sell his practice for a big sum is folly; closing my eyes and staying intertwined with him allows me to continue to see him as this broken down person I've got to save. Just so many reruns. I want to pay off the debt, even though I didn't literally create it. It feels good to contemplate being less intertwined with him. I'm learning how to be involved in a different way. My son was impatient and headstrong when I asked what his involvement was with a cruel prank at school. (A group of youngsters had been involved in a macabre act of painting a dead deer and putting it at the front entry of the school. At first the patient was paralyzed and found herself passively agreeing to go the movies with him and her husband who was snubbing her.) When we got there (the movies), I realised I didn't want to be there and that it would-n't be good for me to stay there with them. In the lobby, I told them I had decided I didn't want to stay and that I would make my way home. (Her son protested some and expressed concern for her safety. She assured them she would travel safely.) When my husband and son got home I spoke to my son and told him I had felt hurt by his earlier response. I also said that I realised he may have been reacting to more than my question about the prank given how tense things are at home, and that I'd welcome him telling me more directly what his feelings were.

A: As you were illustrating to him. I'm thinking that there's something in that spirit that we have yet to attend to—the question of your coming in for a Friday session, as you proposed at the end of last week, but have not reintroduced. I've been wondering whether you're doubtful that such an openly stated wish to me would be welcome.

P: I have thought about it, and I realise that I could come and it would be useful. I don't think I doubt it being welcome by you. I know, though, that I push too hard sometimes, that I can't give myself a rest, and that I want to; I think I can be with myself without too much discomfort.

We agreed to meet next on Monday coming.

Commentary on
Dr Holmes' clinical material

Peter Fonagy

Introduction

My task is far from easy. I am required to illustrate the EPF Working Party's framework for implicit theory outlined by Jorge Canestri using the subtle, intriguing, and detailed clinical material presented by Dr Holmes. There is one important rule to this game. I have to avoid the temptation, ever-present for psychoanalytic clinicians, to offer reformulations of the case. We do this without thinking when we supervise publicly or privately. But then I would be illustrating *my* public and private theories rather than exploring those of Dr Holmes. My task here is not to listen to the patient and hear, or pretend to hear, experiences that the analyst indicated no awareness of. In this presentation I am illustrating something rather different, illustrating the act of listening to the analyst, showing understanding of the analytic understanding. I am trying to uncover the analyst's hidden (implicit or preconscious) assumptions that help explain *her* understanding of the patient's material. Thus I am forced to forgo the usual narcissistic gratification of demonstrating my superior understanding of the patient who just happens not to be here to deny my speculations. By contrast, Dr Holmes is very much here and is undoubtedly able to tell me that my explications of her ideas are not only inaccurate and unhelpful but also reveal more about me than they do about her thinking as an analyst.

My aim is to elaborate Dr Holmes' analytic thinking, not her declared model to which she shows explicit allegiance, that again is the more ordinary way we tend to tease apart our clinical work, but rather point to hidden assumptions behind features of her work. This we think about less often and yet it probably differentiates us from each other more radically than explicit theories do. I should qualify my comments by saying that they were written for the purpose of illustrating our framework and not as commentary on Dr Holmes' way of working. Further, that the comments, while sounding general, can pertain only to this patient in these sessions, not Dr Holmes' general way of thinking or even this patient's experience of the analysis outside of the sessions we heard. So with that preamble let me start by elaborating on aspects of Dr Holmes' preconscious theories as codified in our grid.

Dr Holmes' implicit theory

It is evident from Dr Holmes' material that she respects, by and large, our (and by "our" I mean all of our, not just psychoanalysts) *common assumptions concerning intentionality*, the experience of mental states. She tries very hard not to contravene the patient's naïve understanding of mind. There is very little jargon in her interpretive work. For example, "denial" is restated as "disbelieving what is immediately in front of you" and is presented as explained by its logical purpose of avoiding painful recognition. When "projection" and "enactment" are discussed this is not done in terms of an overly concrete image of putting negative aspects of the self into the object. As part of our work we have reviewed process notes where the naïve understanding of mind were dramatically and repeatedly contravened by analysts working in this way. When Dr Holmes explains that the patient's complaint of her husband's tendency to blame others for his misfortune could be seen as her own unconscious sense of placing a broken part of herself into Bob, this complex idea is contextualised with the common-sense notion: 'it is inconvenient and uncomfortable to be the targeted one, whose fault it is'.

Dr Holmes' work is nevertheless quite markedly couched in the *implicit value-system of her culture*. There is much in this analysis that is specific to a North American context that is assumed and unnoticed but might well be the subject of analysis elsewhere. For example, the patient's realistic concern with money, her clear preconscious wish to be treated "pro bono" on the unscheduled Friday session, and the constraints this imposes on her relationship with the analyst might generate quite a different unconscious exchange concerning analytic fees if the analysis was covered by a socialised healthcare system as it might be in Germany. This is what we mean by the "frame of the frame", the preconscious acceptance by both patient and analyst of the cultural frame within which they work. The "frame of the frame" is evident at very low levels of analysis. The patient consistently defers to the analyst as the interpreter of her thoughts. There is a clear implicit expert–client relationship that is appropriately unquestioned by either party.

The preconscious version of public theory which most analysts use is often an eclectic integration of many often incompatible ideas. By contrast Dr Holmes' thinking appears fairly free of influence from ideas borrowed from groups other than the one that trained her. There is actually a remarkable coherence in the preconscious model that is presented. Only in her introduction, in response to the question "what do I say I do?", is there some indication of a move away from an ego psychological model. When Dr Holmes distinguished her patient's two states of mind, (the one free flowing and the other "stymied by dread of being dropped"), there is a hint of having moved away from the conflict interpretation approach. At times, in the patient's stymied state of mind, Dr Holmes says she speaks to her patient of *her longing for the provision of safety* that a true understanding of thoughts and feelings provides. Here we see her in a Winnicotian world where not insight but the provision of kindness and the recognition and acceptance of the longing *is* the interpretation. This "blip", if I see it correctly, is a reaction to a very specific countertransference of having *herself* lost the patient and is probably driven her longing to recover the free flowing "good analysis". In this way she comes to be attuned to the patient's experience of loss.

An aspect of implicit undeclared eclecticism is rooted in the pragmatic, rapid means-to-ends thinking, which we need to engage in to carry on normal clinical work. As I have said already, it is remarkable how free Dr Holmes' material is from our normal tendency to grab the piece of theory that is closest to hand. She is consistent in using the framework of defence analysis. There is little eclecticism, but equally there is little pluralism. In the Monday session the analyst's interpretation of the patient's puzzlement at her need to "understand" her husband implies a theory of role responsiveness that Dr Jones and Bob play out a fantasy, a role play where stepping out of role is met by rage and blaming. This almost implies an object relations understanding of Dr Jones' persistently masochistic devotion to Bob. But then we hear Dr Holmes return to an explanation of her patient's rumination about her partner's motives as merely a way of avoiding the experience of disillusionment that accompanies her psychological dependence on his enactment of total irresponsibility and untrustworthiness. So the obsessiveness about Bob's motives is not seen as satisfying a need but rather an avoidance of unpleasure.

In looking at any analytic work, it is very easy for all of us to find evidence of the wish to avoid using concepts associated with "alien schools of thought". Harold Bloom talks about the *anxiety of influence*. One aspect of the material we just heard struck me as a possible illustration of this. Dr Holmes at times seems determined to avoid the idea of the negative transference. Many British analysts would take the patient's yawning and moving towards sleep not simply as an indication of conflict but as a denigration of the analyst. The episode starts by the patient gratefully acknowledging the analyst's help in the previous session. She goes on to say that if she did not work so hard at denying her feelings of anger then she would not be able to sleep at night. After this she promptly indicates that she is drifting off to sleep. Here I am not suggesting in the slightest that the analyst's way of dealing with this, by using humour to help the patient see that denial was indeed their shared mental state of the moment, was probably not the best intervention to tackle the situation. I am merely hinting that avoiding the concept of *projective identification* leads to a countertransference denial of the analyst's expectable internal state (i.e., the analyst being placed in the role of the one who is "dropped", left/abandoned).

Another aspect of psychoanalytic cultural variability is the implicit understanding of *the polysemic nature* of language, that each word can have multiple meanings dependent on context. In France, for example, you might well expect the patient's comment about not being able to move on because of her perception of her husband as a replacement for her lost father, to be linked to her castration anxiety. Her reference to "deep down" could be interpreted as referring to her genital area and her expressed wish "to make sure it does not happen again" to be an allusion to the unconscious fantasy of castration. In our explorations of technique we have noted the marked absence of *play on words* in modern English language analytic discourse. We wondered if losing this "royal path to the unconscious" may be to do with the historical fact that few of the leading Anglo-American analysts were native English speakers. The equivalent to polysemy in the Anglo-American tradition is poly-object. This is the hidden assumption of interpreting displacements between the person manifestly talked about and another individual, usually an aspect of the experience of the analyst in the transference. In Dr Holmes' material, Bob is a *poly-object* in Monday's session standing for a range of the patient's internal imagos—the failing care-taker, the bearer of the patient's sense of inadequacy, and the rebuking voice of the patient's superego.

Let us now turn from the relatively safe domain of preconscious uses of theory to the more risky domain of *unconscious use of theory*. By the very nature of these ideas it is hard to use clinical material without being both quite speculative and, far more worryingly, highly offensive. Nevertheless it is unarguably the case that we can at times use theory to reduce the experience of the patient's disturbance on us, to explain away what is deeply perturbing about what we learn. In the case of Dr Jones, we are all deeply upset by her mad and maddening determination to continue to support a highly destructive man that threatens, in a very concrete way, the destruction of Dr Jones' own existence. It is perhaps for this reason that we see Dr Holmes try to *normalise* the patient by focusing attention on her depressive anxieties rather than on indications of her more paranoid–schizoid states of mind. For example, the patient starts the Wednesday session by explicitly pointing to her deep anxieties about her own mind: "It scares me", she says, "the thought that I benefit from acting in the ways we discussed yesterday". At this point she is evidently anxious about the degree to which she can step outside reality. The analyst, guided by the principle of clarifying the conflict by elaborating associations, chooses not to address this deep anxiety but asks her: "I think I would be helped to know what you mean by 'benefit'?" By doing this, she subtly legitimises or normalises the patient's experience and sidesteps the patient's momentary awareness of her madness. But I should immediately point out, that in one sense when we bring *any* theory to bear upon clinical material we do this, in part, to reduce our anxiety about facing the fragmented self- or other-directed destructiveness of our patients. Inevitably, theory explains and will serve to normalise the patient.

Unconsciously, psychoanalytic theory also often comes to the protection of the *analyst's narcissism*. For example, interpretative references to the patient's defensiveness in the session can hide our own sense of inadequacy. When we point to the patient's reluctance to talk about something, or even as in the Wednesday session, point to something that the patient has "not yet attended to" (the Friday session—slip), often we project our own sense of being unclear about what is being communicated on to the patient. We often attribute (and interpret) such unconscious reaction to the patient as the patient's state of mind. In this instance, we might speculate that when the patient discusses her ability to assert her preferences about not watching the movie because of the tension at home, she is also referring to the tension in the consulting room about her request for a free extra session. Dr Holmes points to the patient's avoidance of the issue. In focusing on the patient's scotomisation she may be overlooking her own avoidance of the patient's conflict about asserting her independence and requesting that her concern about the long gap between the Wednesday and Monday sessions be acknowledged.

Moving beyond the topographical vector, the next aspect of implicit theories discussed in Canestri's paper concerned *conceptual issues*. Perhaps the most central aspect here concerns *clinical generalisations* implicit in our thinking about specific patients. Dr Homes' material illustrates several clinical generalisations: that she does not believe in self-disclosure but is happy to speak in the first person ("I was wondering . . .") to support reflection; she considers the external world as important as the transference (there is reference to the patient's "day-to-day" reality); she believes that explanations related to her view of the unconscious determinants of patient's behaviour can be helpful to her; she accepts the occasional need to ask her patient for clarification and that this will not disrupt the flow of free association; and that it might be enough to make an allusion to an unconscious process that is ongoing rather than having to spell out fully the fantasies involved (allusion to the Friday session on Wednesday).

In other ways theory can serve *as countertransference* even in the most coherent of theoretical views. The analyst applies a theory as a reaction to how the patient is at that moment. Thus Dr Homes' countertransference (or more simply experience of her patient) allows her to assume the patient wishes to be analysed. Thus there is room for a concept such as a therapeutic alliance with her. It is clear in the way she interacts with Dr Jones, that she is not made to feel and does not need to assume that the patient is actively precluding an authentic dialogue that could only be accessed by constantly interpreting defences against it, and so on.

Dr Holmes' *implicit theory of change* appears to have at its core the idea that knowledge of the way unconscious mechanisms can function will lead to permanent change. Far less in the foreground, but also present, is the idea that putting the patient in touch with the feelings she is trying to split off will benefit her. Thus, her wish to revive Bob as the proper care-giver, to exclude despairing feelings from her consciousness, and to regain contact with the sense of herself as an unworthy daughter to her mother are feelings assumed to be excluded by a process of repression or splitting that the analysis can overcome. Further, there is an assumption that if the infantile roots of her maladaptive attitudes to her marital situation could be identified, this will liberate her adaptive capacities sufficiently for her to find a more appropriate point of equilibrium in this difficult situation. In the material presented, Dr Holmes avoids personification of the non-conscious parts of her patient's mind; she talks about "deep recesses" and "deep down", but not of an anthropomorphised unconscious. There is an implicit view of the mind as layered. The only exception to this was Dr Holmes' reference to the "rebuking voice" that presumably anthropomorphises the superego. The drift is towards a wish to liberate and integrate the ego by defining and delimiting its maladaptive aspects through conscious insight.

A brief final word about our *action vector*; how does implicit theory emerge from the style of analytic work. It is clear, for example, that Dr Holmes does not believe (as many French psychoanalysts do) that to be ambiguous or enigmatic can be helpful. The style also distinguishes Dr Holmes from object relationship or interpersonalist psychoanalysis. Most of the wording of her interpretations is what we have called "one-person-wording" rather than "two-person wording". Interpretations are targeted at the patient's mental states of hope, despairing feelings, avoidance, fantasy, etc. They are not interactional in the sense of identifying mental states as arising from interpersonal interactions (between patient and analyst or patient and object). For example, in the final interpretation of the Tuesday session, when Dr Holmes describes the complex unconscious fantasy that underpins her patient's irrational commitment to her destructive husband, she states: "You are stuck with your current relationship with your husband because you unconsciously agree with his sentiment that if you are not responsible for the feeling of being broken than you do not have to do anything about it. So by accepting his logic and his example, you are yourself relieved of the harsh self-blame that is already inside your head". We see here that she is careful to avoid attributing mental states to anyone of the "actors" in the scenario (Bob, patient's mother and father) except the patient. Bob's state of mind is inferred but not spelled out from a direct quote from him (in Dr Jones' report). The implicit one person psychology can permeate the style of interpretation. The formulation that is communicated is a comprehensive rendition to the patient of what the analyst has in mind about the mental world of her patient. It is not a depiction of individuals causing feelings to arise in each other either through inter-actions in "day-to-day" reality or in the consulting room.

Conclusion

Did we go beyond Dr Holmes's reply to the rhetorical question "What do I say I do?" The answer is probably, in this case, not very far. The reason for this is of course could be twofold. First, and most impor-tant, is that Dr Holmes appears to work unusually firmly linked to a single, well-established, and coherent set of theoretical psychoanalytic ideas. Second, is that, as is usual for such debates, we were exploring not what Dr Holmes does, but rather what she remembers having done and is able to report to us. Whether further implicit theories would surface from studying more comprehensive accounts of her work remains, for the moment, an open question.

What I hope we were able to illustrate was the intrinsic interest and value in fully exploring the analyst's mind at work. So much of what we do is driven by poorly thought out half-intended actions, many of which are unlikely to fit any decent definition of analytic interpretation. Yet interpretation of our patient's actions is indeed what we do simply by virtue of the fact that any action that we perform with our patients implies to them (and to those studying our actions) an understanding of the experience that we have just been exposed to. This mostly will not be an analytic understanding but a simple human one. Its ordinariness however does not preclude the possibility that it is richly imbued and informed by our clinical experience collected in this setting over years of hard earned struggle. It is harvesting the fruits of these millions of clinical hours of encounters, very little of which is codified in extent theories, which the efforts of the EPF working party is all about. For us to do this however, our first step has to be a comprehensive and atheoretical reporting of the analytic process, so the full complexity of our thinking and experience can emerge and be subject to study.

CHAPTER THREE

Theoretical and clinical reflections on public and private theories

Charles Hanly

The idea of hidden implicit theorising in psychoanalysis is akin to Collingwood's (1946) idea that contemporary historians implicitly express but do not state the latent assumptions of their own epoch when they write the histories of earlier epochs. Hegel (1837) had already announced in his *Lectures on the Philosophy of History* that the owl of Minerva only takes flight at the end of an era. The history of an era can only be written after it is over. The epistemological implication of these German idealist ideas is that when history moves beyond narrative to explanation, the ideas required for the construction of explanations will impose a selection from among the facts made available by the narration that will, unbeknownst to the historian, shape his account of the past into a mirror that will reflect the implicit, unacknowledged value and ideological premises of his own age, which he must inevitably bring to the explanatory task. Hegel's history actually illustrates this epistemological predicament in the writing of history. Hegel was aware of his idealised version of the nineteenth century Prussian parliamentary monarchy that enabled him to "find" in history the hidden purpose of its dialectically inevitable realisation through the conflicts and travail of the eras that preceded it. What Hegel did not grasp was the implicit nationalist, religious, racist values, and ideology that obscured their handiwork behind the ecstatic idea that in the Prussian state was to be found the sublime end of humankind's struggle to incarnate collective and individual human perfection. At the end of Hegel's era, from the perspective of the history of the twentieth century, we are able to see with painful clarity that to which Hegel's nationalist enthusiasm left him purblind.

The psychoanalytic project we are exploring here attempts to improve on historiography, as understood by Collingwood and Hegel, by articulating the current unacknowledged private theories of analysts that are expressed implicitly in their clinical work but are not recognised and articulated explicitly in their publications. Analysts may be using theoretical and technical ideas in their clinical work that differ in varying degrees from the ideas they consciously hold. In principle, the variations can run from the contradictory to the consistent, but nevertheless remain unacknowledged, as such, in the analyst's published theoretical reflections. An implicit contradiction would appear in the work of a classical analyst who explicitly acknowledges drives but who clinically interprets castration anxiety in his male patients as though it were caused only by competitively, abusive fathering aided and abetted by seductively preferential mothering, or by passive, obsequious fathering aided by enviously threatening mothering. Another implicit unacknowledged variation would occur in an analyst whose "official" theoretical position did not acknowledge projective identification but who, nevertheless, sensitively monitored her affective responses to her patient's transferences as a means of forming an impression of her patient's unconscious affect laden phantasies by attending to her own affective responses to the patient. Yet another example would be the analyst who in publications was an advocate of the death instinct but who in clinical interpretations regularly interpreted manifestations of aggressive oral rage as consequences of experiences of traumatic frustration by the mother during the oral stage of development.

This view implies that a training analyst may, in good faith, supervise a candidate according to the official doctrine he/she holds to be true, without letting him/herself or the candidate know what and how he/she actually thinks and practices clinically, even though the supervising analyst may impart clinical vignettes from her/his practice as illustrations which will be selected because they agree with the analyst's "official" theory. It implies that an analyst may engage in controversy as a member of one school of thought with members of other schools of thought advancing theoretical arguments, recommending interpretations, and citing clinical data all the while ignoring certain subtle respects in which his/her operative clinical thinking and interpretive practice has adopted aspects of ideas he publicly opposes. History offers us the examples of the over-heated rhetoric of the twentieth century cold war that obscured a process of reciprocal economic imitation in the contestants, and of the nineteenth century English parliamentary debates in which winning the battle to extend the franchise by means of the Reform Bill of 1832 obscured the continued control of parliament by the aristocracy and landed gentry. It would not surprise us then, to find that psychoanalytic writing and clinical practice might sometimes also bear this same duality.

But if history must go wrong when it seeks to be explanatory, what could persuade us that psychoanalysis can do better? What if there is an inescapable tangle of implicit, unacknowledged, and unexamined assumptions not only in historical explanation, but also in psychoanalytic explanation which is, after all, a species of historical and biographical explanation? What if the analyst who "discovers" implicit theorising in the work of a colleague is him/herself inevitably deploying, without being aware of doing so, his/her own unconscious implicit theorising? If such epistemic tangles must occur in the theoretical thinking of analysts, as subjectivists would claim, must they not also occur in the meta-theoretical thinking of analysts as well? Bias of thought cannot be escaped simply by moving from one level of thought to another. These questions bring us face to face with the current controversy of psychoanalytic epistemology between those who advocate a postmodern version of an ancient subjective idealism and those who adhere to scientific realism. If one assumes that this kind of cognitive entanglement, forming a barrier to objectivity about unacknowledged theories implied by the practice of analysts, is inevitable and inescapable, one is logically committed to postmodern epistemic subjectivism. If one assumes that these subjectivity producing cognitive entanglements can, but need not, occur and when they occur can be overcome, one holds the epistemological position of critical realism. Critical realism lays no claim to infallibility, certainty, or absolute knowledge. It acknowledges all of the difficulties that lie in wait for the investigator who seeks to formulate the theories implied by an analyst's technical orientation and interpretive activities. These difficulties run the gamut of all the usual potentially disturbing subjective influences on the enquiring analyst's capacities for observation and thought, from philosophical and theoretical investments through personality to nationality and culture. "Critical" in "critical realism" refers to a capacity for self-criticism informed by the psychoanalytic understanding of the subjective sources of observational and conceptual error, strengthened by analysis, sustained and improved by self-analysis or by further analysis. In these investigations we need not concede defeat before we begin even if the best we can achieve is corrigible fallibility. There is no doubt about the need for doubt. Nevertheless, we need to be clear about what is doubtful and how doubtful it has to be. What is hidden in the human psyche is not easy to know, but psychoanalysis can teach us what evidence to look for and what explanations of what we see are most probable. No scientific enquiry worth its salt was ever easy. Psychoanalysis need not take second place to history as an explanatory enquiry. It may even legitimately aspire to the epistemic status of great literature by being good enough science (Hanly, 2007).

The Hegelian comparison also raises the question: what if there is a subterranean synthetic process going on out of which, one day, an integrated theory will emerge that will, at last, let the charismatic lions lie down with the charismatic lambs; Hegel's (1837) cunning of history (the tendency of history to bring about unintended consequences) having found its way into the consciously unintended cunning of clinical experience. The question is worth considering, even if history has falsified both Hegel's dialectic of ideas and Marx's dialectic of economic conditions. However, psychoanalysis has taught us not to expect scientific wisdom from unconscious processes. The instinctual unconscious is more likely to produce coherent delusions than reality tested theories. Bohleber makes it clear that no such Hegelian teleological synthesis is secretly at work unconsciously in the clinical work of psychoanalysts, although such processes might well be at work preconsciously. And it would be strange indeed, if the theory of a clinical discipline that had been originally forged out of clinical experience did not advance as a consequence of clinicians finding in their treatment of patients that some of their ideas need revision, and find themselves making observations that would warrant revision. This would be yet stranger, given that the founder of the theory himself

developed the theory out of four major revisions and related technical improvements (Hanly, 2005). And, it would not be in the least
surprising, if it could be shown that Freud was using the structural
model clinically before he formulated it theoretically. Well before *The
Ego and the Id*, Freud was clinically exploiting an idea of the resistance
to interpretations caused by the narcissism of conscience, ". . . in
general it is far harder to convince an idealist of the inexpedient location of his libido than a plain man whose pretensions have remained
more moderate" (1914c, p. 95). But along with these promising possibilities Bohleber justly states that,

> a somewhat broader consideration . . . makes apparent that the further
> development of concepts was by no means always as continuous and
> organic . . . the continuous stretching of the meaning-space of concepts
> did not automatically lead to ever increasing integration of clinical
> phenomena; instead, some clinical insights were also lost and elimi-
> nated from the conceptual meaning-space". (p. 10)

How could it be otherwise, when unanalysed and unresolved conflict,
trauma, and grandiosity in the analyst is much more likely to lead to
a failure of psychoanalytic observing and understanding, resulting in
unreliable idiosyncratic ideas, whether private or published, rather
than in durable innovative improvements in psychoanalytic theory
and technique sustained by clinical evidence? In so far as theoretical
advances originate in unconscious thought processes, these processes,
like the listening of the Freud's (1912e) telephone analogy, must be the
handiwork of the preconscious rather than the instinctual unconscious
(Hanly, 1992). There are two important although difficult tasks of the
EPF study that Dr Bohleber's distinction identifies: the first is to
discriminate between constructive innovations and developments in
psychoanalytic theory and technique on the one hand, and the polarities of inflexible, closed adherence to received ideas and a restless
questing after originality on the other; the second is to shed light on
their conditions and causes.

The following argument offers a general orientation toward these
difficulties. The topographical model offers a differentiation between
the dynamic instinctual unconscious driven by repressed memories
and phantasies that are gratification seeking by any available means,
highly vulnerable to wishful thinking and even to delusional observing and thinking, and the economic preconscious unconscious the

pleasure seeking of which is subject, however imperfectly, to the reality principle, to evidence and logic. The distinction made here is similar to the contrast in clinical work between selected fact and overvalued idea described by Britton and Steiner (1994). Philosophical evidence of the preconscious functioning of logic is found in the ability of people to think logically without being able to articulate verbally and become explicitly conscious of the rules of valid reasoning. The rules of logical reasoning are unconsciously and, for the most part, validly at work in human thought processes. Were it not so, only logicians would be able to think logically. Fortunately, we follow the rules of validity, for example, of the logic of classes, without having to know what they are. (This state of affairs also gives rise to the irony of Hegel and Marx proudly announcing their adherence to dialectical logic using the syllogistic logic we all preconsciously share to justify their deviation from it. If you disagree with this observation, try a thought experiment; construct an exposition of dialectical logic employing dialectical logic.) Fallacious thinking is much more likely to involve material fallacies (breaches of rationality e.g., *argumentum ad hominem, ad baculum, ad verecundiam, ad misericordiam*, etc.) than formal fallacies (breaches of logical rules e.g., affirming the consequent of a hypothetical syllogism or failing to distribute one of the connecting terms in a categorical syllogism). It is probable that the polarities of inflexible adherence to ideas and the restless questing after originality at any price, including the loss of reality, are vulnerable to the primary process thinking of the instinctual unconscious and of hyper-narcissistic conscience. Psychologically, material fallacies bear the stamp of primary process thought activity. And it is probable that constructive, durable developments of theory and technique will be the handiwork of the synthetic activities of preconscious secondary processes of observing, remembering, and thinking submitted to the evidence of observation and subject to logic.

There is a romantic, somewhat mystical, even magical, trend in psychoanalytic technical thinking that is evident in the misunderstanding of Freud's (1912e) telephone metaphor. Freud is himself to some extent responsible for the misunderstanding because he did not specify the meaning of "unconscious" in his statement and his late reflections on telepathy could easily be used to read back into the metaphor a meaning that he had not intended. The metaphor was stated in terms of the topographical model in which there are two types of unconscious processes: those that derive from repression which are subject to primary process thought, and those that derive from the need of consciousness for concentration of attention in order to know perceptually or conceptually. In the metaphor, the unconscious of the analyst refers to the analyst's preconscious, funded as it is with more or less tested theoretical ideas that can be made available for further reality testing, and the patient's preconscious in so far as it is at work associatively finding expressions and creating derivatives of dynamically unconscious processes demanding satisfactions that are unacceptable to the analysand's conscience. The preconscious synthetic activities of the analyst should be governed by the rules of deductive and inductive reasoning the results of which can be made available for explicit logical consideration. To the extent that they are not, the analyst is vulnerable to errors of observation, memory and thought (Hanly, 1992). It can be shown that Freud's major modifications of psychoanalytic theory and technique are the expression of such preconscious secondary thought activity. In addition to the influence of inductive inferences, one can show the role of deductive reasoning implicitly at work in Freud's clinical and theoretical thinking (Hanly, 2005).

Bohleber, drawing upon Sandler (1983), describes the private theory of the experienced analyst as an "amalgam of public theory elements and one's own clinical experience, as well as personal life experience, individual values, and private philosophies or ideologies" (p. 8). This description raises some questions. Are the official theory elements personally selected in the sense that different analysts may favour different collections of public theory elements? If so, may not these public theory amalgams be more or less idiosyncratic? Other analysts may prefer to contribute to an independently existing more unified theory. Does this choice avoid idiosyncrasy only by failing to integrate new ideas and to explore the usefulness of new hypotheses? Dr Fonagy, if I understand him correctly, differentiates between eclecticism and pluralism. Eclecticism may be pragmatic but is indiscriminately and unreflectingly ad hoc—a bricoleur's tool chest of consistent and inconsistent ideas on the negative side of Dr Bohleber's key distinction; while pluralism is pragmatic, discriminating, reflective, and more consistent. Pluralism requires a reasoned discrimination that is not based on an idiosyncratic idea or personal value, but an idea based on reasons (evidence) to which the analyst submits his credulity and which can be impartially recommended to others. A third possibility would be a comprehensive, integrated theory with generally accepted methods for its further development. That a comprehensive theory will be inevitably generated, in Hegelian fashion, out of the dialectics of existing psychoanalytic schools is no more likely than the arrival of Marx's utopia in the near future. But perhaps the English poet Browning was right "our grip should exceed our grasp" despite how difficult it is to imagine a comprehensive theory with which the members of existing schools could be satisfied.

We may reasonably suppose that the public theory elements of a private theory are likely to be the least, if at all, idiosyncratic, because they have been subjected to years of evaluation by many analysts; whereas, the elements deriving from "personal life experience, individual values, and private philosophies or ideologies" (Bohleber, p. 8) would be most vulnerable to individual preference because they would not have been tested in this way. These individual factors may interfere with the capacity for non-judgmental evenly suspended attention clinically and they may motivate theoretical preferences. But this supposition may also mislead. New observations and explanations rely upon individuality even though the pursuit of originality and novelty can all too easily devolve into idiosyncrasy. Dr Bohleber's exposition makes it clear how complex the task of theory building is in psychoanalysis and what open mindedness one needs to bring to the work of studying it. The EPF schema he describes seems well enough designed to take these complexities and difficulties into account.

Perhaps the cardinal feature of the schema is its theory neutrality. This feature raises the question of what theory neutral criteria are available for an inquiry into private and public psychoanalytic theorising. I would like to explore this question a little further. Logic immediately springs to mind because its rules are formal and do not depend at all on the content of descriptive observation statements and on the conclusions (theories) derived inferentially from them. By applying the rules of propositional logic, for example, the principle of non-contradiction, a private theory can be assessed for its coherence. Elements that are in contradiction with or contrary to any of the coherent elements will be idiosyncratic within the total amalgam in the sense of being inconsistent with it. Contradictions may occur in the plurality of public theories as well, as in certain of the elements of

Kleinian theory as compared with Freudian theory, self-psychology, relational psychoanalysis, etc. Contradictions can find their way into the relation between theory and practice. For example, an analyst may explicitly hold a theory of psychic functioning that finds the gratification by the analyst of a conflict generating need in the patient to be counter-therapeutic and may, nevertheless, preconsciously respond with extra-interpretive solicitousness and caring to a patient's defensive regressed need for mothering. In this case, consistency would require a modification of either the clinical theory or the clinical practice. In this way, a formal logical requirement, without in the least pre-empting the outcome, can set in motion an enquiry into the place of the analyst's affective responsiveness in therapy. Clinically, a contradiction in a patient's associations is a reliable indicator of the activity of an unconscious conflict. A contradiction between an analyst's theory and his practice also indicates an intellectual conflict and, perhaps, an unconscious conflict as well, if a resolution of the intellectual conflict is illusive. This use of logic can open up links to be explored between our personalities, our thinking, and our practice.

A second logical criterion consists of employing rules of inference to explore the dependency of the elements that make up a theory, whether public or private. In this way, we can determine what elements are fundamental and what elements can be derived from them. We can also make clear what hypotheses are essential to the explanation of important phenomena. For example, the hypothesis of drive development is essential to the Freudian/Kleinian explanation of moral conscience. A theory that does not include the drive hypothesis is logically required to construct a different explanation of moral anxiety and conscience and its motivating influence on defensive processes. For example, relational psychoanalysis has an obligation to explicitly adopt some form of the common sense notion of how a child acquires its conscience from its parents and their substitutes.

Exploring inferential relations can also help us identify how private our private theories are. If any of the elements of a private theory are private in the sense of not derivable from public theory elements, their privacy does not consist merely of unconscious borrowing, but will have been innovative. In the following example, I would like to illustrate the role of contradiction as a gadfly for theorising and of inference as its means. We can imagine Fairbairn, while still adhering to a public model made up of Freudian/Kleinian

elements, finding himself taking an increasing interest in object relations at the edges of his observation and thinking, perhaps with some
distress and doubt about the primacy of instinct and the pleasure
principle in Freud's theory as though, for him, these premises were
dehumanising and hedonistic ñ a reaction to Freud's drive theory
somewhat akin to critical reactions to Darwin's natural selection. We
can then imagine a gradual transition taking place in which the importance of object relations became increasingly central to his clinical
work until he formalised his "relational turn" in his redefinition of
libido as "not primarily pleasure-seeking, but object-seeking"
(Fairbairn, 1946, p. 31). This redefinition has become a first principle
of relational psychoanalysis. Theoretical pluralism derives from
initially private ideas that are in contradiction with public theories
because if these ideas are fundamental enough, they can become the
underlying assumptions of a new coherent public theory as its implications are progressively worked out. The new theory will have its
own technical recommendations. Dr Bohleber has referred us to the
various and variable individual factors at work in the adoption of the
new theory by individual analysts.

There are other formal criteria such as inferential richness (e.g., a
theory's applicability to other bodies of knowledge) and its explanatory power: for example, its ability to account for apparently disparate
phenomena; as in Freud's uncovering of a common motivational
mechanism in neurotic symptoms, dreams, and parapraxes; as in
Newton's gravitational explanation of the behaviour of projectiles, the
motions of the planets in the solar system and tides in the earth's
oceans; and as in the Fisher/Trivers hypothesis of gender economic
inequalities in the evolution of gender differentiation (Dawkins, 2003).
Initially, a private hypothesis may involve an expansion or a contraction of the explanatory scope of a public theory. This criterion takes
us toward epistemological criteria inherent in the protocol: questions
of evidence for interpretations, the role of theory in the construction
of interpretations and the consideration of how well a private or
public theory tallies with the psychic reality of our patients, and how
effective is its method of therapeutic intervention. As difficult as these
sorts of questions are, they only call for enquiries of the kind that our
analytic conscience daily demands of us in our clinical practices.

I hope that I have already sufficiently underlined the beneficially
theory neutral, meta-theoretical perspective of Dr Bohleber's exposi-

tion. As we leave the more macroscopic level of theory for the more microscopic level of clinical material and its interpretation, can this perspective be maintained? Will Dr Fonagy's private theories distort his analysis of Dr Holmes' analytic work with her patient? Will my private theory disturb my analysis of Dr Fonagy's analysis? If these questions seem to be perilously close to opening a door to an infinite regress it is because they are. The same question can be raised about your assessment of my assessment of Dr Fonagy's assessment of Dr Holmes' clinical material and then about your assessment of my assessment and so on ad infinitum. We avoid the regression by identifying and reflecting on the clinical evidence as impartially as we can and by submitting the result to the best judgment of others.

Dr Fonagy finds that Dr Holmes really does put American Freudian theory to work in her practice coherently and consistently without much evidence of elements drawn from other theories or from innovations of her own. (I prefer the designation of "American Freudian theory' rather than "ego psychology" because I think that it better expresses the current main stream theory in the US that Dr Holmes espouses.) Accordingly, I shall discuss some of the issues raised by Dr Fonagy from the perspective of ideas in transition as analysts search for a better understanding of their patients. These are ideas that may fall, with all the uncertainty it involves, between consistency and contradiction. For this purpose I propose some meta-theoretical descriptive categories that may be useful including: overlapping of ideas (e.g., different terms denoting the same process), assimilation of ideas, modification or redefinition of major terms involving explanatory expansion or contraction, elaboration (explanatory expansion), different use of ideas, evidence for ideas, and the testing of ideas. One purpose of these categories would be to explore the integrative theoretical processes to which Bohleber refers in clinical work. I shall use them to explore the inter-face between Holmes' American Freudianism and the greater pluralism of the approach Dr Fonagy brings to his commentary on her work by reflecting on some of the issues he has raised.

Dr Fonagy finds Dr Holmes' work lacking not in an undesirable eclecticism but in a desirable pluralism; a pluralism that could involve a private amalgam including a Winnicottian use of the provision of kindness as interpretation, a greater readiness to recognise and interpret implicit negative transferences, the employment of the concept of projective identification, an appreciation of the impact of projective identification on countertransference, perhaps, the use of interpretations in a two-person language, and a greater preparedness to recognise paranoid–schizoid states of mind. It is worth noting that, with the possible exception of the provision of kindness as interpretation and paranoid–schizoid states of mind (if the paranoid–schizoid position is implied) these elements are consistent with Dr Holmes' American Freudian theory and practice, and with her focus in these sessions on the analysis of defences. The basic logical problem of eclecticism is that it tolerates explanatory discontinuity even at the unacceptable cost of contradiction and lack of coherence. However, pluralism must, at least, satisfy the same logical criteria and avoid explanatory redundancy (Hanly, 1983).

It seems to me that there might be somewhat more overlapping of ideas with other theories in Dr Holmes' work in these sessions than Dr Fonagy recognises. Dr Fonagy quite rightly stresses the importance of masochism in the patient. It is my impression that, although Dr Holmes does not use the term, and although one could not infer her theory of masochism from the material of these sessions, her interpretations suggest that she is attentive to the patient's masochism. Although she does not explicitly interpret it, she interprets the defences that sustain it in her relation with her husband. These interpretations seem to help her to at least "contemplate being less intertwined with him" within the analytic process even if not in her relationship with him. The question of need arises in the context of the patient's masochistic attachment to her husband. Dr Fonagy ventures that the patient's "obsessiveness about Bob's motives is not seen as satisfying a need but rather an avoidance of unpleasure" (p. 33). But is not this avoidance of the pain of her relations with her parents also a need that is powerful enough to maintain the defences that make her prefer the lesser pain of her masochistic attachment to her husband? Perhaps there is more overlapping of ideas here than at first meets the eye. But even if so, the material does not provide a basis for identifying similarities and differences in the theoretical understanding of masochism—at least not to this observer. I can find no decisive evidence in the material as to whether or not Dr Holmes explicitly or implicitly adheres to Freud's theory of primary masochism and the death instinct or has rejected it publicly and privately.

There is no evidence of an overlapping of a Winnicottian "provision of kindness and the recognition and acceptance of the longing" (Fonagy, p. 32) treated as interpretation by Dr Holmes, but I think that there may be a limited proximity. Dr Holmes reports that "I speak to her of a barely recognisable longing for me to provide safety for her to be in touch with her true thoughts and feelings" (Holmes, p. 25). An American Freudian analyst can consistently hold that an implicit provision of kindness can facilitate the effectiveness of interpretations and strengthen the therapeutic alliance and, as well, that sometimes the analyst's provision of kindness can be counter-productive. For example, if there were hidden sadistic impulses in the patient toward her husband along with her masochism, expressions of kindness could be confusing to her and intensify guilt. The analyst's responses would need to be influenced and modulated by the understanding that guides her interpretations. In that case, the therapeutic usefulness of the analyst's affective responses would depend on the adequacy of her understanding. Rather than making a non-verbal provision of kindness to the longing she perceives in her patient, Dr Holmes interprets it. There is some evidence that Dr Holmes' interpretations do make the patient feel safer by being better able to be in touch with her own feelings and thoughts.

Thus, there are these three theoretical possibilities: 1) the analyst's affects can be interpretive in and by themselves; 2) when they are appropriately responsive, they can be therapeutically useful but not interpretive; 3) they are neither interpretive nor therapeutically useful and need to be neutralised to avoid their interfering bias in the pursuit of sound interpretations. Rationalist philosophers (e.g., Spinoza (1677) thought that affects, other than neutralised *amor intellectus dei*, disturb the clarity and distinctness of thought) have held the third view but I do not think any psychoanalysts have. Freud's dispassion was aimed at fastidious sentimentality and idealisation and not at sympathy as such. The second view is the one that I would attribute to American Freudians. One and two are, at least, somewhat more proximate than opposite, as is the case with the first and third possibilities, although one and two remain inconsistent and could not both be included in a unified theory without significant definitional modifications.

Returning then to Dr Bohleber's distinction, has Dr Fonagy's Winnicott stretched the meaning of interpretation too far by making affective responsiveness interpretive and, thereby, risking the loss of two important distinctions in American Freudian clinical theory: 1) the distinction between insight and feeling, and; 2) the distinction between situations in which an affective response such as kindness is beneficial therapeutically and those in which it is not? Or, have American Freudians preserved a too narrow view of the therapeutic role of affects, in which case, could they not benefit from adopting Winnicott's idea? Integration could be achieved on the Winnicottian side by narrowing the definition of interpretation. Integration could be achieved on what I have called the American Freudian side by enlarging the definition of interpretation. In my view a decisive consideration as to whether or not these ideas of interpretation can be integrated into a consistent theory (public or private) would be whether or not the distinction between useful and harmful affects could be retained.

Dr Fonagy points out that in these sessions Dr Holmes uses "one-person-wording" rather than "two-person-wording". What I will have to say next will reveal clinical consequences of my own theoretical and philosophical investments, which I have sketched above. Dr Holmes' focus is upon her patient and not on a putative patient who is the creation of their dyadic interaction. Although this aspect of Dr Holmes' work can be located in the action vector, it is rooted in some philosophical, theoretical, and technical implicit assumptions that are consistent with her American Freudianism. In terms of the implicit philosophical premise, Dr Holmes is acting as would a critical realist who assumes that the patient brings herself and her traumatic and conflicted life to the analysis. She strives to make her interpretations tally with the psychic and external realities of this epistemologically independent real person. Accordingly, she makes a continuing assessment of how the analytic process is going and, by implication, the soundness of her interpretations by monitoring the way in which the patient responds to and uses them, and what effect they have on the patient's functioning in the analysis and in the world. She allows that the patient, quite on her own, becomes "stymied by dread of being 'dropped'" (Holmes, p. 25), seeing this not as an artefact of their interaction but as something expectable when there are memories of trauma and conflicts that will be revived by the work of the analysis, when it is working, and that will also interfere with the work by generating resistances. Thus Dr Holmes has a pragmatic handle and a perspective on the process that is being generated by the patient and facilitated by the analyst without whom it could not occur. I may be mistaken, but it is my impression that these ideas are broadly shared by Kleinian and European Freudian analysts.

However, explicit indications of countertransference are not apparent in this record. The material includes transference symptoms (e.g., the patient's sleepiness) that could give rise to countertransference. The way Dr Holmes deals interpretively with these symptoms strikes me as a rather robust, steady response to the patient's threatened abandonment of the analyst and the analysis in sleep. In the material, there is no evidence of using countertransference to gain information about the patient. But only Dr Holmes can help us on this point. With this possible exception, to which I will shortly return, I would suppose that Dr Fonagy shares this view of Dr Holmes' way of working, that is, that her one-person-wording does not result from blinkers, but from a thought-out and tested point of view with methodological implications deriving from natural observational science and thought that fully acknowledges that the analytic dyad involves two persons. This acknowledgement does not logically imply that the dyad is co-creative.

Dr Fonagy also makes it clear that Dr Holmes' patient-centred focus includes the object relations that are important in her patient's life. She follows the patient's associations where they lead and when they lead to her relation to her husband, as they often do in these sessions, she interprets the defensive processes at work in the patient that influence her experience of her husband, of herself in relation to him, and her masochistic clinging to him. I see no evidence of any need at work in Dr Holmes to herd her patient toward transference interpretable associations or to attempt transference interpretations on material in a forced or artificial way. The theoretical implication of this mode of therapeutic action is an acceptance of a Freudian constitutional/drive development/object relational etiological model. Dr Holmes is not a relational psychoanalyst. She equitably follows the significance that the patient's free associations attach to drive and object relation factors at any time without consigning precedence, in principle, to either. The only link that I can see with relational psychoanalysis is the importance that the analysis of object relations assumes in the three sessions. But that is surely watered wine to relational theorists. At the same time, it is apparent from the case material that Dr Holmes is not an exclusionary drive/defence analyst; she naturally and steadfastly refuses the straw man some European and American analysts like to substitute for American Freudian analysis.

Next, I would like to consider a near inclusion from a different public theory somewhat disguised by a difference in use. Dr Fonagy correctly, I think, finds the idea of projective identification missing from Dr Holmes' clinical repertoire as a conceptual device for under-standing countertransference where, in Kleinian clinical thought, this use would be typically found. I have doubts that processes of projec-tive identification and countertransference were taking place in the analyst's response to the patient's transference symptoms of sleepi-ness. I am inclined to think that Dr Holmes was able to observe, comprehend, and rather lightly interpret her patient's withdrawal from the analytic work and her, even while forming an impression of its potential for hostility but without having to suffer so painfully the experience of being abandoned by the patient that she had to deny it by means of a phantasy and then, with a rapid bit of on-the-spot self-analysis, undo the defence so as to be able to observe the patient's denial by uncovering her own. (Dare one wonder whether or not an ordinary sympathetic being with the patient relatively free of counter-transference might make such an insight possible without the self-analytic acrobatics required by projective identification?) Dr Holmes' interpretation evoked laughter in the patient, presumably as a conse-quence of its aptness. This discharge of any hostile feelings and the acknowledgement of denial restored the patient to the on-going work.

Dr Fonagy felicitously differentiates theoretical language from clinical language and notes that Dr Holmes excels in her consistent use of clinical language. In her interpretations there is no evidence of a withdrawing, intellectualising use of technical jargon by Dr Holmes. Her interpretations use the vocabulary and syntax that has been worked out between patient and analyst. This vocabulary includes the technical term "denial" but it has become a word that works in the language of the two of them.

The central clinical issue of these sessions is the masochistic entanglement of the patient with her husband. Dr Holmes is working interpretively with their "intertwinement" as the patient calls it. It is rooted, as Dr Holmes understands it, in the patient's identification with her husband's passive aggressive refusal to accept responsibility for fixing what he believes he did not break. His attitude is concretely manifested toward his troubled professional practice and the resulting debt for which he passes the buck to his wife. She is all too ready to take on the responsibility because of her need to maintain her own equivalent to his attitude in her attitude to her own life catastrophes, her need to undo her failed relation to her father, and, possibly, her need to manifest the care toward her husband that she would like to receive from him. Dr Holmes says to her, "Deep down you believe what he in effect says about himself, 'I'm broken but I didn't break myself and so I don't have to fix what's broken'"(Holmes, p. 28). The patient's pursuit of these unconscious needs enables her to rage at him for not keeping her informed and confiding in her so she can take care of his problem that she has made her own even though she knows it is his. His assignment of his problem to her enables him to rage at her for taking over from him and weakening him. The identifications and projections allow the patient to deny her own catastrophes and the affects and wants attached to them. They may also allow her to "better" her husband out of envious aggression disguised as altruistic care-giving. By analysing the patient's defences, Dr Holmes is seeking to set in motion a process of disentanglement so that her patient can find out.

Dr Fonagy notes that the processes at work in her patient's relation to her husband are understood by Dr Holmes, in terms of projective identification—one might say of reciprocal projective identification. Is it possible that Dr Holmes understands the work of projective identi-fication in her clinical language without using the term in her theo-retical formulation of it? If so, Dr Fonagy has enabled us to identify a paradigm of Dr Bohleber's concept, central to the EPF project, in the implicit invention or amalgamation, by Dr Holmes, into her own American Freudian theory, of a concept from Kleinian theory at the working level of clinical practice and thinking.

Conclusions

So far as space and self-knowledge has permitted, I have set out some of my own guiding ideas in this meta-theoretical commentary on a commentary. These ideas are for the most part, perhaps entirely, in agreement with Bohleber. What insidious, repressed unconscious wishful thinking has biased my theoretical and clinical reflections must be left to the reader to judge. It will be readers who will have to decide whether the commentary merits use or oblivion. However, in doing so, the reader too will have to consider not only what biases have compromised my understanding of Dr Fonagy's commentary on Dr Holmes' process notes, but also what biases may be influencing their reading of my commentary. If psychoanalysis has anything in the least true to tell us about human observation and thought about human nature, it is that psychoanalysts must eschew *ex cathedra* theorising. I take this proposition to be a fundamental premise of the methodology of Canestri's valuable programme for an *in situ* enquiry into psychoanalytic theorising that relies for its success upon the psychoanalytically informed reflexivity of psychoanalytic thinking.

References

Britton, R., & Steiner, J. (1994). Interpretation: Selected Fact or Overvalued Idea? *International Journal of Psycho-Analysis, 75*: 1069–1078.

Collingwood, R. G. (1946). *The Idea of History*. Oxford: Oxford University Press, 1994.

Dawkins, R. (2003). *A Devil's Chaplain*. New York: Houghton Mifflin.

Fairbairn, W. R. D. (1946). Object-relationships and dynamic structure. *International Journal of Psycho-Analysis, 27*: 30–37.

Freud, S. (1912e). Recommendations on psychoanalytic technique. *S.E., 12*: 111–120. London: Hogarth.

Freud, S. (1914c), On narcissism. *S.E., 14*: 73–102. London: Hogarth.

Hanly, C. (1983). A problem of theory testing. *International Review of Psycho-Analysis, 10*: 393–405.

Hanly, C. (1992). *Method in Applied Psychoanalysis. The Problem of Truth in Applied Psychoanalysis*. New York: Guilford.

Hanly, C. (2005). Deductive reasoning in psychoanalytic theorizing. 2005 Freud Anniversary Lecture, New York Psychoanalytic Institute (unpublished).

Hanly, C. (2007). On fictional truth (unpublished).

Hegel, G. W. F. (1837). *Lectures on the Philosophy of History*, J. Sebree (Trans.). London: Bohn, 1861.

Sandler, J. (1983). Psychoanalytic concepts and psychoanalytic practice. *International Journal of Psycho-Analysis, 64*: 35–46.

Spinoza, B. (1677). Ethics. In: J. Wild (Ed.) *Spinoza Selections*. New York: Scribner, 1930.

CHAPTER FOUR

The case of Albert

Samuel Zysman

Introduction

During the IPA Congress in New Orleans in 2004, the EFP Working Party on Implicit Theories organised a discussion panel where the "map" was introduced as a working tool in their ongoing research, meant to uncover and classify the contradictory unconscious theories acting in the analyst's mind during the sessions. Thanks to their invitation I had then the opportunity to read a short paper with the title "Theories as objects". In it I commented on the "map" (or "grid") and its application to clinical material that was then presented, trying to enlarge the metapsychological approach to the problem of different theories coexisting simultaneously in the analyst's mind. Shortly afterwards I was invited a second time to a similar panel to be held at the Rio de Janeiro IPA Congress in 2005, but this time it was not as a discussant but as the presenter of the clinical material that both the panel members and the audience were to discuss, upon which the "map" would be put to the test again.

What the readers of this book will find here is exactly the same material discussed then, with only two exceptions: some minor corrections, necessary because the first version of material originally spoken in Spanish showed the existence of errors leading to misunderstand-ings, and a greater concern to preserve the patient's identity. Of course, as it always happens after a public presentation I disliked some of my own interpretations and I felt tempted to suppress or at least modify some of them, perhaps just to look retrospectively smarter. But I decided to run the risk of acting honestly and did not permit myself to introduce any cosmetic repairs in the form or in the substance of what was actually said and done both by my patient and me in the analytic sessions; the transcription of what happened is as truthful and accurate as is humanely possible.

Perhaps I should stop here with the introduction and let the read-ers go straight to the material, but although it may seem just a personal need with a possible cathartic goal, I feel it necessary to add some comments about this presentation because they may be relevant to the investigation itself.

With the passing of time and successive discussions of different materials I came to think that the functioning of unconscious contra-dictory theories might well be sustaining some customary traits in our way of presenting material for open discussion. My comments will leave aside on purpose the well known difficulties that happen regu-larly in supervisions, however related to our investigation they may be, as for instance the selective forgetting or remembering of some material, or the difficulties to find the time to just sit and write down a session in all its details. I want basically to concentrate here on two intertwined phenomena that usually appear when we have show what we do privately in our offices to a big public, such as the audience in a Congress or the mass of readers of books and journals. One of them is the tendency to substitute a fully detailed transcription with "illustrative" vignettes or with a sort of personal description made by the analyst where some selected pieces of true session material are included. Frequently the listeners or the readers of such material can reconstruct fairly enough in their minds what was going on between the patient and the analyst and this may be enough for the occasion, but at other times people can be left with the impression that the analyst has everything so clear—even his own mistakes—that possible different views of the presented clinical data can hardly find space. To put it in other words, the possibility to validate or refute the analyst's working hypothesis—which matters much more in a research situation—are smaller in comparison with the possibilities that open up when the "transformations" (in Bion's sense) entailed in any kind of transcription are less, more accessible, and easier to follow.

The other related problem I have in mind is the existence in us all of a strong tendency to mistake the examination of clinical material in search of unconscious (implicit) theories with a clinical supervision. In this case, the difficulties to retrieve unconscious theories and submit them to a conscious validation process come from the fact that such process has occurred—with faults, if at all—in the "supervisor's" own mind, where no lack of unconscious theories is to be expected. In short, and notwithstanding the feelings that accompany the publishing of my own material, I am advocating fully detailed presentations, at least when it comes to an investigation. I hope the following one may serve as a good opportunity to look for unconscious theories in spite of, or better still because of, my stripping it to the bones and letting what was right or wrong surface equally.

Presentation

Albert is nearing his twenty-first birthday and for the last couple of years he is in psychoanalytic treatment, on the couch. Three times a week were agreed at first but at his own request a fourth one was added a year ago, so he has four consecutive sessions Monday to Thursday. We had already gone through a *first period of analysis* three times a week starting when he was a child aged less than ten, and until he approached fourteen, sessions took place in the play room. After that and until he reached sixteen, we moved to my office were he mostly talked or made some drawings in face to face sessions. He had been reluctant to accept this change, as he usually mistrusted unknown places. He had been referred to me by a colleague who knew I was a child analyst. He was treating the father, and had been asked to look for someone "able to deal with a difficult case". The patient presented at that time a bizarre, almost psychotic picture, where complicated obsessive rituals consumed a lot of time and had to be helplessly endured by the family, to the point of exhaustion. All this seemed to have started when he was around six, a couple of years after his only sister, Sara, was born.

Albert attributed secret meanings to numbers, which complicated the situation further because one single error in the performance of his rituals meant starting all over again and repeating it a given number of times. Strange conducts like hitting glasses or dishes on the table, sitting down and getting up many times, or banging with his fists or his head on the table added to this unbearable situation. He had queer ways to roll his eyes or turn his head, which his parents used to refer to as his "tics". When talking, some bad thought could cross his mind at any moment. He had then to engage in a special ritual touching his mouth and his palate with his tongue a number of times in a precise order, lest one or both of his parents might die. Worse still, he entertained conscious paranoid fears: when his parents went out at night he had to wait sleepless for them to come back, then when they finally did he was afraid they were not his real parents but impostors, which again prevented him from sleeping.

In spite of all this, he was a bright and agreeable child. He was well aware of his condition and he complained about his state which brought him much pain, and about his feeling unable to stop acting in this way. His performance at school seemed to be unimpaired and he obtained good marks. The problem was more with other children: he was sure they laughed and said dirty things behind his back and this made him feel miserable and a fool; he had very few friends.

Before coming to see me, he had a non-analytic treatment but with no good results. He willingly accepted the possibility his parents offered him of a second chance, and thus we started with a great deal of hope on the side of the patient and the family. On my side, I had no doubts that I was to work with a very sick boy whose disturbing obsessive defences I could only understand as the worrying façade of severe underlying psychotic traits. I thought, however, that there was a possibility of helping present. Thus, I agreed with his parents to have three sessions a week, because at that time they lived at a distance from Buenos Aires and the patient would only agree to come in his mother's company, which was one more disturbance in her complicated life. Both parents are professionals, and while the mother keeps working in her profession, the father gave it up a long time ago and went into business.

This first period of treatment lasted some six years and had to be stopped because of the father's severe economic problems that led him practically to bankruptcy. An important debt began to develop because of unpaid fees, and when this situation became visible in Albert's paranoid fears about what my real feelings towards him might be, I decided the time had come to stop and wait for a while. For the time this situation might last, an interruption was agreed with the parents and with Albert himself too. Also, that I would be available to see him if he felt in need of it and I offered to charge only a reduced fee to facilitate this. This period lasted in all nearly three years, but it was only in the first one that I received no news from the patient or the family. He then began to call me from time to time and ask me for single sessions, mostly to sort out acute anxiety states related to his paranoid fears and to what he called "my low self esteem", which had much to do with his feelings towards his friends in sexual matters. He had made some friends and even started dating girls, but he still had no sexual relations and resorted heavily to masturbation. As his family's economic situation had begun to return to some degree of normality, and both parents wanted very much to help their son and find some relief themselves, the frequency of these sessions consequently started slowly to grow. At nineteen years old, and after more or less three years since the beginning of the interruption, Albert asked his parents to resume his treatment. I could only agree with this idea, because I was already feeling that single, isolated sessions had run out of whatever use they might have had. Thus, what we may call the *second period of analysis* formally started, at first three times a week and, almost a year ago and at his request, we added a fourth one. In the meantime, important changes had occurred.

Albert had entered the University, at the Engineering Faculty, where he does quite well specially in electronics and computational systems. He still complains of being backward as compared with his friends, but this time not on sexual matters. He started having sexual relationships and he even has a girlfriend, but what he feels now is that he should be recognised as one excellent and admired student. He entertains some almost delusional phantasies about his great capacities, but, in a symmetrically opposed way, he may feel again at times he is a fool, with a "low self esteem". Then he resorts to compulsive masturbation to recover his lost "self esteem". Obsessive rituals are still present, the outstanding one now is to go to bed, but rise frequently to make sure the main key of the gas supply in the kitchen is properly shut; any error committed in the coming and going can force him to start all over again. However, it is worthwhile to say that he started to develop some ability to refrain from performing this ritual and he feels much better when he does.

On the other hand, a big change took place in the family in the past two years. The parents split due to the father's infidelity. He tried to hide and deny this situation (he is having an affair with a much younger woman working at his office), but he finally had to admit it in the midst of a confrontation in front of the children. The mother then moved with both of them to a smaller place in Buenos Aires, and according to Albert she is depressed and drinks too much. Albert does not feel comfortable at home, he can not stand seeing his mother in this shape, but at the same time he developed a growing feeling of rage and mistrust towards his father. He always kept his sessions very punctually, but lately a rebellious attitude began to appear and to develop into a more hostile transference relationship. His efforts to exert a firm control over the session and over me are strong. He accepts interpretations on one level while continually trying to argue back on another.

May 19th 2005. Thursday session

Patient arrives punctually. He lies down on the couch but does not stretch his legs completely. He lies down more on one side, but moves all the time as if he could not find himself a comfortable position. This is a common feature in many sessions.

Patient: It was hard enough for me to come today, I hesitated a real lot. I realise that lately most of the time I don't feel like coming; many times I don't see the point of it, a lot of trouble for no results. I'm not sure it is just my fault, I wondered what to talk about today and I was trying to figure it out all the way from home. What I feel is: I have to come for I don't know how much longer and still my head is full of doubts. Today, for instance, on one hand I want to speak about Julie (his girlfriend), but on the other I know what is going to happen. I'd have to admit I have to tell her to go to hell, she betrayed me and I caught her kissing another guy, this idiot who is after her. I know there are a lot of better girls, but I can't make up my mind because actually I'd feel I'm a fool. I did not control her and I knew she is dangerous when she drinks too much. So, if I let her go, I see myself staying again alone, hiding myself in my room at home, which I hate, playing games in my PC, and masturbating. I can see no solution to this, I am not well with her but I can't afford to leave her!

Analyst: From the moment the session started you kept showing me that you can't find a single place to feel comfortable and the same happens to you with people: it's bad to be with them and still worse to lose them, a bad girlfriend is better than nothing. In the end all places and all people are the same to you if you feel you can't be in control, your doubt as to what to choose to speak about today is also because you need to feel in control of what may come out in the session. Your last resource is trying to control everything in your mind through masturbation.

P: But am I not right? Is it not true I caught her kissing the other guy? Why should it be my fault? Why can't I leave her? I should be able to punish her at least, but she told me she would not obey orders. This is what this therapy does not fix; we always arrive at the same conclusion: you tell me I can't make up my mind and that's all, you leave everything to me! And I know there are nicer girls, a lot of them, I could enjoy life, I have the right to it, I'm young and I have enough time to settle down, really Julie is not so beautiful. At first I thought she was the most beautiful girl in the world, but after a while I found out: I don't like her bottom! And then she is unreliable. All my friends keep telling me: why don't you leave her and go out and fuck all the girls you like? So here we are: I don't get the proper help, why don't you stop idling and try to do something for a change? I wonder if another analyst would not help me more!

A: Your wish, as it turns out, is to be in control of everything, and you want both to keep and also to drop—anything and anybody—because all is beautiful when you don't have it, but something happens and it changes to the worse after a while when you get it. You are convinced you have such a right and you blame me because you expect me to endorse this idea and, like Julie, I don't take your orders. So also therapy was beautiful to you once and now it is ugly.

P: (After a few minutes silence) I agree. It is true there are moments when I look at the girls everywhere and I think about fucking any of them. But then I think I will come to the same point in the end. I know I will always think I missed something better and I will want to change. Really I believe I deserve the best. Did I ever tell you how it was when I was small? You already know that I spent all day with my mom, because my dad went to his office very early and came back very late. Quite often I did not even see him. I stayed at home at first mostly with mum, then with the lady working at home. I had all sorts of toys, always the best, the newest, because when we went out and I asked for a toy they always bought me what I wanted. I played with them for perhaps a few days and then, if we went somewhere and there was a new toy in a store I had just to signal what I wanted and say: now![1] It was immediately bought and all the previous toys, many only touched once or twice, went on the upper shelf of a closet and I never played with them again.

A: So, you still want to say "*ahola!*" (now) and every time get a new toy, be it a girl, or an analyst, or even an interpretation. And what seems to go wrong with any of them and makes you feel you have to start all over again is that you can no longer decide to send them to the closet so easily. You need people but you can't admit it; people resist and make you feel you are not their master, so the only thing left to you would be to destroy them and to find others, which you can not afford either. You said mom and dad bought new toys all the time, it was the magic that helped you to feel really above all others, and this is what you still expect from people.

P: I feel I'm crazy, I'm afraid I will end up mad! I feel I have to apologise to everyone because many times I feel hate and I don't know why. I cannot sort this out!

A: It frightens you to feel how much you can hate me because, as you see it, I am not helping you get a new toy nor do I behave like a toy. You probably wish me to utter the "magic words" you are waiting for. And the punishment for your hatred is being here and feeling it's your analyst who is driving you crazy.

P: I feel I have to continue talking about yesterday's subject. It was really a gross subject. Do you remember I told you my father was at home a couple of nights ago? He came to visit us and stayed for diner and my mum told him to stay for the night, it was late and it would not be very wise for him to travel back home alone.[2] I know mum wants him to come back and give up his affair, so I understand she tried in a way to show her interest in him. But, well, I see my father now as some sort of an arsehole, completely disconnected from reality. What are his activities nowadays? He does not work, he goes around the city at night taking photos in tango houses: he's got a friend from among the tango people who is also a dancer, they go to all tango houses and they have taken some 2,000 photos, can you believe it! They will supposedly publish a book with them but meanwhile my father is socially very busy, he has many new "friends" and he has no time for anything else. I can tell you, if I think about my mother, she makes me feel angry, sad, and tender to her, all at the same time. Towards my father I can only feel I'm angry, his presence bothers and disturbs me. I saw him sleep that night at home on the sofa and I almost felt sick, I asked myself: what is he doing at home? What the hell is he doing? I hated him, we are better off living without him, when he is not at home I feel I am a clever guy and I stop thinking I'm stupid, when he is at home I feel it is me the arsehole, the stupid one as I felt at school, my self esteem falls down.

At this point the patient stops and is silent for a while, but he turns on the couch from one side to the other several times, until he finally remains quiet on his right side.

P: I'm feeling uneasy, I don't know how to say this but I thought I had an erection. I felt excited when speaking about my father. Sometimes when I have an erection and I try not to masturbate I feel better if I can pull my penis into the left side, I think I can control myself better. It is awkward to be telling you this.

A: What seems to make you feel uneasy now is to be found out feeling so excited when you can display your father's image as an arsehole. This makes you feel so strong and clever; you are the real master, dominating us all with your hard on. You said "I thought I had an erection", but it looks you really had it and you resorted to your own method of trying to pull your penis to the left; all you had to do was to roll from one side to the other on the couch. Perhaps you thought I'm also an arsehole and I would not understand what is going on here.

P. I'm not only concerned about my dad. I also talk a lot with Sara about mum. Mum is also not well. We think she must be sexually frustrated, sometimes when I come back home late I find the door to her room open, she is asleep and the TV is on, but not just on, some porno movies are on the screen and sometimes we have found empty glasses as if she had been drinking. We ask ourselves: did she watch and masturbate? To think about this also excites me; I get excited thinking about her excitation.

Silence.

P: I remember seeing her asleep once with her legs spread open and this makes me remember I saw a porno movie myself with a woman showing her legs spread, you could see everything. Just as my sister when she was very small and mom had to wipe her arse, she had her legs up and wide open, all her holes were there to be seen, they were at one's disposal. In this movie I told you about, there was a man who introduced one finger into the woman's arse, she then felt as though she was paralysed, she could do nothing, she surrendered to him, and was completely dominated and he was in total command. Sometimes I have phantasised doing this to Julie; it excites me a lot to think I can be in total control of her and do whatever I like.

A: So this seems to be the story in the end: mum's body is your ultimate and secret toy, the best in the world, all others may attract you for a while but they are disposable. To possess it can make you feel you're the master of the universe. For this purpose, it is more convenient to have an father–analyst who is an absent, stupid arsehole. While you listen to me engaged in some idiotic psychoanalytic activities, as your silly father does with his photos, you get excited watching your private porno film in your own mind and you can masturbate in my presence. You feel like you are entering mum's body through any of its holes and you finally have control over her and she is yours only, "*ahola!*" (now!). You began the session asking me for help, but at this point you feel it's better to keep me at a distance.

The session finished a few moments later.

May 23rd 2005 Monday session

P: Today I also came here wondering what I would talk about. What I want is to be able to talk accurately. So I'll talk about what happened during the last couple of days; it mostly has to do with Julie, because I have her on my mind all the time. But I'll start from last Thursday. After leaving here I was supposed to sit down and concentrate to study analysis.[3] But what was I to do? Because I also had to go to the faculty to take another course, but if I were to do that I would not have time enough to prepare myself for the analysis examination. So I decided not to go to that course and study instead. When I was trying to figure out what to do I remembered what you once told me, about my difficulties with this analysis, here. I was confused, mixed up, because I'm very behind with analysis but at the same time I'm also behind with the other courses I have to take. At last I decided to study. But when I was approaching the faculty's library with that intention I asked myself: why go to the library? Why not sit comfortably and do the same at home? I can keep my privacy in my own room and study very well. OK, this is what I did, I tried hard to study until Sunday and I realised it was madness and I could not make it. I had lost so much time that I would need more than a few days, so finally I said to myself enough! Give it up!

In the afternoon Julie called. I was glad; I felt I'm fond of her. I asked her how she was doing and she told me: not well. She told me she's tired of the situation between us because she can never go out with her friends alone because of what happened[4] and she has to spend the weekend alone at home. It is ridiculous, it was she who made me doubt. And with this she made me doubt again, I thought she might go out without telling me and start all over again. This made me feel insecure and I started feeling I wanted to jerk off. But I refrained from it, I told myself it has to be possible to feel secure and yet not jerk off. I felt in this way I would not lose contact with reality and this made me feel good.

At night Julie dropped in at home. The possibility to fuck was in the air. My dad's office is near home and there would be no one there Sunday night. Julie does not like the place much but I started convincing her and she finally accepted. But before going she wanted to see if she had any e-mails, which she did, and I saw she deleted all except one, it was from that same guy who caused us our entire problem. Why haven't you deleted this one also, I asked. Oh. I don't know, I did not realise it was this guy's, she said. I thought she did it on purpose. And then it all went wrong again! I thought: I can choose not to make a fuss of it, but I can also raise the problem. But it is no good! Either way I would not feel well. When Julie saw I was getting upset and angry she confessed that she had been chatting with the guy and she told him everything about us and the guy said he wished us luck. Then I went really crazy! You stupid arsehole! I told her, stupid cow! What did you do? Why did you have to talk about us with him? And that piece of shit, who does he think he is? He must be insane to wish us luck, out of his mind! He may go to hell!

I'm afraid she is lying to me again (now a bit calmer). She told me the guy asked her if I know who he is and she asked him if he is afraid of me, and he said well, he may want to punch me in the face. No, she said, he is not violent!

You see, I think she is a real idiot. But, if I were sure she will not lie to me again I could try to forget . . . you understand? I know who I am . . . although often it does not look so, that guy may think I'm a jerk. Well, OK, but what I really wanted to say is this: before this situation exploded I had tried to keep my head clear, I did not want to fall into these thoughts: I'm a fool, I'm not well, I have to masturbate, etc. But then all went wrong, I wanted to fuck her but if so I had to keep calm, if I felt angry I would not like to fuck. Perhaps I should fuck first and then get angry? This might have been a solution, but it did not work, I could not do it, it would just be to have physical relief. I decided to tell her the truth, I would not fuck because if I did she would understand that nothing matters a lot and she would act in the same way again. So I told her: don't you imagine you tell me such a stinking story and I don't mind!

A: The story you are telling me is that your weekend was lousy, "all wrong", you could not rest and everything you wanted to keep apart reappeared, and especially this: what are you to do with this analysis, here.

This guy you talk about seems to be the same idiot that your father and I were to you last Thursday. And what drives you crazy is that I want to know about you, while you think you can do very well in your own place with no one bothering you. You may even choose to do your own analysis very privately including masturbation or not. And still worse, how do I dare to wish you luck or to be helpful, who do I think I am? I must be insane. So it must be up to you to decide if you come to analysis here or you do it alone, and if you come it has to be only with one purpose: to stop feeling you are fooled and to gain again control. As you said speaking about Julie, it's not out of love, you only come here to get relief, this is the truth you're telling me.

P: Well, in the end I did masturbate, I was hot, but I do not know if I did it because of that or because I felt insecure, or both.

A: You say "in the end", but you also said you had to refrain from it before Julie's arrival.

P: (interrupts) Yes, yes . . .

A: You ended doing what you wanted from the start: if you want to find really safe relief, you're the only one who can give it to yourself.

P: Well, no, not at all. Why do you say this when I told you I felt glad to see her and I wanted to be with her? I felt a tenderness towards her but I could not say "everything is OK", could I? Julie finally agreed with me and besides, many people masturbate. I could not fuck her when I was feeling so bad.

A: It seems you feel I am just criticising you and therefore you have to defend yourself. In the beginning you felt glad to have her, but in the end it became a question of what is the best procedure to avoid feeling you are laughed at, the arsehole in the story. What turns out to be the most important thing to you is to investigate: who is thinking I am an arsehole? Then tenderness fades away and what remains is feeling hot, so jerking off looks the only and best solution.

P. Well, it was the physical part of it that remained. I admit I could not make love, I just could have fucked to find out if that made me feel secure again.

A: When the session started you said something about wanting to talk accurately, so I gather you were aware of some difficulty with what you feel about what is happening. All the doubts you have: what to do with Julie; to study analysis or to give up; to study at home or at the library, they all point to the main question: shall I trust my analyst and speak accurately with him? Will he think I'm a fool if I include all my feelings? Would it not be better to fix things myself?

P: I don't know, you keep telling me the whole problem is I trust nobody, I have to investigate everything, and all that matters is not to be an arse-hole. But I don't know, when did I start to feel like that?

A: You told me a while ago that you felt like a fool yelling at Julie in outrage. But peeping into Julie's e-mail also seemed to excite you.

P: I did not do such a thing, it was just impossible not to see, she was actu-ally showing me that e-mail. Why do you say this to me?

A: Both things may be true, to peep and to be shown, and both are excit-ing. And the quarrelling seems to be part of the fun.

P: (Silence for a while) I just had something like a dream. In our house at the country club there has been for a long time a huge piece of cloth that belongs to my mother, I never knew what it was for. But I remember I liked to touch it. Remember I told you I always liked the feeling of some special kind of cloth, like silk or satin for instance, or the stuff of the panties my sister wore when she was small? I was also small then and I wanted to put them on. I just imagined Julie and I were wrapped in this cloth, like hidden inside, and then I felt hot and I was fucking her right there. But something happened to her, perhaps with the movements a bit of shit came out of her arse and soiled the cloth, and this excited me more.

A: The images you tell me about are like porno movies that you like to replay in your mind. To see that shit comes out of Julie's arse is like seeing your sister's arse and her shit, and you feel the one who can make it come out. To imagine that you can be inside her panties and do the same as she does, this excites you very much. It also excites you to be inside that cloth because it is like being inside your mum and have her all for yourself. Then each one of you can give their shit to the other which is also very exciting.

P: I can not understand you, I don't know why you say this excites me! I told you that what I wanted was to fuck Julie. Finally I had no choice but to jerk off.

A: To say you don't understand me is, at this point, to put a great distance between us. You need to keep me at a distance because in this movie you did all what you wanted and you felt excited and you liked it very much. This is what you were not sure if it was safe to let me know. When you say Julie is lying, or talking nonsense, it may be that in some way you like this and are excited by it because to you her mouth is functioning as her arse, and you can imagine you're exchanging shit. And keeping your inner images and feelings from me may also serve the purpose of inducing me to give incorrect interpretations, which is also exchanging shit.

Notes

1. The patient actually said "*ahola!*" which is a small Spanish child's way of pronouncing "*ahora*", which means now.
2. The father still lives alone in the country club house, that in a way is a safe place, but the road to it at night it is not equally so.
3. He is referring to the third level of mathematical analysis, which is causing him difficulties.
4. The quarrel about kissing another guy. Albert asked her not to go out alone, which she accepts under heavy protest.

Commentary on Samuel Zysman's clinical case

Paul Denis[1]

The case presented by Samuel Zysman lends itself rather well to the study of the analyst's explicit and implicit theoretical presuppositions because of the frequency and the clarity of his interventions.

Of course, much of what we can say based on a clinical history of this complexity, necessarily too briefly reported, and on the account of only two sessions, is entirely conjectural. We are well aware that this constitutes a stage in an analysis, a sort of snapshot, and that many fantasmatic configurations in the transference and resistances left aside in the two sessions in question will have been the object of the analyst's interventions and interpretations at other times. What I am going to try to present is rather like a school exercise and cannot in any way constitute a valid clinical viewpoint on Albert's case, less still an analysis of Samuel Zysman's practice.

If we consider the fourteen interventions made by the analyst in the course of the two sessions that he has reported to us, the "mapping" that has formed part of the investigative method enables us clearly to distinguish some explicit theoretical and technical trajectories.

In what is for many psychoanalytic groups a highly classical way, the analyst works from the here-and-now of the sessions: "From the moment the session started you kept showing me that . . .".

In a highly classical—and explicit—way, the analyst refers to the transference and the Oedipus complex at various points during these two sessions, saying for example at the end of the first session: "Mum's body is your ultimate and secret toy . . . To possess it can make you feel you're master of the universe. For this purpose, it is more convenient to have a father-analyst who is an absent, stupid arsehole".

This interpretation might constitute the classic example of a "mutative" interpretation as described by Strachey.

The analyst also works explicitly on the psychic conflict, on the drive–defence pair, in particular on the patient's need for domination, for mastery. "You need people but you can't admit it; people resist and make you feel you are not their master, so the only thing left to you would be to destroy them and to find others . . ." This way of working is explicitly connected with the theory of obsessional neurosis and the theory of the drives and the erogenous zones; it also takes account of destructivity. However, the reference to the transference does not appear directly, which implies an underlying theory that favours, at that point at least, the interpretation of content over that of the transference impulse.

In the register of the drives, the analyst again refers to anality and, like Freud with the Rat Man, indicates the confusion between the anal and oral zones, but explicitly in reference to the transference:

> When you say that Julie is lying, or talking nonsense, it may be that in some way you like this and are excited by it because to you her mouth is functioning as her arse, and you can imagine you're exchanging shit. And keeping your inner images and feelings from me may serve the purpose of inducing me to give incorrect interpretations, which is also exchanging shit".

This is therefore classical to the extent that the register of the drives, as well as the transference dimension, is very explicitly taken into account.

However, it seems to me that it is in the divergence, whether subtle or more obvious, from classical precepts that we can anticipate the emergence of the analyst's own implicit or possibly unconscious theories. Of course, these divergences or deviations from the classical technique or theoretical perspectives explicitly accepted by the analyst are largely dependent on countertransferential impulses. However, we sense here an analyst who is at ease with his patient, and during the sessions presented the analyst's countertransference does not seem to have posed him any insoluble problem. Moreover, the material presented to us provides scant basis for the hypothesis of phobic avoidances on the part of an analyst who is not averse to dealing with the rawest material as it arises.

For the good of the cause, we will thus consider matters from the— biased—angle of the divergence that can be noticed between the classical aspects of Zysman's interventions and their more personal elements in this particular case.

One of the "personal" aspects of Zysman's technique is the relative frequency and the length of his interpretations. Far from seeking a sparse method, the analyst reveals his generosity with words. We may suppose that this generosity relates to an implicit theoretical register: to support the patient with a form of narcissistic reinforcement by verbally testifying to a continuous interest in what he is communicating to his analyst.

A further aspect emerges in the choice of material addressed. At certain points, for example, the analyst directly takes account of his patient's behaviour during the session. The usual recommendation, at least in France, is to refrain from making interventions concerning the patient's behaviour—gestures, delays, small actions—during the session unless the patient talks about them himself. The analyst chooses to intervene concerning the patient's motor behaviours:

> You said "I thought I had an erection", but it looks as if you really had it and you resorted to your own method of trying to pull your penis to the left; all you had to do was to roll from one side to the other on the couch. Perhaps you thought I am also an arsehole and I would not understand what is going on here.

We can certainly imagine here a countertransference impulse of mastery, induced by the patient—to show him that nothing escapes the analyst and he is neither an idiot nor an arsehole—but, apart from a possible impulse of that kind, we can perhaps link this type of intervention to a theoretical and technical position concerning the analysis of behaviour in the session: this would be a matter of translating the meaning of the patient's *behaviour* and according it a meaning. This technique was suggested by Wilhelm Reich for breaking the patient's "character armour"; if Zysman's intervention is partly influenced by Reich's technique, the theory that guided the analyst would not be all that unconscious.

However, we may think that the analyst is implicitly acting as if the motor behaviour as well as the verbal elements should be interpreted and that this—personal?—theory originates from his practice in child analysis, in which the young patients' motor play and behaviours are the object of the analyst's interventions. But we must also consider the narcissistic aspect of character organisations and it seems to us that it is the weight of the narcissistic symptomatology that leads the analyst to make interventions concerning behaviour here.

There is a further element that may give us pause for thought, namely the explanatory or clarificatory quality of the analyst's relatively long interventions. Their interpretive quality is of course apparent, but their formulation points to an implicit theoretical choice. In this context, the following interpretation (already quoted) has been given:

> When you say that Julie is lying, or talking nonsense, it may be that in some way you like this and are excited by it because to you her mouth is functioning as her arse, and you can imagine you're exchanging shit. And keeping your inner images and feelings from me may serve the purpose of inducing me to give incorrect interpretations, which is also exchanging shit.

The transference dimension is addressed here in two stages: first, an extra-transferential interpretation—"when you say that Julie is lying you like that because it is exchanging shit with her"—followed by the transfer of this interpretation to the relationship with the analyst. In this impulse, the criticisms indirectly addressed to the analyst through the remonstrations made against the girlfriend—concerning whom it is said that it is better to have one like that than none at all—are bypassed. Some analysts would only have said: "better to have a bad analyst than no analyst at all", hoping that the patient's associations would be stimulated from the side of the transference and that, at the same time, the relationship with Julie would be extricated from the negative lateral transference that is displaced on to her. The analyst's implicit theory, at least at this point, would be to foster the understanding, the access to the conscious part of the self, and the patient's desire for narcissistic mastery that is leading him to seek to induce misinterpretations.

Furthermore, the analyst prioritises the study of everything the patient may be feeling in the session, especially excitation, as well as fantasies of possession and megalomaniac fantasies, but he makes few interventions concerning the patient's *feelings*, the affects themselves. The analyst's idea is that the patient is seeking a form of control, of mastery, over his feelings. This desire for mastery is probably linked to the patient's obsessional pathology, but also to the mother's alcoholism and the father's lying . . . but essentially to a megalomaniac ambition for domination that relates to the narcissistic register.

When he indicates what is happening in the session, the analyst makes no reference to any positive feelings that the patient may have towards him. It may well be that the analyst's position here is that of interpreting the hostile aspect of the material as a defence against excessively positive feelings, and a desire for submission towards the analyst would have a seductive quality and induce an increased proximity that would assume a homosexual quality for the patient, which he would be unable to tolerate or would risk inducing an uncontrollable affective attachment.

Can we imagine here an implicit theory on the analyst's part concerning how to deal with homosexuality in the treatment? It seems highly probable. In fact, the most classical Freudian theory links jealousy with homosexuality and we can be certain that Samuel Zysman subscribes to this perspective, which is revealed by clinical practice to be correct on a daily basis. The implicit theory would be to refrain from addressing homosexuality directly in order to be gentle with this patient's extreme susceptibility and avoid wounding him, which would risk triggering a persecutory impulse and impeding the rest of the treatment. It is probably the same perspective that is directing an intervention such as the following: "You probably wish me to utter the 'magic words' you are waiting for. And the punishment for your hatred is being here and feeling it's your analyst who is driving you crazy".

The request for invigorative homosexual penetration present in the request for "magic words" is left aside in favour of an interpretation that demonstrates the patient's narcissistic needs and his disappointment, but avoids emphasising the conflict between fear and the desire to be penetrated by the paternal power. The alternative might have been: "You would like to receive my power through some magic words but this desire makes you feel that you're subjugating yourself to me, and then you want me to go to hell".

The analyst chooses to prioritise the narcissistic axis over the homosexual trajectory.

The trajectory favoured here also emerges in an intervention by the analyst concerning Albert's relationship with Julie: "As you said speaking about Julie, it's not out of love, you only come here to get relief, this is the truth you're telling me". Moreover, the patient talks about "fucking" rather than "making love". Fucking relates to narcissism: taking action, being the stronger one, being independent; making love implies a loving exchange and consequently giving the object considerable power. The analyst demonstrates the force of the narcissistic striving: "but you also said you had to refrain from it [the desire to masturbate] before Julie's arrival. . . . You ended up doing what you wanted from the start: if you want to find really safe relief, you're the only one who can give it to yourself".

Unquestionably the patient tends to organise himself in a narcissistic mode and the necessity for the analyst to take this tendency into account is expressed in various interventions he makes. These are probably ultimately based on an implicit theory of narcissism and its interpretation in the treatment. In fact, almost all the analyst's formulations incorporate a narcissistic dimension: the analyst emphasises the lack of a "place to feel comfortable", and then the desire for mastery and the importance attached to masturbation, not as a link with internal objects but as a means of re-establishing a narcissistic equilibrium: relief. When the analyst interprets explicitly at the Oedipal level, he simultaneously emphasises the patient's narcissistic ambitions. "Mum's body is your ultimate secret toy . . . Possessing it can make you feel you're master of the universe. For this purpose, it is more convenient to have a father–analyst who is an absent, stupid arsehole". An ultimate secret toy is a narcissistic possession; being master of the universe is the fulfilment of a megalomaniac narcissism. The accuracy of Zysman's interpretation is corroborated by the fact that the patient enacts his fantasies of playing with the mother's body by watching pornographic films as she does, a deferred incestuous activity, to have the same masturbatory pleasure as her, with her. The incestuous register conflicts with the Oedipal register and contributes to a particular form of narcissistic organisation.

Beyond the "classical" aspect of the analyst's drive-related, Oedipal interpretations, an implicit theoretical trajectory can be seen to emerge: analysing the characterological aspects of narcissism, reducing this narcissistic armature. The homosexual dimension, of which it might be wounding for the patient to become aware, is respected but also fuelled in the transference by the analyst's generous verbal support, but it does not form the object of direct or indirect interpretation. We may suppose that the implicit theoretical trajectory has emerged as a result of the analyst's perception of the weight of the narcissistic symptomatology and has adapted to this in some sense.

Marion Milner taught us that perception is not an innate function but results from a form of creation. Sensation is innate, but perceiving requires us to establish a link between one or several sensations and a play of representations. That is why perceiving is creating.

During the analytic session we have no immediate perception of what is happening in the patient's mind. We only have "psychic sensations" generated by signals that originate from the patient, by what is said to us and how it is said to us.

Understanding what is happening in the patient's mind, in his preconscious and his unconscious, is for us the result of a form of perception, a specific act of perception: the psychoanalytic perception. This results from a creative impulse that links our "psychic sensations" to a set of representations. Some of these representations are organised into a system that constitutes our theory.

In a way that is obviously too simple, we can compare our theories to an optical device that enables us to perceive the innermost core of the latent content of the patient's discourse. This perspective highlights the instrumental character of the theory, as a mode of perception. The link between the psychic sensations we experience in the session and our theory gives rise to psychoanalytic perception.

For each of us, our implicit theory is something we have forgotten exists and it has come neither into our view nor our understanding. It establishes itself in us insidiously and ends up becoming part of us, during our personal analysis and our experiences of supervision. We acquire our implicit theories in the same way that children who are beginning to speak acquire grammar by talking with their parents.

They are unaware of the existence of grammar, but they construct correct sentences.

Our explicit theories are those that we are aware of having established in ourselves. We remain conscious of using them, in the same way that we are aware of using our glasses, even if we sometimes look over the frames or we forget that we are wearing them.

Theory enables perception to occur, but only in its own domain. The width of the angle and the depth of the field are limited by theory itself. The metaphor of the optical device also reflects the fact that we cannot perceive everything at the same time and that we can only have an approximate and incomplete image of one angle or one aspect of things. The complete and precise psychoanalytic perception is something that we have to mourn, just as—in the domain of translation—we have to mourn a translation that would give an exact equivalent from one language into another. Every optical device allows perception in a certain field but simultaneously prevents vision in the other possible fields. Corrective lenses do not enable us simultaneously to see from close up and far away.

The underlying problem in every psychoanalytic treatment is the following: what is escaping the optical device of our theory? As Charcot said: "Theory is all very well, but it can't stop things existing!" What we do not perceive nonetheless exists in the patient's mind. To grasp it and to touch what lies beyond his theoretical field, the analyst has to create a new device: to make a discovery. That is to say, he must avoid restricting himself to his theories or, more precisely, allowing himself to be restricted by his theories; he must know that other things exist beyond his theories in a way that leaves open the field of discovery. Clinical practice should not merely verify the accuracy of theories; it must deploy theory in order to discover and modify the theory. The psychoanalyst must listen to Hamlet: "There are more things in heaven and earth, Horatio, than are dreamt of in your philosophy".

Note

1.   Translated from the French by Sophie Leighton.

CHAPTER FIVE

Unconscious theories in the analyst's mind at work: searching for them in clinical material*

Werner Bohleber

In this work we want to arrive at a deeper understanding of how the analyst uses psychoanalytic theory in his clinical work. We want to offer greater theoretical illumination to the cognitive–affective space of the preconscious in which the public and the private implicit theories and their content and motives are established.

Listening to a patient perception, reflection, and communication of psychic states, motives, and tendencies are normally formulated in the language of a sophisticated common sense psychology (Reder, 2002). With this language we are able to understand ourselves and the communicated material of the patient at first in a more or less naïve way. However, at the same time psychoanalytic concepts come to our mind. They are functioning as preconceptions that focus our attention on particular and very different aspects of the clinical material. This process has the structure of a hermeneutic circle, which can be traversed by various theory segments in generating new meaning. We thereby place the patient's statements in a theoretically determined "contextual horizon" (Boesky, 2005), that we can change and that can be expanded in practice.

---

*Panel presented at the 46th IPA Congress, Chicago, July 29–August 1, 2009.

This process of translating theory into practice is tied to the individual mind and results in a subjective adaptation of theory. The concepts of public psychoanalytic theory we work with are not as well defined concepts as perhaps in other scientific disciplines but they are elastic (Sandler, 1983). Its meaning can be enhanced or changed. Beyond that the analyst forms with growing competence a pool of preferred concepts and theories which can come from different theoretical traditions. In these adaptations personal world views, ideological elements, and elements of a common sense psychology are also amalgamated. Our theoretical knowledge is a mixture of an implicit use of official theory which is intermingled with the analyst's own private implicit theories. I cannot go into more detail here.

The peculiarity of psychoanalytic practice, with its use of theories that bear the stamp of the implicit and personal, should not provide grounds for approaching them with scholarly suspicion. Rather, these facts—it was Sandler (1983) who first has pointed it out—impart its concepts with an elasticity and a fluid field of meaning, which makes it possible for creative analysts to devise an initially implicit expansion or reformulation of a concept, the practical testing and confirmation of which can then lead to the formulation of an explicit and public concept or to a corresponding partial theory.

However, private theories can have another side. They are not always a creative resource, as they may also have a highly idiosyncratic significance. This increases the danger that personal convictions which are no longer scientifically valid and communicable can take over. In addition, we often encounter an inflated idealisation of certain theories or concepts. The personal convictions expressed in private theories shape the meanings the analyst assigns to the clinical material and also determine his emotional response to it. In doing so, private theories can serve as an important indicator of the analyst's countertransference (Purcell, 2004). This must be analysed instead of being further theoretically elaborated.

In clinical work with the patient a great deal of what takes place is routine for the experienced analyst. When asked, he at first has difficulties explaining his mode of operation, focusing of perception, conceptual considerations, and formulations of interventions. They must first be subjected to an introspective enquiry in order to become accessible at least partially. Hence, at work here are theory elements, models, and individual beliefs on which the analyst orients himself, along with mindsets and convictions operating largely implicitly or preconsciously. Therefore a substantial part of implicit theories or elements of theoretical thinking can only be discerned by an observer.

The Working Party on Theoretical Issues of the European Psychoanalytical Federation (EPF)[1] has assumed the task of more closely examining analysts' private implicit theories. We developed a tool, a vector model, a so-called "map" which we hope can help to bring better theoretical illumination to the cognitive–affective space of the preconscious (Canestri, Bohleber, Denis, & Fonagy, 2006).

I would like to conclude by saying that the aim of such an analysis of implicit theories is not to demonstrate a different or seemingly better understanding of the analytical session, but instead to use the analyst's reactions and interventions to hypothesise about the way in which he was thinking theoretically and which implicit theories he applied either consciously or unconsciously. Such an approach might, at first, seem unusual because in the discussion of cases we are simply not used to this. In clinical workshops using this method, however, it quickly became apparent that after a phase of adjusting one's approach and shifting the focus of attention, the perception and retrograde study of implicitly operating theories in the analyst's deliberations and interventions led to new approaches to clinical procedure and to a new awareness of the value of theory in everyday practice. This we now hope to demonstrate by presenting and discussing clinical material.

Note

1.   Members of the Working Party are Werner Bohleber, Jorge Canestri (chair), Paul Denis, and Peter Fonagy.

The case of Floppy

Lilia Bordone de Semeniuk

Case history. Floppy

Floppy is an attractive twenty-six-year-old woman who started her treatment with me three years ago. I have been seeing her three times a week, Mondays, Tuesdays, and Thursdays. Her former treatment, with a male analyst, was interrupted due to the analyst's illness (supposedly a depressive syndrome). Then she asked her father what to do he advised her to look for a new analyst, a recommendation that she accepted without hesitation.

When I asked her about the reasons for seeking psychological help, she described them in the following order:

1. Problems in her work: she is currently devoting her time to making women's clothing, in association with her brother and a friend of his. She feels she is disorganised and not efficient enough in her work as well as in other activities.
2. Vocational doubts: she started studying to become a journalist, but after a while she was not sufficiently convinced whether she liked it or not.
3. The meaning of her mother's premature death: she died when Floppy was two years old, and even though she was not sure of

the illness which ended her mother's life, she thinks it was a cerebral tumour.

Her father, a clinical psychotherapist, is described as a person always concerned with the welfare of his children, with whom he has good communication.

Floppy's siblings are a thirty-year-old sister and a twenty-eight-year-old brother. She also has two half siblings from a second marriage of her father that occurred not very long after her mother's death. For this reason Floppy is only five years older than her younger brother.

She says she has a good relationship with every member of the family, although she criticises her stepmother for the preference she shows towards her own children. In the sessions she referred to her as mother and seemed to feel real affection for her.

Floppy used to describe quite vividly home scenes where she enjoyed watching mother looking for chocolates or little presents she had bought for her own children and that Floppy had hidden.

She had moved to live with her boyfriend three years ago. They are planning to get married, even though they went through two short separations as a result of differences in the way they see life. From her point of view, "it is difficult to live with a person who has so many more advantages than oneself", emphasising the financial help G is getting from his family, which she lacks.

At the age of nineteen, she became pregnant by a former boyfriend, and had a provoked abortion. She speaks about this fact without the slightest emotion.

She stressed her intention to call me before, but did not because she had lost my phone number. She did not link this with her already mentioned "disorganisation". Just before the end of the interview, she excused herself because she had come to meet me "being such a mess" in a clear reference to her appearance and to her clothes. Needless to say, this did not coincide with my impression. We agreed to begin the treatment the following week, even though the summer vacations were coming soon.

In the course of the treatment Floppy talked about the difficulties she had in reaching her ideal: to be able to earn enough to live on modestly at first but progressing to become a real self-made woman, somebody quite busy, with an excellent income.

Ideas about becoming a journalist had been given up some time ago. In secret, she expected some recognition from her father in relation to her efforts not to be financially dependant on him.

She offered an image of the boyfriend as being selfish, demanding, and not very respectful towards her, although she never complained about him openly. She admired him for being able to keep his job which allowed him to earn a living and to make plans.

As a patient she was respectful of the sessions, asking for a change only occasionally. She seemed to be at ease in her hour, bringing associations and dreams quite frequently. I felt fairly comfortable treating her, but this feeling was often interrupted by the bothering impression that I was not going deep enough and by the fact that Floppy used to respond to transferential interpretations by saying something of this sort: "It is like my boyfriend says; analysis is OK, except when the analysts begin with that story of what is going on between you and them".

Session: Tuesday, November

She comes in punctually. Immediately, she asks me to allow her to go to the bathroom "to pass water". Once she is back, she lies down on the couch and starts talking.

Patient: Fine, I am fine. The truth is that today I don't have anything to complain of . . . I don't have anything to be very happy about either . . . in fact, I am a little anxious, but . . . I can bear it.

Analyst: In another recent session you wanted to go to the bathroom at the end; today it is at the beginning. Is that perhaps because you feel at home here, telling me, as if to your mummy, that you have to go to the bathroom before doing anything?

P: I have just had a milk shake to pass the time. I felt like going to the bathroom before coming here, but I thought: the restroom at the bar can be dirty, can be ugly. Then I thought: I can go during the session, but: how can I tell you? Would I ask for permission, or should I go on the way? This is something I don't like because I know it can be interpreted that I am too direct, or too sincere.

(Pause)

P: When I was a child, my father worked at home. He had some patients who always wanted to go to the bathroom, and we lived in a two storey home. My father's office was downstairs and there was no toilet there, so the patients had to climb the stairs if they needed to go to the toilet. So we children had to be careful to keep the doors closed and we couldn't go to the bathroom whenever we wanted.

A: Maybe you are afraid I am not willing to receive your urges, so I would be happier if you only talk about them. On the other hand, you seem to feel pleased if you can use my bathroom without caring about other people.

P: Some years ago, when Bob (her associate in the shop and her father's patient) used to come late some mornings, he used to step right into the bathroom. I knew by that time he was coming from my father's session, and I thought he didn't dare to use the bathroom. This isn't my case, although it is not so easy for me because I don't know whether to go or to ask you for permission. I know in the session everything has a meaning

A: It seems now you want to hear an interpretation that doesn't sound like a cliché.

P: I was telling you I am rather anxious. In my previous analysis, at the end of the sessions, I would cross the street to the drugstore and always had something: a juice, a sweet. It was almost a ritual. It happened one day that my analyst saw me, I felt ashamed because he was seeing my oral anxiety. I don't eat when I come here, but, if I remember well, one Tuesday morning before coming I went to McDonalds, and many times ... I go to the gas station just round the corner and I buy a sweet which is almost a synonym of fatness. Today, while passing the time, I walked into the bar and saw a guy having a shake. I couldn't resist and ordered not only a shake but also a big toasted sandwich, really big. Then, I thought: it is OK, I had only a hamburger for lunch, and I was hungry. However, when leaving the bar, I thought I am a glutton!

A: The little Floppy who was ashamed of being exposed to her former analyst, is present here today and is afraid I shall think she is insatiable to the point of filling herself with food; but, on the other hand, she doesn't want to run the risk of remaining hungry.

P: Then what is the meaning of eating after a session? Maybe, I am not satisfied?

A: Maybe, you are telling me I am not rewarding enough, like your former analyst, and your mother, who didn't stay with you for long.

(Pause)

P: I was thinking of a dream I started telling you last session and we couldn't finish it. You know, many times when bringing a dream I believe I have it clear enough, because I have already thought about it. I know it sounds omnipotent, but . . . it's so. Anyhow, I'll tell it to you again.

I was with some girl friends and Jules, a boy, Deborah's neighbour, comes. They became friends in the square when taking their dogs for a walk. Deborah has a Setter and Jules a Dobermann. Well, I meet Jules and tell him I am looking for a dog. Then he tells me that his bitch is giving birth, and I can go for the puppy in two hours. He is a generous guy, and he was giving me a . . . a giant dog.

Last weekend we went with G (boy friend) to a dog breeder; I was astonished to see the number of breeds they had.

That guy, Jules, has the same name as my ex-boyfriend and he also has a very small dog, quite old. And yesterday, when I was telling you the dream, I almost told you I met this ex-boyfriend, but decided afterwards not to do so.

It's funny, it came out all of a sudden, I didn't mean to tell you . . ..

A: Sometimes, you feel it's better to keep some events or ideas to yourself. Maybe, you are afraid this work, the work the two of us are doing, is something small, not enough, like that little dog you mentioned before.

Perhaps you expect to obtain from me something impressive like the Dobermann Jules gave you.

P: Does it mean I feel I can do all this work by myself? Could be, but sometimes I feel fascinated when you tell me things I have not thought about.

(Pause)

P: Do you remember my friend Val, the girl who works at night? She found a small dog in the street two months ago. Well she is now twenty-two years old, and she says she can't have a baby for at least five years. Then the small dog is like a palliative for the wish to have a baby; she says she can't get pregnant until she has a stable job and a good salary. My boy friend and I are looking for a dog, with the excuse of it being a guardian for our home; we know that it is necessary to educate him, to teach him not to break things. I say to G and to myself that having a puppy is a good training for having a baby later on. But it is also a way of postponing it.

In the dream, I was able to have a dog in two hours.

A. Number two is being repeated . . . I think you would like me to hurry up with your treatment, maybe to have your mind and emotions developed in a short time; let's say a short time like the two hours that went by between you talking to Jules and the meeting with the puppy.

But what happens if, in the middle of the process, an aspect of yourself comes out that tears everything apart, or is quite greedy?

P: I am giving myself two years in which to establish myself in my work. Even when I know I have even less time left.

A: We are already near the end of the first year of treatment. Your mother died when you were not quite two years old .You seem to feel you have to be established before two years pass, perhaps fearing something wrong may happen between us.

(Pause: Floppy says something in such a low voice that it's impossible for me to hear it.)

P: There is something else to tell you. I went to pick G up at his job; I took him to the homeopath who gave him an injection. I left him there and when I came back, he was asleep. I explained to the doctor I had to take him to his analyst, and he answered that G was exhausted and needed affection.

My father had told me the same!

When G came back from his analyst he was much better. Once again he started talking about his job, complaining that he is not appreciated enough and that nobody tells him what to do.

He has the feeling of growing up detached from his family, and now he is telling everybody I am at his side. I am happy to hear that.

A: Being so needed by G is a good way of forgetting your own needs

P: Could be true, because when G asked me to pick him up, I had a moment of doubt and reviewed my agenda for the following day. But if he needs me, it is worth leaving my things aside. But the girl who is in charge of the sales can't take care of all the clients.

End of session

Commentary on
Lilia Bordone de Semeniuk's
clinical case

Dieter Bürgin

F irst of all, I want to express my gratitude to Lilia Bordone for having offered us such interesting material to work on. It is a strange thing to have three people looking at one's clinical work in search of unconscious theories.

Reading the material of this session about a twenty-six-year-old woman who seems to be a traumatised child (loss of the mother at the age of two), a traumatised adolescent (interruption at the age of nineteen; isolated emotions), and a traumatised young woman (loss of the former analyst—a man—because of a depression), who has a psychotherapist as father (burden or chance?) on whom she seems to be quite dependent (she again and again asks him what to do), and who is not settled in her professional identity, I first followed the steps of the analyst who had the "impression that I was not going deep enough and by the fact that Floppy used to respond to transferential interpretations saying something of this sort: 'It is like my boyfriend says; analysis is OK, except when the analysts begin with that story of what is going on between you and them'."

What does "deep enough" mean? Why did the patient not respond to transference interpretations? I will limit myself to the first hour of the presented material. Using the idea of the vectors Bohleber has described, and following my own first ideas, I thought that the *time-factor* might be an underlying structure on which several preconscious concepts of the analyst might be fixed.

Already the beginning of this analysis is very quick: one interview, then analysis starts immediately during the following week. The session begins with an acting, a bodily urge (asking to be allowed to go to the bathroom). The patient then talks of being fine, having nothing to complain about, being a little bit anxious . . .

Immediately (urgently?), the analyst makes her first intervention, taking up descriptively the urges of the patient at the beginning and at the end of the sessions (recently at the end, now at the beginning). Then she mentions a transference aspect: feeling like being at home, talking of bodily urges as if to mother. ("In another recent session you wanted to go to the bathroom at the end; today it is at the beginning. Is that perhaps because you feel at home here, telling me, as if to your mummy, that you have to go to the bathroom before doing anything?".) The theme of having or not having time for something, of working or of being at leisure stands, in my way of hearing, at the centre of what is said. It shows up in body language (urge and action, recalled from procedural memory).

The patient talks then of having killed time in a bar before coming to analysis. She already evaluated whether to go to a rest room, rejected this (dirty, ugly), decided to go before the start of the session and evaluated in phantasy whether she should ask for permission or go straightway. She hesitated, because she feared interpretation ("I know it can be interpreted").

Then follows a childhood memory: being restricted in going to the bathroom, and keeping all doors closed because of father's patients (i.e., a conflict between an evacuation need and an obedient inhibition in respect to father's law).

The analyst follows immediately with a second intervention. ("Maybe you are afraid I am not willing to receive your urges, so I would be happier if you only talk about them"). In the second part of the intervention she points to a transferential aspect (idealised good mother) ("On the other hand, you seem to feel pleased if you can use my bathroom without caring about other people").

Time, which might let feelings come up to be felt, was killed! Now the urging factor is combined with a question of authority and power of the external object.

Again, but in another form, the time-theme (urge to evacuate) comes up: Bob, the patient's partner and her father's patient, when coming from his sessions had not dared to use the bathroom, and in the office headed straight for the toilet. During the session, says Floppy, everything has a meaning. She says that during the session, not before or at the end, things have meaning.

The analyst intervenes a third time ("It seems now you want to hear an interpretation that doesn't sound like a cliché"); this might reflect an implicit private theory of hers that the patient would like to get something special, for example, that silence would not be supportive enough for this patient (topographic vector, conscious but not public) and that therefore she would have to follow the patient very closely with her interventions.

Now, the analysand speaks about her former analysis. After the sessions she used to drink or eat something. Today too, while waiting, she could not resist the temptation to eat before the session. She fears being fat.

Nevertheless, the *time factor* seems to be intensively present on the side of both protagonists. Both might share a preconscious agreement, that waiting would be negative. The dialogue seems to be characterised not so much by a mutual listening to listening or a quiet emotional searching and sharing, but more by an exchange in which, as in a competitive tennis match, the first goal is not playing together, but scoring against a competitor. The theme "urge to go to the bathroom" is now exchanged to an "urge to eat or drink"—no longer evacuation, but ingestion!

Nearly always, the analyst puts the material directly in the transference. It seems that she has the conviction that only then could change occur (implicit theory of change; conceptual vector, e). A technical generalisation seems to exist that any dynamic described by the patient implicitly refers to the analyst (conceptual vector, subgroup c). Interpreting *in* the transference, for example, seems to be of minor value for the analyst. This might be a personal conviction or a loyalty to the analytic school the analyst came from. In any case, the analyst continues transference interpretations, even when she remarks that the patient dislikes this way of intervention. Floppy probably does not fear what in the French tradition is called "the violence of interpretation", but might resist an unconscious influence she feels when the analyst follows her own concept (in the sense of *theory operating as a superego activity* (topographical vector, preconscious theory, and theorisation)) and submits her to the analyst's own needs, like the father did with his children.

In the following interpretation, the analyst takes up the "shame of exposure" in the previous analysis and links it—again directly in the transference—to a hypothesised phantasy of the patient. ("The little Floppy who was ashamed of being exposed to her former analyst, is present here today and is afraid I shall think she is insatiable to the point of filling herself with food; but, on the other hand, she doesn't want to run the risk of remaining hungry . . ..") The patient reacts to the analyst's intervention by asking herself about possible meanings. Is she unsatisfied? She is now herself in search of meaning. But she remains very obedient, taking up exactly the way the analyst understands things.

Following this, the analyst feels perplexed and touched (why?). And then she mentions two forced separations: one from the *former analyst*, who fell ill, and the other one from the *mother*, who died, and links it to the fact that *this analysis*, too, might not last long enough (the separation from the baby, i.e., the interruption, is not mentioned). ("Maybe, you are telling me I am not rewarding enough, like your former analyst, and your mother, who didn't stay with you for long."). The wording the analyst uses here is drawing a timeline of points marked with unfulfilled desires, starting with separation from mother, then the forced separation from the former analyst, and finally ending with the not having enough time with the current analyst.

The patient does not react directly. But she turns to a dream, taking up an interrupted slope of understanding, mentioning that the work on this dream was not finished in the last session because the session ended (". . . I'll tell it to you again"). In the here and now, a blocked movement between her and her current analyst is mentioned. Unfinished business emerges. Interruption of the time-flow—and therefore separation—appears, but also the wish to take things up, to explain what was not explained (to mother, the former and the current analyst).

The following dream might give some explanation concerning the reactions of the patient to the interrupted relations, if we assume that the sequence of significants tells a lot about underlying unconscious meanings.

In the dream we find a group of people ("some girl friends"), Jules, and Deborath. They have a common and shared theme, a third thing: dogs! The patient gets included in that third thing "dogs" by her wish to have one. The analyst is not waiting for what would follow, but asks immediately for associations. By that, the patient has to produce material, cannot be generous herself in offering more details or be greedy in withholding them. So the patient continues the dog-breeder story, going first to the last weekend, then speaking of yesterday, and coming, at the end, to the present: she willingly and consciously withheld some information from the analyst (having met an ex-boyfriend). Even now, she had no intention of telling this, but "it came out all of a sudden". A bunch of mixed feelings (retention, expulsion) is manifested in an attitude of being obedient and not-obedient at the same time.

The analyst follows the patient with her intervention. ("Sometimes, you feel it's better to keep some events or ideas to yourself"). Then, she turns to a possible deception about the common work. ("Maybe, you are afraid this work, the work the two of us are doing, is something small, not enough, like that little dog you mentioned before."). And then, she addresses a possible wish of the patient ("Perhaps you expect to obtain from me something impressive like the Dobermann Jules gave you"). The movement goes from a narcissistic acceptance of the shared work and ends with an unfulfilled wish from the patient. The patient's reaction is a little bit angry–irritated (Could be, but sometimes I feel fascinated when you tell me things I have not thought about). Then she continues with the theme of having to wait for a baby (five years!), that a small dog can function as a palliative to the wish of having a baby, and that it is good training for having a baby later on. Small dogs you can get "in two hours"—in the dream!

Now, the analyst reflects upon the question of time and speed. ("I think you would like me to hurry up with your treatment, maybe to have your mind and emotions developed in a short time; let's say a short time like the two hours that went by between you talking to Jules and the meeting with the puppy"). By this, she interprets a wish of the patient, addressed to the analyst that she could "hurry up with your treatment". At the same time, she points to the fact that intrapsychic events of the patient might appear. ("But what happens if, in the middle of the process, an aspect of yourself comes out that tears everything apart, or is quite greedy?"). We can wonder if slowing the speed of "spending meaning" by the analyst might paradoxically speed up the analytic process, in the sense that the patient might find her own pace in "analytic working".

The patient speaks now of a clear cut timetable. ("I am giving myself two years . . ."). The analyst links the time of analysis to the age of the patient when her mother died (under two years) and a potential anxiety. ("We are already near the end of the first year of treatment. Your mother died when you were not quite two years old .You seem to feel you have to be established before two years pass, perhaps fearing something wrong may happen between us."). Following this intervention, the patient is no longer withholding, but speaks ("in such a low voice that it's impossible for me to hear"). Floppy is obedient (she speaks, is not withholding) and non-obedient at the same moment (speaks but cannot be heard)—an elegant solution!

At that moment, the analyst—contrary to her asking for associations after the dreams—does not take up her not-hearing of the spoken words; thus, the utterance of the patient remains a non-communicated communication.

The patient changes the content and the theme: her boyfriend is in need of help from her. The analyst points to a defensive attitude of the patient. ("Being so needed by G is a good way of forgetting your own needs"). This intervention is confirmed by the patient.

Separation, a concept insolvably linked with time, appears often in this material, but it remains unclear at which level it is conceptualised by the analyst. She interprets more drive derivatives (wishes, desires, and urges) than defensive activities (only at the end of the session) and she does not stick on a particular stage of development; she seems to be more disposed towards a flexible (mainly Kleinian?) conceptual "patchwork", but shows that she has to a major extent integrated various theories in a personal way.

I cannot search for implicit theories in the given material without asking about my own implicit theories. As in any observation, the observer's side cannot be excluded; in any comment the commenter's way must be taken into consideration too. The patient has implicit theories, the analyst also, and the third person, trying to find out what would be the analyst's implicit theories, brings in his own preconscious theories that are guiding his search.

Why did I take up just these time-linked factors? It reflects my personal and conscious way of listening to both analyst and analysand. In my personal conviction rhythm plays an enormous role in enhancing the analytical process: rhythm as a musical element that governs emotional exchange and shared (or only partially shared) emotionality as the sound of the interchange. This is a developmental perspective which is influenced by infant research, child, and adolescent development.

Commentary on Lilia Bordone de Semeniuk's clinical case

Beatriz de León de Bernardi

The role of psychoanalytical theories in the mind of the analyst throughout his/her practice has been a topic of constant reflection in the psychoanalytical community. In the mid 1980s I participated, as a candidate, in a group of the Uruguayan Psychoanalytical Association that studied clinical materials at two different times. The first time we heard the clinical narration, seeking to free ourselves of our preconceptions, attentive to the psychoanalytical ideas that could emerge in our minds. These first comprehensions were called "fantasy theories", by Marta Nieto (Nieto et al., 1985) because of the fact that they integrated the language lived by the patient with the broad and blurry psychoanalytical ideas—clinical generalisations as we would call them nowadays (map of implicit theories)—that arose in us. The second time, the experience was in an already functioning reflexive group process, the material was analysed from different psychoanalytical theories trying to discriminate how each approach shed light on the material in a different way. This experience, that marked my later development as a psychoanalyst, came about in a context that was worried about the incidence of theoretical pluralism in our practice, but also gathered ideas formulated by thinkers such as Liberman and Bleger, among others.

Bleger (1969) pointed out that "developed and explicit theory doesn't always coincide with implicit theory in practice" (p. 288). And his main interest was taking care of "the divergence between psycho-analytical theory and implicit theory [in the practical task], the latter not being totally formulated nor assimilated in the psychoanalytical theoretical body" (p. 289). Reflection upon these aspects was initiated in the 1960s and continues up until now (Duarte, 2000, etc.), but it is without doubt after the distinction formulated by Sandler (1983) between public theories (explicit) and private theories (implicit) that the reflection was generalised, pondering on what we really do with our patients and in which way psychoanalytical theory operates in our practice.

I would like to thank Lilia Bordone de Semeniuk for the richness of her clinical material that will allow us to reflect upon the technical and theoretical models that implicitly guided her interventions. As an instrument of analysis I will partially use "the map of private (implicit, preconscious) theories in clinical practice" elaborated by Canestri, Bohleber, Denis, and Fonagy (2006) which includes vectors that describe the different aspects of implicit theories in practice: the topographical vector, the conceptual vector, the action vector, the object relation of knowledge vector, and the developmental vector.

Lilia's clinical material shows her actively intervening, naturally including herself in her formulations. Her first three interventions place Floppy's physical needs as part of the story of her bond with her, "In another recent session you wanted to go to the bathroom at the end; today it is at the beginning".

Lilia follows the patient's affective movement moment by moment and the emotional context is the central clue in her interpretations, "Maybe you are afraid I am not willing to receive your urges" and "It seems now you want to hear an interpretation that doesn't sound like a cliché".

The needs of the patient of having to go to the toilet or eat, are experienced by the analyst as requests carried out by a daughter to her mother, in the intimacy of the home. She tells Floppy so using open metaphors and comparisons, of a polysemous character, "you feel at home here, telling me, as if to your mummy". The sequence follows a regressive path and ends with the fifth intervention which connects the patient's bodily needs and current fears with her experiences related to the disappearance of her mother and her previous analyst,

"Maybe, you are telling me I am not rewarding enough, like your former analyst, and your mother, who didn't stay with you for long".

At the beginning of the session theoretical and technical ideas of the Kleinian framework referred to the maternal bond come to my mind: ideas such as unconscious fantasies, anxieties and primitive defences, traumatic situation, separation anxiety, pre-Oedipical, continent, enactments, etc. There is a special relation in the analyst's thinking, with the way of working and the ideas of significant authors from the Rio de la Plata tradition such as W. and M. Baranger on the dynamic field (1961–1962), Racker on complementary roles in the transference–countertransference relationship (1953), Alvarez de Toledo on "associating and Interpreting"(1954), Liberman (1970) on the analytical communication (conceptual vector). I think that these ideas, transmitted transgenerationally in a public or tacit way in supervision experiences and analysis, affects the way in which the analyst conceives the inter-subjective relationship. (Object relations of knowledge vector. Transgenerational influences. Psychoanalytic process.)

It is interesting to consider the concrete forms of communication which in this first sequence are frankly interactive. This coincides with the influence of the above mentioned contributions and allows us to infer an implicit coherence in her way of working, (coherence *vs.* contradiction vector). The metaphor of the home: "you feel at home here" and the reference to the patient's way of talking: "telling me, as if to your mummy" used by the analyst express, in a condensed manner, her experience of the bond with the patient, in which emotional experiences and primary relations with the patient are acted, as well as the analyst's answer to them. These forms of communication suppose different expressive manifestations in addition to their referential content and show the functioning of the mind of the analyst at an unconscious–preconscious level. Metaphorical formulation allows the connection of multiple unconscious enactments that take place between the patient and the analyst, with rudimentary aspects of the analytical theory, which allow a reflexive attitude towards them (action vector: listening, wording or interpretation, behaving). The analyst's perplexity seems to show a special moment of insight on the meaning of the patient's anxiety: a moment of great permeability of the analyst's mind towards unconscious aspects of the patient and herself (topographical level).

We can infer the implicit "Theory of Change": it is through the modifications in the current bond with the analyst that the patient's pathological reaction modes which express past experiences of traumatic separation can be transformed. Interpretations seek the integration of the emotional experience and a global conception of transference is inferred where new and old intertwine in a dialectic spiral (Pichon-Rivière, 1998). Without doubt countertransference (also in a broad sense) gathers the patient's form of talking and her affective tone which leads the analyst to be placed, complementarily, in a maternal role (Racker, 1953).

I would like to refer to the second moment of the session introduced by the narration of the first dream. In it, the analyst keeps the same attitudes towards her patient as in the beginning: she appears as emotionally close, trying to verbalise the patient's fear and seeking to assure the stability of the treatment: " Your mother died when you were not quite two years old .You seem to feel you have to be established before two years pass, perhaps fearing something wrong may happen between us".

In this second moment we can find some of the analysts suppositions about the effect of the mother's illness and death when the patient was only two years old, a time in which her physical needs (oral, anal, and urethral) were intrinsically united to the exchange fantasies with the mother, with the concomitant emotional tone (love and aggression) (developmental vector).

In spite of that, the theory of change and the interpretative goals are modified in the course of the session, opening up into new directions. The analysis of the dream, and probably the memory of the psychoanalytical process (in the same session the patient refers to her father's prohibitions in the use of the bathroom), lead the analyst to also consider aspects of the patient's bond with her father, with her current partner, her future projects, and the issue of her maternity. We notice that there is a change in the focus, the goal, and the theory of change implicit in the analyst's interpretations, which seek to modify Floppy's attitudes of neglect and abandonment of her own desires for those of her father and boyfriend.

Apart from having an attitude of "maternal" care towards the patient, the analyst seeks the discrimination of the patient's idealised aspects related to the masculine figure, confronting it with her attitudes of submission: "Perhaps you expect to obtain from me something impressive like the Dobermann Jules gave you." And in the tenth and last interpretation of the session the analyst condenses a couple of her interventions: "Being so needed by G is a good way of forgetting your own needs."

Leaving a place for her physical needs at the beginning of the session gives way to personal desires and aspirations in the present. The analyst takes into account more evolved aspects of Floppy's psychic development that lead us to infer a constellation of ideas that differ from the previous one, these last ones closer to the Freudian conceptual frame (superego, ideal ego, idealisation, desire of the other, subjugation, masochism, and Oedipal).

Additionally in this second part of the session the analyst includes the patient's current relational world. The father and the boyfriend not only exist as a blurry representation of the patient's internal world, but they are also considered with their own existence, from where they exert pressure over the patient. The analyst's interpretations implicitly seek to allow the patient to put a brake on them. I think that the dynamic (intrapsychic), situational and dramatic points of view, to use Bleger's terms (1978), integrate the conception of the analyst's analytical process in that moment with more current developments, for example Berenstein and Puget (1997) on the role of the present context and the surrounding reality.

A risk in the use of the map is that it can lead us to wish for exaggerated specification of the inferred ideas. This will lead us to lose the blurry and open character with which ideas arise in the session. To a certain extent these ideas work as intermediate formations, "fantasy theories". In this way metaphors used by the analyst on some occasions integrate enactments and unconscious fantasies between patient and analyst, with rudimentary theoretical aspects that arise in the session.

I deem it is also necessary to maintain an outlook on the whole session in order to follow the diachronic movement (not only a synchronic analysis in a determinate moment) of the communication so as to be on the alert for the simultaneity of imperative direction, of "lines" that impact the analyst with different "strength". If the session started with a strong tone of the patient's urgent claims to the analyst, leading her to be placed in maternal countertransference, we can also see announced from the beginning, like in a melody, the different important thematic chords related to the father. "When I was a child, my father worked at home . . . So we children had to be careful to keep the doors closed and we couldn't go to the bathroom whenever we wanted". These stay latent in the analyst from the beginning until they are installed in a stronger manner in the second part of the material. But the multiple superposed interpretative lines add density and depth to the analytical communication and interpretation.

Considering the session as a whole allows us to ask ourselves, finally, about the dark zones of the material that are left out of the map. These zones seem to be detected by the analyst even though they aren't worked on in this session. ". . . she was not sure of the illness which ended her mother's life, she thinks it was a cerebral tumour" ". . . she excused herself because she had come to meet me 'being such a mess' in a clear reference to her appearance and to her clothes. Needless to say, this did not coincide with my impression". The patient's inhibition of curiosity about the process of her mother's illness and the causes of her death stands out. Is this aspect linked to her anxieties and her experience of mess and disorganisation? With her way of relating to her father? With her disaffected experience of her abortion and her doubts about her femininity and her future maternity? Does this dark zone constitute a real tumour in her mind? These questions lead me to conceptions about the patient's mental functioning modes and her ways of perceiving her own reality (Bion, Fonagy).

In this analysis we have seen—taking into account the different vectors in the map—that different notions converge in a "patchwork" manner in the material's main interpretative lines. This conceptual network not only supposes convergent interpretative lines, but also diverging ones which arise from the comparison of different moments of the session. The exercise of mapping the implicit theories used on our practice carried out individually or in a group after the sessions, also allows visualising the interplay of the alternative hypothesis, and inferring the deliberative processes which latently contribute to the clinical investigation of the analyst and the process changes.

Commentary on
Lilia Bordone de Semeniuk's
clinical case

Peter Fonagy

The big and refreshing difference between standard psycho-analytic commentary on case reports and our efforts to map implicit theories in clinical practice is that the focus in the former case is on the patient, at what the patient is *"really* trying to communicate", whereas in unearthing implicit theories the concern is with the analyst's preconscious and unconscious mind (Canestri, 2006; Canestri, Fonagy, Bohleber, & Dennis, 2006). Normal clinical supervision will self-limit through the patient's inaccessibility to the supervisor. Getting it right is judged by the quality of the fit between the report and the formulation. The task is relatively easy as the material is treated as text, the person interpreted by the supervisor is not there to respond, directly or indirectly, to indicate dissatisfaction. In exploring implicit unconscious theories, by contrast, we work directly with the source. The analyst is here to tell us that our presumptions are inappropriate. Both concern unconscious thoughts and feelings, but while simple clinical commentary aims to illuminate the patient's communication, the effort of this panel is trying to unearth the preconscious and unconscious forces which drive the therapist's work both in terms of her relations to public theory and as these become more or less relevant during the unfolding of a single session.

Floppy's analyst provides us with the material from which we may attempt to identify preconscious theories, unconscious influences upon the use of theories, her cultural world-view, and her implicit theories of change. My remarks will focus around these core aspects to mapping the analyst's mind at work. Let me start by saying that the clinical material is not only wonderful for this purpose but it is also a credit to the imaginative and enthusiastic engagement of both parties in the exploratory adventure of this psychoanalysis.

In her first intervention on the Tuesday session, the analyst remarks on her patient's change of habit and links it to what appears to be a countertransference experience. She feels that the patient is somehow making herself at home, as if conversing with her mother, triggered perhaps by having been invited as it were to witness and contemplate her patient's bodily functions. She is assuming that the act is significant, that she is intended to be the receptacle of the patient's evacuation, and that the act suggesting urgency is somehow linked to this. In her second intervention she is quite explicit about her experience of being required to accept a patient's urges. She responds to the patient's description of feeling intruded upon by her father's patients as a defensive response on the part of the patient, turning passive into active, having been intruded on Floppy becomes the intruder.

There is something in this interchange which speaks to a set of assumptions implicitly shared by patient and analyst about the primitive, drive driven nature of enactment. The analyst assumes in her comment that her patient is pleased about enacting familiarity that is a gratification of a need or something that generates pleasurable affect. The patient accepts that "everything has a meaning" but somehow this raises an issue of boundaries. It is as if this was a paternal dictum from the psychotherapist father that she expects the analyst to share because of her "father psychotherapist". This touches what we in our mapping have talked about the object relations of knowledge. The relation of analyst and patient to analytic theory is clearly entering both the transference and the countertransference of this session. The analyst feels and is seen to feel, an attachment to her "thinking–talking" (not acting) parental heritage, a link which she is not about to allow her patient to sever.

Non-consciously the analyst is clearly aware of the transgenerational aspect of this commitment to a search for meaning but perhaps less conscious of the incestuous phantasies that accompany it—hardly surprising considering that the primal scene was probably fantasised by this patient to occur in father's consulting room—extending to the upstairs lavatories. The patient continues her concern with Oedipal boundaries, describing feeling being caught by her previous analyst stuffing herself. Her current analyst takes a position on our developmental vector, talking about "Little Floppy" and emphasising her somatic experiences at the boundary. She may well be right and the patient's wish to fill her stomach before the session may be a defence against feeling left hungry, deprived of boundary-breaking contact. But the patient will have none of this pretence of childhood and forces the analyst to abandon her developmental preconceptions by asking a very adult question, based on a piece of syllogistic reasoning: "Then what is the meaning of eating after a session? Maybe, I am not satisfied?". The analyst reports feeling perplexed which is less likely to be due to the searching nature of the patient's questioning (the simple answer is of course "could be") but by being knocked off the perch of her assumptions about the current developmental age of her patient. Little children worried about toilets and filling themselves up with food do not ask searching questions based on syllogistic reasoning.

At this point the analyst switches implicit theories and starts seeing the material in relation to the trauma of the patient's loss of the first analyst. She abandons the pseudo-drive theory formulations of the first part of the session, moves along our preconscious topographical vector into the domain of object relations: attachment and object loss. The patient is as confirmatory about this as any patient could be and tells the analyst her experience of "unfinished business" in relation to the dream of the previous session. Suddenly the toilet urgency and food and boundary issues appear in a different light to both patient and analyst. It is now all to do with *temporality* of their joint experience. The dream is about acquiring a giant puppy in a magically rapid way without going through the normal time consuming pre-requisites. The analyst now firmly in an object relations mode identifies the patient's anxiety about not receiving enough in the time they share together.

The analyst's sensitivity to the patient's state we assume enables the patient to get closer to her underlying anxiety about her wish to have a child. Is the analysis progressing fast enough for this to be possible? Interestingly here the analyst switches theoretical frames again and makes the strong assumption that the anxieties in the present about time make most sense in the context of the patient's biography: the early loss of her mother. Her theory of therapeutic action at this point seems to be putting the patient in touch with the potential anxieties she may experience in any new attachment relationship given the historical reality of the early loss of her object. The analyst's implicit theory is "Given your history, I well understand why you should expect to loose me too, hence your urgency, your need to get inside the private parts of my house, my mind; boundaries mean loss to you and frighten you". Note, that she avoids taking up the unconscious fantasies that might surround the loss for which there is also ample material in the session (the orality and anality of the first twenty or so minutes and the puppy dream linking to fragile and old objects).

This shift in analytic conceptualisation yields the most challenging transferential material in the session. Floppy talks about her boyfriend who she has to transport to *his* analytic session, having had a stress-relieving physical intervention (acupuncture). Plausibly, Floppy is talking about herself and her desire to be transported by her analyst, to be shown concern as she is showing concern. We are vividly presented with a Mahlerian struggle about separation–individuation, about existing separately or a part of single fused unit, about looking after in order to be looked after. The analyst moves theories again and becomes slightly relational in her orientation, asserting that getting engaged with the needs of others may help distract attention from painful unmet needs within. She resists the pull towards more primitive content and places the conflict in the context of current relationships. This could be because we are approaching the end of the session and separation, and there is unconscious resistance of primitive theories imposed by her guilt about abandoning her patient at a time when her wish is for blissful stress-free sleep on her analyst's couch.

References

Alvarez de Toledo, L. (1954): The analysis of "associating", "interpreting" and "words". *International Journal of Psycho-Analysis*, 77(2): 291–318, (1996).

Baranger, W., & Baranger, M. (1961–1962). The analytic situation as a dynamic field. *International Journal of Psycho-Analysis, 89*: 795–826, (2008).

Berenstein, I., & Puget, J. (1997). *Lo vincular. Teoría y clínica psicoanalítica.* Buenos Aires: Paidós.

Bleger, J. (1969). Teoría y práctica en psicoanálisis. La praxis psicoanalítica, *Revista Uruguaya de Psicoanálisis, XI*: 287–303.

Bleger, J. (1978). *Simbiosis y ambigüedad. Estudio psicoanalítico.* Buenos Aires: Paidós.

Boesky, D. (2005). Psychoanalytic controversies contextualized. *Journal of the American Psychoanalytical Association, 53*: 835–863.

Canestri, J. (Ed.). (2006). *Psychoanalysis: From Practice to Theory.* London: Whurr.

Canestri, J., Bohleber, W., Denis, P., & Fonagy, P. (2006). The map of private (implicit, preconscious) theories in clinical practice. In: J. Canestri (Ed.), *Psychoanalysis: From Practice to Theory* (pp. 29–43). Chichester: Whurr.

Duarte, A. S. L. de (2000). "Mas allá de la información dada": cómo construímos nuestras hipótesis clínicas. *Revista de la Sociedad Argentina de Psicoanálisis, 3*: 103–120.

Liberman, D. (1970). *Lingüística, interacción comunicativa y proceso psicoanalítico.* Buenos Aires: Ed. Galerna.

Nieto, M., et al. (1985). Investigando la experiencia analítica: una propuesta (Investigating analytical experience: a proposal). *Revista Uruguaya de Psicoanálisis, 83*: 117–135, (1996).

Pichon-Rivière, E. (1998). *Teoría del Vínculo* (Vol. 19). Buenos Aires: Nueva Visión.

Purcell, S. D. (2004). The analyst's theory: A third source of countertransference. *International Journal of Psycho-Analysis, 85*: 635–652.

Racker, H. (1953). A contribution to the problem of counter-transference. *International Journal of Psycho-Analysis, 34*: 313–324.

Reder, J. (2002). From knowledge to competence. Reflections on theoretical work. *International Journal of Psycho-Analysis, 83*: 799–809.

Sandler, J. (1983). Reflections on some relations between psychoanalytic concepts and psychoanalytic practice. *International Journal of Psycho-Analysis, 64*: 35–45.

Supervision in psychoanalytical training: the analysis and the use of implicit theories in psychoanalytical practice

Jorge Canestri

The objective of this work is to propose a comprehensive reflection on the concept of supervision and on its function in psychoanalytical training. Particular attention will be given to the use of the analyst's implicit theories in clinical practice. An example of a supervision will be analysed using a conceptual instrument that is the result of qualitative research carried out within the European Psychoanalytical Federation.

Studying the history of a concept, following its progress and its transformations, and critically analysing its links to theory, are useful exercises in any discipline. But in psychoanalysis, characterised as it is by a growing theoretical pluralism and affected by an insidious terminological Babelisation, the application of the critical-historical method is absolutely essential. This is also the case when considering supervision.

As we all know, supervision originates from the Freudian awareness (1910d) of the intimate relationship between "helping others" and "self-knowledge"; that is, it is a derivation of analysis. The direct derivation of supervision from the analyst's analysis was at the origin of the bitter discourse between the Hungarian School and all the others. The debates at the Four Countries Conference (1935 and 1937), and the discussions relative to the difference between *Kontrollanalyse* (analysis of the student's countertransference) and *Analysenkontrolle* (own analysis) did not succeed in opposing the arguments of Kovacs (1936) who emphasised the advantages of a first supervision by the analyst of the candidate, and which were: an intimate knowledge of the candidate's problems, and the possibility of analysing in depth, using the analytic method, the difficulties at the base of the candidate's specific reactions when facing the vicissitudes and pathologies of his patients. I do not mean that the disadvantages were not obvious (in fact, they brought about the eventual general abandoning of the Hungarian system, except for the Lacanian analysts); and that is, that this practice risks accentuating a dyadic and narcissistic closure between the analyst and the candidate (the function of the supervisor as "third"), and does not allow for a revelation of the possible (and in fact inevitable) blind spots of every analysis. It is important to point out that this "therapeutic" aspect of supervision, that apparently went out of the door when the Hungarian system was refuted, comes back again through the window masked by solutions that are even more debatable. One example alone is the unanimously criticised proposal of Blitzsten and Fleming (1953) that favoured meetings between the analyst and the supervisor of the candidate in order to consider the problems emerging during supervision.

If the literature seems to agree on the bipolar nature of supervision—therapeutic on the one hand, and teaching/learning on the other hand—then this bipolarity itself immediately becomes revitalised. Solnit (1970) conceptualises supervision as ". . . less than therapy and more than teaching". The suspicion arises that this therapeutic–transformative aspect may be hidden but still present, and that this may be due to the "underlying theoretic void" of supervision (Manfredi & Nissim, 1984).

And the learning function is not any clearer. Psychoanalysis has not developed a theory that takes it fully into account—only partially. I would like to make it clear that in this case I am not speaking about a theory of knowledge in the wide sense (psychoanalysis does possess theories or, more precisely, partial models of knowledge (Freud, Bion, Green, etc.)), but about a theory of learning of psychoanalysis, as a theory and as a practice, that would allow for a discussion of the didactic function of analysis, supervision, and seminars in the training of the psychoanalyst.

If these propositions are realistic, then perhaps it would be useful to go back and formulate the routine questions: what is the method and what is the object of supervision?

In *Die Psychoanalyse als Methode*, Herman (1963) affirmed the priority of method over contents: ". . . it could be stated, paraphrasing a famous saying: the method is everything, the content is nothing". However, it is easy to ascertain that while the method is well-defined and characterised in psychoanalysis as a therapy, it is very difficult, if not impossible, to specify the method of supervision if the object and the purpose are not clearly defined beforehand. In his excellent "Critical digest of the literature on psychoanalytic supervision", DeBell (1963), after giving various definitions of supervision, concludes by rightly emphasising how "purpose and method are inextricably entwined". Moreover, the supervision method is generally defined negatively: one must not use the interpretation even when recognising unconscious dynamics in the supervisee; and the rule of abstention and the rule of the analyst's neutrality are not in use.

Let us ask ourselves about the object. "What" do we supervise? In what is called "classic theory" the object of the supervision is the patient and the analytical work. The supervision should allow a binocular vision of the patient, a transmission of "know how", and a growth of the analytical instrument. But of which patient are the supervisor and the supervised talking about? Jacobs, David, and Meyer (1995) hypothesise that it might be ". . . the person constructed through the sensibilities of the therapist", that is, a fantasmatic patient.

It is, however, essential to take into consideration that contemporary psychoanalysis has made a,

> change in outlook that has progressively moved the analyst's focus from the life events and pathology of the patient to an analysis of the situation, the relationship and the analytic process. The complex configuration resulting from the working together of analyst and analysand—differently conceived of according to the various psychoanalytic theories—has ended up creating a new object for study . . . a new and unique figure of intersubjectivity. (Canestri, 1994)

Some of the concepts elaborated and developed during the last fifty years;

- countertransference, conceived of as a useful instrument for clinical work
- projective identification, conceived of as pathological projective identification and also as a means of communication capable of bringing about states of mind
- an enlarged concept of transference and the enactment, intended as an action in which, mainly through the components of the super-segmental level and those of the third channel (gestures, facial mimicry, and attitudes of the body)[1] of communication, the other is influenced and involved in a particular intersubjective sequence

are central points for more adequate elaboration of the complex configuration of psychoanalytic work. Even if the "thing" supervised seems to be the same, that is, patient and analytical work, in actual fact the shift of accent is not without its consequences. In the light of these concepts, the deeper comprehension of the complex transference –countertransference relationship oversteps the boundaries of the therapeutic field to penetrate into supervision.

In reality, this widening of the field is progressive. Ekstein in 1960 and Wallerstein in 1981 began proposing problems relative to the process of supervision which is conceived as a specific sphere; on the other hand Searles (1955) describes supervision as a relationship in which a proportion is obtained: supervisor–candidate as candidate–patient. Searles' "reflection process" in "The informational value of the supervisor's emotional experiences" brings the supervisor/supervisee relationship right to the forefront, asserting that the emotional reaction of the supervisor to the therapist's presentation is caused by the fact that the therapist unconsciously communicates in a nonverbal manner what he does not understand about the unconscious communication of his patient. The same idea is stated by Arlow (1963): ". . . the supervisor acts like the analyst in the psychoanalysis of a psychoanalysis".

Years later, in the same theoretic area (North American psychoanalysis), the concepts of enactment and of parallel process would develop. The concept of "parallel process" implies that there are enactments in the supervisor–therapist relationship of dynamics which characterise the therapist–patient relationship. The patient–therapist–supervisor triangle, apparently equal to itself, in fact, is profoundly different. The dynamics taken into consideration increase the complexity of the object and change the configuration of its limits. The fact that the triangle may become a "therapeutic rhombus" (patient–candidate–training analyst of the candidate–supervisor), a pentagon (including the institution), or any more complex polyhedral figure varying according to the number of elements involved, does not change the essence of the problem. The key is not to be found mainly in the number of the intervening elements, but in the conceptualisation of the dynamics running between them. This allows us to understand how the deepening of the problem leads to the discovery of new elements and new dynamics: such as the paper by Stimmel (1995) on the transference of the supervisor on the candidate, which goes beyond the parallel process itself.

In a different theoretic area, that of the Kleinian trend, the progress of the configuration of the object of supervision, even though obviously inspired by a different conceptual basis, shows noticeable affinities with the preceding one.

If the concept of projective identification is taken into due account, consideration of its effect on the conceptualisation of countertransference becomes inevitable. It is not necessary to give further specifications, but I would like to remind, as an example, of Grinberg's concept of projective counteridentification (1970, 1986), Liendo's concept of counterprojection (1971) (every counteridentified becomes in its turn a potential source of counterprojections) and the emphasis given to the "factual" messages and to the logic traps in clinical work, in order to get a glimpse of the complexity which is created in the configuration of the object.

For a moment, I would like to go back again to the age-old confrontation on supervision as a "therapy" *sui generis* and on to suggest interpretations to the candidate who is having countertransference problems. I take it for granted that every increase in knowledge always has therapeutic effects and that discrimination between therapy and knowledge risks, in our field, being at the least a misplaced problem. However, this reformulation does not absolve us from facing some of the difficulties of supervision in other terms. Nor does it save us from the embarrassment of discriminating (Perrotta, 1978) between interpretation intended at the first level as a hypothesis of work on some material (to offer to the candidate) and interpretation (second level) intended as a therapeutic formulation to the patient.

Following the Freudian concept of countertransference (know yourself to help others), it is quite simple to recognise that the place to solve the candidate's persistent manifestations of difficulty in countertransference—such as those on certain themes, or with certain patients and accompanied by selective blindness—is in the analysis of the candidate. The intervention of the supervisor could easily limit itself to sending the supervisee back to the correct place (that is to analysis).

However, if the preceding notations on widening the concept of countertransference have any meaning, the complexity of the situation that then arises rapidly shows that this solution can only be partial. I must say from the start, that the concept of projective counteridentification must be reviewed and limited in its range (see Etchegoyen (1986), and that projective identification has been used and abused, and that "... the effects of projective identification and of projective counteridentification, as all the other aspects of countertransference are always related to the "*loci minoris resistentiae*" of the specific analyst" (Manfredi & Nissim, 1984). In spite of this, the point does exist. Sending the analyst into analysis at each step forward reinforces the idea of the omnipotence of analysis and ignores its inevitable blind spots; it denies the multiplicity of stimuli deriving from clinical practice and the material impossibility of considering them all in the analysis of the candidate; it implicitly affirms that all the *loci minoris resistentiae* could disappear after a successful cure—thus contradicting all evidence.

But above all it denies the theory itself in its complexity. If the notations that we have made regarding the change in outlook in contemporary psychoanalysis are true, what psychoanalytic theory affirms is that clinical work is the result of a relation in which everyone inevitably puts into play their own characteristics and their own limitations. It is an ethical as well as a scientific necessity that the analyst be aware of this, and that he is able to administer them wisely (Freud, 1937c). This does not allow us to reduce the complexity by sterilising the analyst's participation, for better or for worse, or to deny in the supervision what has been laboriously achieved in clinical work. Experience repeatedly teaches us that to refuse to interpret the exact compromise of the candidate's countertransference—regarding not the blind spots of countertransference, but the responses to the projective identification and to the enactment of the patient—in order

to return him to analysis, results in an ulterior return from the training analyst to the supervisor. If the supervisor cannot interpret and
the analyst cannot supervise, the candidate and the patient remain in
the trap of the pathology of non-decoded transference–countertransference. This all forms a logical trap from which we must escape, as
Liendo (1971) and Perrotta (1978) rightly point out.

In the endless discussion about whether the analysis or the
supervision is the place delegated to interpret and resolve these
countertransference obstacles (not the stable blind spots of the countertransference), I would definitely side with supervision. As Kernberg
(1965) says:

> When dealing with borderline or severely regressed patients, as con-
> trasted to those presenting symptomatic neuroses and many character
> disorders, the therapist tends to experience rather soon in the treatment
> intensive emotional reactions having more to do with the patient's pre-
> mature, intense and chaotic transference, and with the therapist's capa-
> city to withstand psychological stress and anxiety, than with any
> particular, specific problem of the therapist's past. (p. 43)

Rolf Klüwer, in his paper for the Standing Conference on Training
(1981) defined two forms of countertransference: the "helpful countertransference" (*hilfreiche Gegenübertragung*) and the "resistant
countertransference" (*widerständige Gegenübertragung*). To work on
countertransference phenomena as they appear in the supervisory
situation, trying to transform the second form into the first, is a useful
indication in the sense of what was said above. The helpful countertransference is "a specially effective instrument in teaching [and]
promote the learning process".

What is the meeting point of the ideas of Wallerstein, Searles,
Arlow, Stimmel, and others on one side, and of Grinberg, Perrotta,
Liendo, and others on the other? *The proposal to create a bridge between
the two elements of the therapy–teaching bi-polarity and to bind supervision
to the theory of psychoanalysis.* One cannot affirm on the one hand the
existence of projective identification, of counteridentification, of enactment, and then leave out the unconscious of the analyst and not *interpret*—analytically—all the variations and the vicissitudes of his work
relationship with the patient. The sensation of a theoretic void accom-
panying the supervision is largely due to such a dissociation between

what we accept in theory and in clinical practice and what we accept in the practice of supervision. Arlow's definition of supervision as the psychoanalysis of a psychoanalysis, seems to be more adequate than others in describing a new state of things. In it, the object changes again. It would not be possible to think of supervision as a psycho-analysis without attributing to it its own dynamics and without presuming that it would reveal something of the other psycho-analysis—that of the analyst with the patient. My previous reference to Searles and the "reflection process" puts this quite clearly. The subsequent notion about the parallel process conceptualises it. The proposal—both in analyses of the North American area and of the Kleinian area—is not only to consider the dynamics of the supervisor –supervisee relationship as forming part of the process of supervision in which the analyst–patient dynamics are analysed, but also to accept that the supervision relation *is* the place of enactments expressing the dynamics of the analyst–patient relation. If, for example, the theory of projective identification–projective counteridentification truly describes a certain state of things, then it is reasonable to think that the counteridentified analyst becomes a source of counter projection over his supervisor in whom he provokes some responses. Moreover, it is not necessary to adhere to Kleinian theory in order to accept this new delimitation of the object of supervision; in fact, the concept of parallel process did not originate in the Kleinian area.

This all makes it quite clear that the Hungarian approach to super-vision, that proves to be inadequate for the reasons set out, does, how-ever, contain a grain of truth: it is not possible to dissociate the practice of psychoanalysis from the practice of supervision without leaving the latter deprived of a theory. The deeper one goes into the contents, the clinical aspect, and the psychopathology of contemporary psycho-analysis, the more this dissociation proves to be inadequate.

What conclusions should be drawn from these successive delimi-tations and characterisations of the process and of the object of super-vision, that take into due account the relationship between purpose and method that, as I said before, are inextricably entwined?

Supervision can be seen as a field of variable dimensions. The con-figuration of this field ensues from the vertex of observation chosen by the supervisor, and it derives directly from the theory that informs the supervision and from its pre-established goals. The field can include: the patient, the analytic relationship, the patient–analyst–supervisor relationship, the supervision relationship as "analogon" of the analytic relationship, the relationship of patient–analyst–training, analyst–supervisor–institution, etc. The theory that informs the choice of the vertex can, like every theory, turn out to be unsuitable for the purpose or insufficient to recognise the complex therapeutic and intersubjective reality that it has to confront. It is up to the ability, the flexibility, and the awareness of the supervisor to take note of this. The element that usually forces him to modify the field is the psychopathology of the patients; in fact, it is not by chance that psychoanalytic theory has developed a change of outlook in consonance with the acceptance in analysis of psychotic, borderline, and narcissistic pathologies. As I have said above, it can also happen that the vertex of supervision is dissociated from the theory that the supervisor applies in his clinical work. This contradiction is not without consequences, inasmuch as it leaves the supervision itself faced with a theoretical void. The advantage of the know-how on the strategic understanding of the complexity of the process is a manifestation of this void; moreover, it risks fostering a tendency to imitation, to mannerisms, and to dependence in the supervisee ("I'm not sure *why* I do what I do, but I know very well *how* to do what I do").

But the field is also shaped according to the pre-established goal. If the objective is well individuated, the supervisor can operate a cutting of the field; that is, he can choose the variables that he will take into consideration and decide on those that he will deliberately leave out.

Here I am going to give a brief example to illustrate the concept.

In one of the Component Societies of the IPA there used to be a monthly seminar of group supervision for associate and full members. During one of these meetings, an associate member presented some extremely interesting material from a seriously disturbed patient, in which there appeared an anguished and very worrying dream. When the material had been read, the supervisor asked the participants—as she usually did—for their thoughts, fantasies, and reflections about the material. There followed a long silence. The supervisor then pointed out that that silence was linked to the most significant problem of the patient: her tremendous sense of emptiness.

Shortly afterwards, the visit of another senior analyst, who asked for the presentation of clinical material related to what she wanted to develop theoretically, made it possible to reconsider the same sessions in another supervision. Her interventions were mainly about the formulation of the interpretations and she made constant reference to the theoretic concepts explained in the previous conference.

The difference between the two supervisions is to be found not in an understanding of the material, that was very similar, but rather in the delimitation of the field operated by each supervisor. The diversity of purpose conditioned the difference of method. I should like to describe how each of these fields could be shaped.

In the first case we are faced with a group or "collective" supervision that has certain particularities: according to the first type of intervention described above, what is most obvious is that the countertransference response *of the group* to the presentation of the material is the fulcrum of the supervisor's interpretative work. The supervisor interprets the silence that emerges from the group as the "analogon" of the void of the patient. The implicit theory would say that the material induces silence in the group, that this is the equivalent of the essential void of the patient, and that the decoding of this countertransference and its interpretation *to the group* allows for a deeper investigation into the work on the material and for an understanding of the case. This theory naturally has other implicit supportive hypotheses, both on the nature of the mechanisms taking place as well as on the comprehension of the group dynamics. I think it is important to emphasise how this intervention shapes the field of the supervision like a parallel process that includes the institution and the dynamics of the group, and is centred on the group itself and not on the analyst and the analysis of the patient. This is functional to the pre-established goal—that of sharing the clinical work of each member of the group and discussing its coordinates.

The way of handling group dynamics exemplified in the first supervision is very similar to that of the operative groups (Pichon-Rivière). I think that these groups can be incorporated very advantageously in the analytic training with various objectives such as: supervision of clinical material, teaching of theory and technique, investigation of implicit and personal theories in clinical work (Canestri, 1994, 2006), and analysis of difficulties emerging during the learning process and in the comparison between psychoanalytic theories. I will not go any further into the characteristics of these groups here. I only want to say that after having clearly explained the task, the coordinator or appointed leader will take into consideration the dynamics of the group at its various stages (which have a relationship with Bionian hypotheses on group functioning) in order to analyse the "emergence" of the group as the expression of the bond that the group has established with the task. The "emergence", therefore, will be every element that functions as a possible starting point through which a given situation acquires meaning (analytically speaking). The specific goal of this type of group is the integration of disassociated aspects of the work of symbolisation and of the affective dynamics of the teaching process. In the case of the first supervision, the group "emergence" was the initial silence after reading the material of the session. The "emergence" indicates the bond that the group had at that moment with the task: to understand the material and elaborate it. The interpretation of the first group "emergence" constitutes a first moment of synthesis conceptualising the action of the group and enriching symbolisation and affective integration. The group process can be re-launched through discussion in the direction of a new synthesis.

In the case of the second expert analyst who supervised the same material, the supervision developed as an individual supervision before an audience. The established task was to illustrate certain theoretical and technical principles of the supervisor, that is, her concept of analytic work. In a case like this, the supervisor–lecturer obviously limits the field according to the goal.

This type of seminar and this kind of collective supervision provide the suitable surroundings to investigate the implicit and personal theories in clinical work that were mentioned above. The implicit and personal theories, that I have already had the chance to highlight (Canestri, 1994, 2006), following a pioneering idea of Sandler, are the result of a variety of factors. One of them is the development of the theory that leads to the creation of various dimensions of significance, dimensions that vary from one psychoanalyst to another. Sandler, author of the concept, underlined the importance of working to make explicit the implicit concepts that psychoanalysts use in their practice:

> With increasing clinical experience the analyst, as he grows more competent, will preconsciously (descriptively speaking, unconsciously) construct a whole variety of theoretical segments which

relate directly to his clinical work. They are the products of unconscious thinking, are very much partial theories, models or schemata,
which have the quality of being available in reserve, so to speak, to be
called upon whenever necessary. That they may contradict one
another is no problem. They coexist happily as long as they are unconscious. (Sandler, 1983, p. 38)

The following consideration of implicit theories draws on some
conclusions that were reached within the Working Party on
Theoretical Issues project. The above quotation reminds us how the
special relationship between praxis and theory in psychoanalysis
characterises our discipline and illustrates its specificity.

As Sandler says, the psychoanalyst, "as he grows more com-
petent", when he listens to the experiences that his patients tells
him, does not apply simple derivations of the theories that he
knows because he has learnt them, that is, what we could call "official
theories". Rather, he preconsciously and, descriptively speaking,
unconsciously constructs "theories" or models adapted to the circumstances of his clinical work with that particular patient. We
should not underestimate the quantity of elements of every type and
origin that contribute to the construction of these "theories" or partial
models.

These elements may include: the specific contents of the analysts'
unconscious and preconscious; his *"Weltanschauungen"*; the psychology of common sense; his adherence to a psychoanalytical group or
school, the quality of this adherence, and the relationship he has with
the psychoanalytic "authorities"; his scientific and pre-scientific
beliefs; his personal re-elaboration of the concepts of the discipline; his
countertransference, etc. The list could be much longer and is always
open to new influences. On account of the specificity of clinical practice, psychoanalytical concepts are never formed once and for all, but
are continually being transformed and re-elaborated.

A serious analysis would reveal that although the analyst at work
may have declared his adherence to a particular theoretical model, his
comprehension and interpretation were in fact being guided by what
Sandler called partial theories, models, or schemata, that were largely
constructed using concepts deriving from different theories and
integrated unconsciously. The analysis of what *really* occurs in practice must be complementary to the normative capacities of the "official" theories.

In order to investigate this particular movement *from practice to theory*, we need to work out a programme to confront some of the major problems of psychoanalysis in such a way that they can be explored *within* our analytical practice. We also need to elaborate a specific methodology that allows for conceptual research, but that also has a solid empirical basis.

A programme such as this was developed by the Working Party on Theoretical Issues (WPTI) of the European Psychoanalytic Federation, and led to the creation of "The map of implicit (private, preconscious) theories in clinical practice". This piece of qualitative systematic research was based on a study of the following: a) clinical reports of analytic work; b) our own clinical experience; and c) our own negotiation of public theory in a wide range of contexts. Based on these experiences we identified a number of categories (vectors) that we considered relevant to our understanding of the way concepts are used in psychoanalytic practice. This qualitative research was aimed at providing a new perspective on how theory and practice are related in psychoanalysis. The "map" is a fairly organised delineation of today's patterns of analytic thinking about clinical material, that may either not be talked about publicly or are literally outside of the individual's awareness. In the map, "theory" is defined as a three-component model:

public theory based thinking + private theoretical thinking + interaction of private and explicit thinking (implicit use of explicit theory).

Concerning the configuration of "sets of dimensions of meanings", Sandler proposes that ". . . it is also possible to look with profit at the dimension of meaning of a theoretical notion or term *within the mind of any individual psychoanalyst*" (1983, p. 36, my italics). The psychoanalyst would thus be transformed into an "instrument", and the careful study of the analytical situation into a laboratory for studying the "formation of unconscious theoretical structures" in *status nascendi*.

Sandler says:

Such partial structures may in fact represent better (i.e. more useful and appropriate) theories than the official ones, and it is likely that many valuable additions to psychoanalytical theory have come about because conditions have arisen that have allowed preconscious part-theories to come together and emerge in a plausible and psychoanalytically socially acceptable way ... It is my firm conviction that the investigation of the implicit, private theories of clinical psychoanalysis opens a major new door in psychoanalytic research. (p. 38)

The map of implicit (private, preconscious) theories in clinical practice is shown in the Appendix of this volume. It may be useful to refer to this to assist in understanding the clinical material that follows. A more detailed and conceptually developed version appears in Canestri, 2006.

In order to illustrate the use of this instrument I will include a brief clinical example of a psychoanalytical session. I have made some comments that are related to the vectors of "the map".

Clinical example

Methodology

This is an example of collective supervision, coordinated by a supervisor. The analyst presenting the case read a brief summary of the patient's history and the four weekly sessions. The analyst's interventions were analysed using the "the map". All the members of the group, usually about ten, contributed to this analysis in an effort to identify the implicit theories used by the analyst. The intention was to avoid transforming the work into a supervision of the quality or the pertinence of the analytical interventions, but, rather, to identify which were the real instruments that the analyst had used without knowing it. These seminars of collective supervision lasted four hours each, and during this time the theories used (both implicit and explicit) were discussed, as well as their internal coherence and possible integration. The coordinator was thus able to teach and discuss the theories starting from the clinical practice, and not vice versa.

F's case

F is a thirty-five to forty-year-old man. Married. He has a five-year-old daughter. He is a computer programmer. His analysis began four years ago because of difficulties experienced in relationships. With a group of friends he created a software company and is now in transition between a dependent and an independent job. There is a common element in the histories of the patient and the analyst—both were born prematurely due to a genetic disposition of the mother. The patient's first period of life was difficult.

Session 1

The patient arrives thirty minutes late.

> *Patient*: (He comments, with an air of defeat, that he was busy chatting on the landing outside the office with some colleagues. And he adds: a conversation about work that was just as useless as it was repetitive.)
>
> Perhaps there is some part of me that didn't want to come, but contrary to what usually happens, I was aware that I was wasting my time.
>
> *Analyst*: I wonder if, rather than a part of you does not want to come, it could be a part that is afraid to come to the session?
>
> Perhaps there is an anxiety that makes you experience the session and the relationship with me in the same way as that with your firm and your managers, or as, in the past, you experienced the relationship with your family and your parents: that is, passively, without any motivation, as if your hands were tied or you felt like a "dead body" (slip of the tongue). In earlier sessions, when comparing your present incapacity to communicate to your firm your intention of leaving, and your previous incapacity to communicate to your parents a view or intention that was different from theirs, you said that it was as if you couldn't express your needs, your intentions, and your thoughts.

The analyst begins his interpretation speaking in the first person and consequently reveals something about himself, in this case "I wonder if". Generally this type of intervention could be considered as a meta-communication of supportive action, trying to get the patient to reflect, something like "you will make progress in your understanding of yourself". From the point of view of the "the map" there are two vectors to refer to:

2. *Conceptual vector: c. clinical generalisations* (from a technical point of view) and *d. psychoanalytic process*, where we could find several indications about the analyst's theories of change: That is, it is helpful to transmit to the patient that we are working together introducing the interpretation by a "prologue" (I wonder if); putting the patient in

touch with the feelings that the patient is trying to split off is therapeutic ("to be afraid" of in this case), to elaborate alternative self
representations in order to help the patient to adopt an observing role
vis-à-vis the self, implicit ideas about the intersubjective relationship
between patient and analyst, etc.; and, 3 *Action vector, c. wording or
interpretation*, including the elements I described before (prologue)
and *b. formulating*. In formulating we must consider the role of theory
in the analyst's mind and in the interaction with the patient. In this
case it is clear that theory could serve to contain the patient and the
analyst. The analyst said: "I immediately realise that I had a slip of the
tongue—'dead body' instead of 'dead weight'—and I imagine that
behind this slip of the tongue of mine there could be both a second
interpretative level as well as my countertransference reply, both
unconscious. In reality, concerning the interpretation, a theory comes
to my mind, about the traumatic experience of the patient's birth.
Regarding my possible emotional reaction towards the patient, I feel
that his incorrigible tendency to be late made me feel the anxiety of
being useless, devitalised, and discouraged, as he had always felt:
perhaps behind the aggressive component implicit in my interpretation ('you are a dead body') there is hidden my need to free myself
from this anxiety by externalising it and putting it into the patient".

In this case the reference is to *1. Topographical vector, c. unconscious
influences upon the use of theories*. Theory is used to solve a countertransference problem: the aggression against the patient is displaced
onto theory (but cannot avoid the slip of the tongue). The patient's narrative evokes anxiety which is sidestepped by bringing in a protective
theory. It is also a response to the analyst's sense of helplessness. There
is a massive use of the patient's history and of the analysis' history.
Many other considerations are possible, but I am just trying to make an
example of this kind of work on the clinical material.

> P: On this subject, I think there was a period during which I felt more free
> . . . I remember the time I spent in X (a town), when I was in my last year
> of university . . . I had won a scholarship . . . at that time I felt happier.
>
> . . . But it is as though, as the years went by, I could not maintain the deter-
> mination I had in that period . . .
>
> It is as if I had forgotten that in order to feel well I needed and still need
> to "do" things . . . to dedicate a part of my life to doing what I want. This
> is why at the beginning of the analysis I told you that perhaps I no longer

knew what I wanted . . . Today I know something more about what I want . . . not everything . . . But, like I feel today . . . I feel incapable . . . I am afraid of achieving it . . .

A: Perhaps you are trying to make me understand that at the basis of what you want, there is your need to be an independent individual . . . However, the possibility of being one frightens you . . . And so it is as if you could not recognise and use the dependence in order to reach your final goal of becoming independent, of feeling adult . . . of being able to feel on an equal level and, finally, to be able to separate yourself from your parents, from your managers . . . or from me and from the analysis.

Also in this interpretation elements can be identified—relative to the *wording and formulation*—that are similar to those identified in the previous interpretation. In this case there is the more evident addition of having aims for the patient as outcome that impact on how the patient is treated: there is a "direction of the cure" for the patient (2. *Conceptual vector, d. Psychoanalytic process*).

P: . . . Yes . . . and I'm thinking of this new job opportunity . . . Here they would give me six months with a salary . . . because they have considered that my situation is more difficult than theirs . . . I would have to leave my present job . . . and if things don't go well? . . . I would be risking more than them . . . So they decided to meet me half way by giving me six months wages guaranteed . . . these months should show whether the work is getting along well . . . otherwise, like they did, I should have to think up an alternative activity that would bring in some money . . . Francesco, for example, is a computer consultant and writes programmes . . . the other partner has a business of distribution and assistance for printers and hardware components . . .

And then, . . . I'm always scared that after having left my job I might discover that the same tensions come up again towards my new partners . . .

A: I wonder if you are not thinking that these people represent an example of the independence that you, too, are trying to achieve. They put at your disposal a limited period of time, six months, so that you can get a good idea of the situation . . . and individuate strategies that will protect you from possible risks.

But this doesn't reassure you enough . . . and does not make you feel safe from separation and independence anxieties . . . because once again you feel like a child, you can never communicate to others that you want to be equal to them: . . . once again there is something that you can't communicate . . . and that has to do with shame . . . with feeling humiliated . . . And probably these feelings are what you felt as a child in relation to your parents.

Perhaps in analysis, too, you feel that I don't allow you to feel equal, I give you a limited period of time that was not decided by you . . . that doesn't correspond to your needs . . . that doesn't make you feel safe from your anxieties . . .

But you cannot communicate to me that the time I offer is not sufficient for you . . . even if you would like to not need to be in analysis . . . that analysis makes you feel too infantile and ridiculous . . . dependence makes you angry . . . because it is equivalent to a humiliating submission . . .

In other words, how can you make me understand that you are confused and would like to say that the time analysis offers you is too short . . . and at the same time you don't want to do the analysis because you feel grown up and are embarrassed to do the analysis . . .

And so I think that your coming late, like your failures in your relationship with the firm, or your silences as a child, are the only implicit way to communicate your uneasiness . . . to make me understand that you are ashamed to reveal to me that you need the analysis . . . that you need to be helped to become independent.

The analyst added during the discussion: "My last interpretation recalls the considerations Sandlers make in their reflections on the 'model of the 3 boxes and of the 2 censures'. They collocate shame as the typical expression of the second censure, that is activated by the unconscious ego and by aspects of the superego (ideal—narcissistic ego)". This was not an implicit theory, but an explicit mental reference of the analyst who felt himself in trouble.

The first noticeable thing during the discussion was the extraordinary length of the interpretation; it seemed to be out of proportion considering that the patient had arrived half an hour late and there were only about twenty minutes of the session left. The duration of the interpretation suggested that the analyst was taking revenge on the patient for being late, but it was also a response to his feeling useless, devitalised, and discouraged (countertransference). A more careful analysis that, due to space restrictions, I cannot provide here, would allow us to identify the explicit theories that the analyst said he was inspired by, as well as the implicit ones. "The map" 2. *Conceptual vector, b. clinical concepts*, hypothesises that the analyst at work uses and combines middle level concepts to manage a clinical situation, normally borrowing concepts from different theories. He can do this in a meaningful way or can also make an incredible patchwork. In this case it is clear that the analyst uses theoretical segments deriving from Winnicott's concepts (original environmental deficits), from Kohut (failure of the self object), from Sandler (shame and humiliation related to the three box model), etc. It is equally clear that the analyst strongly relies on genetic hypotheses, as though attributing to them a greater probative value or a greater persuasive value for the patient. The analyst's theoretical choices (explicit and implicit) definitely influence his interpretation of some phenomena: right from the first interpretation he avoids the aggressive and competitive aspects of the patient's behaviour, that could lead to the formulation of an interpretation relative to castration anxiety and aphanisis, in order to favour separation anxiety and separation–individualisation processes.

We can now leave this example here. I would like to emphasise how this type of supervisory seminar allows simultaneously for the supervision of the material in order to identify the analyst's implicit theories in his clinical practice, as well as working on theory by moving from practice to theory. In this sense it proves to be an extremely valuable training instrument.

Discussions

Discussions about the nature and function of supervision have usually opposed the therapeutic to the learning–teaching aspect. What I have so far endeavoured to show, among other things, is that this type of opposition does not include the specifics of the field of supervision. An awareness of this false opposition, however, must not deceive us regarding the poverty of our ideas on the teaching and learning of psychoanalysis. Using the word "education" applied to psycho-analysis, when training is being discussed at international events, immediately provokes a rising of defences. It is said that psycho-analytic education is different from education *tout court*, but this it is not to say that we do not have a consistent theory on its specificity, or many suggestions for improving it.

Supervision as a part of the training process is a centre of teaching. All the literature on the subject emphasises this. But what kind of teaching? And what is the relationship of supervision, as a teaching process, with theory?

I mentioned before the risk of not applying to supervisory work the same theoretic principles that guide the clinical work of the supervisor, whatever they may be, because the supervisory work would be left without a theoretic basis. If the analyst, for example, is working with the concept of projective identification and projective counteridentification, he will inform the supervisee that in the process of supervision the candidate can counterproject onto him the identifications that he has unconsciously acquired. He will illustrate how supervision can be the centre for a parallel process whose dynamics can reflect the dynamics of the candidate's relationship with his patient, and when it will be necessary to interpret it, thus avoiding incoherence with the clinical theory that he is teaching in the supervision. This teaching is usually implicit and part of the process; the supervisor can explain it and conceptualise it.

There is another relationship between supervision and psychoanalytic theory that is of a different nature. Perhaps DeBell has best stated that one of the tasks of supervision is to make a "translation of the clinical material into theoretical forms and the reverse". From this point of view, supervision appears as a privileged place in which to link theory and practice: to methodically explain what theoretical hypotheses can be drawn from the clinical material; to show how the theoretic choice informs the reading of the material and conditions it; to emphasise the aspects of the clinical reality in which the chosen theory proves to be insufficient or contradictory; to discover the use that is made of ad hoc hypotheses in order not to abandon a theory; to investigate the presence of implicit or personal theories; and to accustom the candidate to consider every interpretation as a work hypothesis derived from a certain theoretic model.

I think that these ideas are implicit in the concept of supervision as teaching. However, I must say that when they are brought to the attention of colleagues, they usually meet with strong resistance. More often than not, the risk of intellectualising supervision is mentioned, confusing a defensive mechanism with thinking in theoretical terms. I think that Green is right when he emphasises that the frantic research for a common ground that does not exist results in a negation (in terms of defence mechanism) of theoretic discussion, and in a naïve but no less blameful approach to the "common empirical base" of the clinical material, as though this material were not already completely conditioned by an underlying theory (Green, 1993). I do not think that we must underestimate the consequences of such a choice, above all the training of manneristic "artisans" unaware of why they do what they do. Even if considering psychoanalysis also as an art, this must not be confused with artisanship.

Some provisional conclusions to these considerations could be individuated:

a)   Supervision determinates its object and its method according to the delimitation of a field of a variable size, conditioned by the vertex chosen in function of the theory and of the goal.

b)   Planning a conceptual link between "therapy" and "teaching" seems to be a necessary condition to avoid the theoretical void of supervision. In recent years literature appears to be oriented in this way: for proof, the concepts of parallel process, of "analogon" between supervision and analysis, and of the psychoanalysis of a psychoanalysis.

c)   Supervision could be the preferred place to deepen, investigate, and work on translating theory into practice and practice into theory. For certain goals (like this one for example), some particular delimitations of the field could be better than others, for example, to work on theory in group supervision is easier than in individual supervision; on the contrary, to manage the countertransference problems of the analyst is easier in individual supervision than in the group.

d)   A thorough analysis of the implicit theories that the analyst uses in his clinical work, facilitated by the use of the instrument described before, that is, "the map of implicit (private, preconscious) theories in clinical practice", proves to be of great assistance in supervision. As well as having a relevant function in helping to discover "if we do what we think we do", a careful study of the implicit theories also trains the analysts to link working hypotheses (interpretations) to theory and to compare their respective theories and clinical methods. The maieutic and didactic function of the "map" is thus integrated with its heuristic function. As Sandler said, "the investigation of the implicit, private theories of clinical psychoanalysis opens a major new door in psychoanalytic research" (Sandler, 1983).

Note

1. Verbal communication uses at least three different and co-present channels. The first channel, or *segmental level*, includes phonology, morphology, syntax, and stylistics. The second channel, or *super-segmental level*, includes tone, accent, pauses, silences, intonations, and the various expressive connotations. The third channel includes gestures, facial mimicry, attitudes, and positions of the body.

References and Bibliography

Arlow, J. (1963). The supervisory situation. *Journal of the American Psychoanalytical Association, 11*: 576–594.

Balint, M. (1948). On the psychoanalytic training system. *International Journal of Psycho-Analysis, 29*: 163–173.

Balint, M. (1954). Analytic training and training analysis. *International Journal of Psycho-Analysis, 35*: 157–162.

Baudry, F. (1993). The personal dimension and management of the supervisory situation with a special note on the parallel process. *Psychoanalytic Quarterly, 62*: 588–614.

Blitzsten, N., & Fleming, J. (1953). What is supervisory analysis? *Bulletin of the Menninger Clinic, 17*: 117–129.

Blomfield, O. H. D. (1985). Psychoanalytic supervision—An overview. *International Review of Psycho-Analysis, 12*: 401–409.

Bokanowski, T. (1989). La chasse au snark du supervisé. *Etudes Freudiennes, 31*: 75–80.

Canestri, J. (1994). Transformations. *International Journal of Psycho-Analysis, 75*: 1079–1092.

Canestri, J. (1999). Psychoanalytic heuristics. In: P. Fonagy, A. M. Cooper, & R. S. Wallerstein (Eds.), *Psychoanalysis on the Move. The Work of Joseph Sandler* (pp. 183–197).12.68 ptic supervision: clinical approach. New contributions by candidates. Sixth IPA Conference of Training Analysts, Amsterdam, Netherlands.

Casullo, A. B., & Resnizky, S. (1993). Psychoanalytical supervision: a clinical approach or shared clinical reflections. Sixth IPA Conference of Training Analysts, Amsterdam, Netherlands.

Corrao, F. (1984). Sulla supervisione. *Rivista di Psicoanalisi, 30*(4): 581–586.

Crick, P. (1991). Good supervision: On the experience of being supervised. *Psychoanalytic Psychotherapy, 5*: 235–245.

DeBell, D. (1963). A critical digest on the literature of psychoanalytic supervision. *Journal of the American Psychoanalytic Association, 11*: 546–575.

Deutsch, H. (1935). On supervised analysis. *Contemporary Psychoanalysis* (1983) *19*: 53–67.

Dewald, P. (1987). *Learning Process in Psychoanalytic Supervision: Complexities and Challenges.* Madison, CT: International Universities Press.

Dick, M. (1987). Contribution. In: P. Dewald (Ed.), *Learning Process in Psychoanalytic Supervision: Complexities and Challenges.* Madison, CT: International Universities Press.

Eitingon, M. (1923). Report of the Berlin Psychoanalytical Policlinic. *International Journal of Psycho-Analysis, 1–2*: 254–269.

Eitingon, M. (1926). An address to the International Training Commission. *International Journal of Psycho-analysis, 7*: 130–134.

Ekstein, R. (1960). A historical survey of the teaching of psychoanalytic technique. *Journal of the American Psychoanalytic Association, 8*: 500–516.

Emch, M. (1955). The social context of supervision. *International Journal of Psycho-Analysis, 36*: 298–306.

Eskelinen de Folch, T. (1981). Some notes on transference and counter-transference problems in supervision. *Bulletin, 16*: 45–54.

Etchegoyen, H. (1986). *Los Fundamentos de la Técnica Psicoanalítica.* Buenos Aires: Amorrortu.

Ferenczi, S., & Rank, O. (1924). *Die Entwicklungsziele Der Psychoanalyse.* Vienna, Leipzig, and Zurich: Internazionaler Psychoanalytischer Verlag.

Fleming, J. (1987). The education of a supervisor. In: S. Weiss (Ed.) *The Teaching and Learning of Psychanalysis. Selected Papers of Joan Fleming, M.D.* New York: Guildford Press.

Fleming, J., & Benedek, T. (1964). Supervision. A method of teaching psychoanalysis. *Psychoanalytic Quarterly, 33*: 71–96.

Fleming, J., & Benedek, T. F. (1966). *Psychoanalytic Supervision: A Method of Clinical Teaching.* New York: International Universities Press, 1983.

Freud, S. (1910d). *The Future Prospects of Psycho-Analytic Therapy. S.E.,* XI: 139–152.

Freud, S. (1937c). *Analysis Terminable and Interminable. S.E.,* 23: 209–253. London: Hogarth.

Gardner, M. R. (1994). *On Trying to Teach. The Mind in Correspondence.* Hillsdale, NJ, London: Analytic Press.

Gardner, R. (1993). Reflections on the study group experience and on supervising. In: The American Psychoanalytic Association, *News from COPE* (pp. 6–7).

Gediman, H. K. (1983). Review of *Becoming a Psychoanalyst* (1981), edited by R. S. Wallerstein. *Review of Psychoanalytic Books,* 2: 415–428.

Gediman, H. K. (1986). The plight of the imposturous candidate: learning amidst the pressures and pulls of power in the institute. *Psychoanalytic Inquiry,* 6: 67–91.

Gediman, H. K., & Wolkenfeld, F. (1980). The parallelism phenomenon in psychoanalysis and supervision: its reconsideration as a triadic system. *Psychoanalytic Quarterly,* 49: 234–255.

Glover, E. (Ed.) (1935). The Four Countries Conference. *International Journal of Psycho-Analysis,* 17: 346–354.

Gray, P. (1993). Reflections on supervision. In: The American Psychoanalytic Association, *News from COPE* (pp. 8–10).

Green, A. (1993). Diálogos entre analistas: Cuestiones del psicoanálisis. *Review de Psicoanálisis,* L: 4–5.

Grinberg, L. (1970). The problems of supervision in psychoanalytic education. *International Journal of Psychoanalysis,* 51: 371–383.

Grinberg, L. (1986). *La Supervisione Psicoanalitica.* Milan: Cortina Raffaello, 1989.

Grotjahn, M. (1955). Problems and techniques in supervision. *Psychiatry,* 18: 9–15.

Haesler, L. (1992). La distance adéquate dans la relation entre superviseur et supervisé: la position du superviseur entre enseignant et analyste. *Bulletin,* 38: 35–49.

Hermann, I. (1963). *Die Psychoanalyse als Methode.* Koln und Opladen: Westdeutscher Verlag.

Hoffman, I. (1992). Some practical implications of a social-constructivist view of the psychoanalytic situation. *Psychoanalytic Dialogues,* 2: 287–304.

Isakower, O. (1957). The analyzing instrument in the teaching and conduct of the analytic process, edited by H. M. Wyman and S. M. Rittenberg. *Journal of Clinical Psychoanalysis* (1992) 1: 181–194.

Isakower, O. (1963). *The analytic instrument*. New York: New York Psychoanalytic Institute.

Israel, P. (1992). Les supervisions collectives: Quelle place dans la formation du psychanalyste. *Revue Français de Psychanalyse, 56:* 537–544.

Jacob, P. (1981). Application: the San Francisco Project—the supervisor at work. In: R. S. Wallerstein (Ed.), *Becoming a Psychoanalyst: A Study of Psychoanalytic Supervision*. New York: International Universities Press.

Jacobs, D., David, P., & Meyer, D. (1995). *The Supervisory Encounter*. New Haven: Yale University Press.

Keiser, S. (1956). Panel Report. The technique of supervised analysis. *Journal of the American Psychoanalytical Association, 4:* 539–549.

Kernberg, O. (1965). Notes on countertransference. *Journal of the American Psychoanalytical Association, 13:* 38–56.

Klüwer, R. (1981). Some remarks on supervision. *Bulletin, 16:* 55–59. European Psychoanalytical Federation.

Kovacs, W. (1936). Training and control-analysis. *International Journal of Psycho-analysis, 17:* 346–354.

Kubie, L. (1958). Research into the process of supervision in psychoanalysis. *Psychoanalytic Quarterly, 27:* 226–236.

Langer, M., Puget, J., & Teper, E. (1964). A methodological approach to the teaching of psychoanalysis. *International Journal of Psycho-Analysis, 45:* 567–574.

Lawner, P. (1989). Counteridentification, therapeutic impasse, and supervisory process. *Contemporary Psychoanalysis, 25:* 592–607.

Lebovici, S. (1970). Technical remarks on the supervision of psychoanalytic treatment. *International Journal of Psychoanalysis, 51:* 385–392.

Lewin, B. D., & Ross, H. (1960). *Psychoanalytic Education in the United States*. New York: Norton.

Liendo, E. C. (1971). La estrategia del narcisismo. Su doble trampa y su doble coartada en la comunicación psicoanalítica. *Review de psicoanálisis, XXVIII:* 2.

Liendo, E. C., & Gear, M. C. (1974). *Semiología psicoanalítica*. Buenos Aires: Nueva Visión.

Manfredi, S., & Nissim, L. (1984). Il supervisore al lavoro. *Rivista di Psicoanalisi, 30*(4): 587–607.

Martin, G. C., Mayerson, P., Olsen, H. E., & Lawrence, W. (1978). Candidates' evaluation of psychoanalytic supervision. *Journal of the American Psychoanalytical Association, 26:* 407–424.

Moreau, M. (1977). Analyse quatrième, contrôle, formation. *Topique, 18:* 63–87.

Ornstein, P. (1967). Selected problems in learning how to analyze. *International Journal of Psycho-analysis, 48*: 448–461.

Perrotta, A. L. A. (1978). Psicoanálisis y supervisión. Intento de unificación teórica. *Review de psicoanálisis, XXXV*(5): 973–1017.

Quinodoz, J.-M. (1992). Le déplacement du transfert dans la supervision. *Bulletin, 38*: 50–54. European Psycho-Analytical Federation.

Russell-Anderson, A., & McLaughlin, F. (1963). Some observations on psychoanalytic supervision. *Psychoanalytic Quarterly, 32*: 77–93.

Sachs, D. M. (1993). Opening Plenary Address. Sixth IPA Conference of Training Analysts, Amsterdam, Netherlands.

Sachs, D. M., & Shapiro, S. H. (1976). On parallel process in therapy and teaching. *Psychoanalytic Quarterly, 45*: 394–415.

Sandler, J. (1983). Reflections on some relations between psychoanalytic concepts and psychoanalytic practice. *International Journal of Psycho-Analysis, 64*: 35–45.

Schwaber, E. A. (1983). Psychoanalytic listening and psychic reality. *International Review of Psychoanalysis, 10*: 379–392.

Searles, H. (1955). The information value of the supervisor's emotional experiences. *Psychiatry, 18*: 135–146.

Searles, H. (1965). Problems of psychoanalytic supervision. In: *Collected Papers on Schizophrenia*. London: Hogarth.

Shevrin, H. (1981). On being the analyst supervised: Return to a troubled beginning. In: R. S. Wallerstein (Ed.), *Becoming an Analyst: A Study of Psychoanalytic Supervision*. New York: International Universities Press.

Skolnikoff, A. Z. (1997). The supervisorial situation: intrinsic and extrinsic factors influencing transference and countertransference themes. *Psychoanalytic Inquiry, 17*: 90–107.

Solheim, K. O. (1988). Les aspects spécifiques de l'utilisation du contre-transfert dans la supervision. *Bulletin, Formation Psychanalytique en Europe. Deuxième Monographie du Bulletin. Encore dix ans de discussion* (1993): 63–68.

Solnit, A. J. (1970). Learning from psychoanalytic supervision. *International Journal of Psycho-Analysis, 51*: 359–362.

Stimmel, B. (1995). Resistance to awareness of the supervisor's transference with special reference to the parallel process. *International Journal of Psychoanalysis, 76*: 609–618.

Tesone, J.-E. (1991). Controle collectif: intéret et difficulté. *Actes du XIe Pré-Congès I.P.S.O. Buenos Aires*. pp. 493–500.

Valabrega, J. P. (1969). Les voies de la formation psychanalytique. *Topique, 1*: 47–70.

Vlietstra, D. (1995). Rapport sur la supervision. L'avis des candidats. Amsterdam, Netherlands.

Wallerstein, R. (Ed). (1981). *Becoming a Psychoanalyst: A Study of Psychoanalytic Supervision*. New York: International Universities Press.

Weiss, E. (1975). *Lettres sur la Pratique Analytique*. Paris: Privat.

CHAPTER SEVEN

Theories as objects: a psychoanalytic inquiry into minds and theories*

Samuel Zysman

Introduction

In the quest for gaining self-knowledge and to understand its place in the universe, mankind has been making momentous steps forwards since its origins. Even before modern neurobiological studies started to appear in the second half of the past century, the amazing ability of human consciousness to focus research activities on itself was already at work: in the beginning, as one of the great human philosophical concerns. Then, during the nineteenth and the early twentieth centuries Charles Darwin and Sigmund Freud made two outstanding contributions from the scientific field to this endeavour. We owe Darwin not only for his revolutionary formulation of the general laws that govern living nature. Also, and no less important, we owe him both the humbling recognitions of our being part of the

* This chapter was first presented as a discussion paper in the Panel on "Mapping implicit (private) theories in clinical practice", at the 43rd IPAC, New Orleans, March 2004. A revised Spanish version of it was discussed the following year in an APdeBA scientific meeting. A series of joint discussion meetings on the subject was held in 2005 and 2006 with Dr Horacio Etchegoyen and the late epistemologist and logician Dr Gregorio Klimovsky. Both are given here due thanks for the careful reading and the valuable suggestions.

zoological realm under such laws, and of the existence of evolutionary links between man's cognitive capabilities and the similar ones present in other species.

In his own time and also based on meticulous observations, Freud introduced concepts no less revolutionary. He started from the practical problems he met with in his clinical practice and proceeded to put forward sets of growingly complex descriptive and explanatory statements, and to evolve successive models of the mind. All this came in time to be integrated into a theoretical corpus known as "the psychoanalytic theory"; we know, however, that various theories, each one claiming separately for themselves the true fidelity to Freud's teachings, appeared during his lifetime and multiplied later.

In his early efforts to develop a comprehensive theory of mental functioning, he introduced his hypothesis based in the most advanced neuroscientific data available at that time and formulated them in neurological terms (Freud, 1895a). For reasons we can guess, he later abandoned that language in favour of a purely psychological one; he consistently employed it in all his following works to make public his theories and most of it is still in current use. The perusal of them, however, allows us to perceive in the background many traces of a permanence of the neurological explanations of his clinical psychological findings.

I consider it important to mention here these different languages because of what I want to put forward in what is to follow. First, and in relation to the production of theories, I wish to stress the central place given to different kinds of thought with their underlying logics and in general to cognitive processes throughout Freud's work, as an inherent, ongoing mental activity. His clinical observations permitted him to state that its results can be inferred, also that they may be stored and sometimes retrieved, and they always have some impact—for better or worse—on the ensuing cognitive development. Freud's enduring interest in these topics can be followed both in the neurological language of the Project and in the psychological language of his subsequent psychoanalytic magnum opus. This is nothing to be surprised at, given that the psychopathology he studied continually referred to problems such as conscious and unconscious thought, remembering and forgetting, truth and its distortions related to underlying mental illness or health, and so on.

Second, it can be said that although the different languages are two, the matter they deal with, organise, describe, and try to explain is one and the same. It consists basically of huge amounts of empirical data obtained in the psychoanalytic clinical setting and also in everyday life. At this point, we could base ourselves on the evident adequacy and the extraordinary helpfulness of the psychological vocabulary for the advancement and communication of Freud's work to assume its inherent superiority for such task. It would be pure speculation to try to imagine what Freud could have done if our contemporary neurological knowledge were available during his time. In all probability, he would have engaged in the task that contemporary psychoanalysis tries to face: to establish links to related fields of research. For now what we know is that after abandoning the Project Freud kept looking for a way to express his ideas at the highest possible level of explanation, which prompted the introduction of metapsychology with its particular language and related terms.

As this paper intends to deal psychoanalytically with theories as such, not focusing for now either on their epistemological value or on the qualities of the concepts they contain, resorting to metapsychology seems to be necessary and the only available language to formulate statements about our study matter. Its sophisticated meta-theoretical vocabulary should suffice to theorise about theories and their place and role in the human mind. This approach calls, however, for a degree of tolerance to what might be seen as one more blow to human narcissism, namely that we have to accept that psychoanalytically speaking there are not extraterritorial rights for theories when it comes to study them as mental contents. This does not mean in any way a lack of respect for what theories stand for, neither within the psychoanalytic field nor in general. On the contrary, from my perspective two positive consequences can be expected from this approach. On one hand for psychoanalysts as such, on the other as a very specific interdisciplinary contribution linking our own developments with those taking place in other fields that focus research on similar matters.

Psychoanalysis and cognitive development

The perspective I want to introduce in this paper is based on the application of psychoanalytic theories to the process of constructing theories. From its inception psychoanalysis had to deal with problems linked to normal and pathological thinking, distorted and false explanations based on equally distorted perceptions, truth and lies, learning, and much of what Money-Kyrle (1961) studied in his book *Man's Picture of His World*. It can be said as well that Freud, when he defined psychoanalysis as a post education, or Bion when he introduced in the 1960s and 1970s what can be considered his general theory of normal and pathological thought, were very much following the same path.

At the same time different epistemological developments appeared to deal with theories, basically as very sophisticated and advanced products of our conscious minds. Their main concerns were the validation criteria, the internal coherence and solidity of theories and their capacity to explain facts and establish regularities in a given field of research. The existence of mental steps necessary to construct them, and the possible relationships among those steps and their "final product", was acknowledged but it was scarcely studied because it was considered a matter for psychologists and of no consequence to the epistemological goals in themselves. However, the psychoanalytic theoretical field also expanded in such a way as to provide wide possibilities to study theories starting from the opposite end, that is, the beginnings and the development of the whole process and not just the final results.

In this way the extension and depth of the psychoanalytic knowledge of the mind and its functions sustain its application to the understanding of what theories are, their construction and the ways they are put to use, and to formulate statements about them both as the products and contents of our minds. The title of this paper reflects and materialises in some way these opinions.

In 1973 the Argentine analyst Jose Bleger gave the therapeutic aims of psychoanalysis, which are accomplished by widening the knowledge of ourselves, the name of "maieutic" according to the classical dictum *"nosce te ipsum"*. Following this idea we can also hold that the study of cognitive development in general is essential to improve the results of our clinical work. In it, this development which includes both the conscious and unconscious functioning of the mind, also embraces our capacity to make inferences from psychoanalytic observations, and the ensuing explanations and generalisations that we use to formulate interpretative statements that are sustained by other statements of a different level called "theories".

In this way the necessity of examining epistemologically the structure of the existing analytic theories becomes evident, and this was perhaps one of the most important trends in our science in the second half of the past century. But another one that set in afterwards was— and continues to be at present—of no less importance. It focuses on the theories, or fragments of them—conscious or not—that analysts have in their minds while working. This gave place to a research project of the Committee on Theoretical Issues of the European Psychoanalytic Federation called the "Mapping of private (implicit) theories" (see Canestri, Bohleber, Denis, & Fonagy, 2006), accompanied more or less at the same time by David Tuckett's investigation on compared clinical methods (Tuckett, 2008). Similar projects started also in other regions. Among them one with a different metapsychological perspective that opens the possibility to identify as well implicit theories or fragments of them, but tracing their origins to what is classically defined as the dynamic unconscious (Zysman, Villa Segura, Bordone de Semeniuk, & Pieczanski, 2009), very much related to this paper.

I wish to draw attention now to the fact that all theories, whatever their level of abstraction, their logical internal coherence, and their explaining or predicting power might be, are also—in the first place and undoubtedly—products and contents of our minds. What follows from this is the possibility to sustain that in such condition they partake in one way or another in the "normal" psychic functioning, including what we usually call the "defence mechanisms". Being so, it seems just reasonable to say that they fall under the laws that current psychoanalytic theories have put forward as ruling such functioning. In other words, a solid internal logic or even the brilliance of any given theory does not mean that it belongs to a realm totally apart from ordinary psychic life. Quite to the contrary, it does mean that theories can be thought of as the outcome of long and complex processes with different degrees of development, success, and stability, where psychic conflict and its inherent mechanisms have had to be sorted out in such a way as to make this result possible.

If we follow this approach the basic psychoanalytic theories of the unconscious, of infantile sexuality, and of the transference, as central to a psychoanalytic understanding of the mind, cannot be neglected. And it is to be noted as well that when a good balance exists between the functions of the mind involved in cognitive activity we usually do not pay much attention to them, but it would be a mistake to conclude that they are absent.

Even in ordinary everyday life, any statement addressed by one person to another entails some "theory" related to the subject dealt with in the sentences employed, although such "theories" seldom reach a scientific level. What usually happens when they actually do so, and especially if they are valued by researchers of the same field or have managed to draw respect from the community at large, is that they attract more interest because of the increase in knowledge they produce than by the psychic steps leading to their explicit formulation. My intention is to put forward the idea that the comprehension of these steps can be important to understand the scope and structure of a theory, and maybe more so if we deal with psychoanalytic theories. Recent studies in biology and neuroscience related to cognitive processes point to the existence of close connections between the emotions and higher psychic functions as conscious reasoning, these notions are clearly consistent with already existing psychoanalytic theories. My point of view is that psychoanalysis has much to offer to this kind of research, and much to learn from it when it comes to its own theoretical developments. To these ends the peculiar regularities of the analytic clinical situation offer many relevant data.

In a previous paper (Zysman, 2006) where I followed many of Money-Kyrle, Bion, and Piaget's ideas, I picked up some of their points of view and linked the theories about human cognitive development coming from psychoanalysis to others coming from ethology and genetic epistemology. I accepted the statements of the existence from the start of a permanent cognitive activity of the human mind with early and probably innate roots, and, from an evolutionary biological point of view, essential for survival by means of cognitive development itself. I named this early activity "theorising" and I defined the child as a "small researcher" (*petit chercheur*, Zysman, 1998). I wish to stress here the expression *theorising activity* because while many psychoanalytical schools accept (although with great differences) the existence of an early psychic development with some kind of inherent cognitive capacities, to link it to such a complex process as the construction of what we call a theory may look to many people an unacceptable exaggeration.[1]

Because of their accessibility and rich research possibilities, I chose the infantile sexual theories not so much because of their role in sexual development, but especially as an example of the construction of a theory under the conditions imposed on cognitive capacities by the ongoing instinctual conflict. In their study some very interesting facts appear: a) according to most existing definitions they can be called theories, which is how Freud himself denominated them[2]; b) their being flawed with gross errors and distortions and therefore unsuitable to give a proper picture of the reality of sexual facts is precisely what points to their being part of an inner (sexual) psychic conflict and the activity of the defence mechanisms (the cognitive aspect present in instinctual drives, (Money-Kyrle, 1968)); c) as they invariably appear as a transference phantasy in the material of the patients of all ages, they are for us the *via regia* to the theories they elaborate about their own early conflicts. Symmetrically, they can be equally useful when we face the analysts' own conflicts, that become apparent through their countertransferential involvements. So, we can expect the study of the analysts' interpretations to give us access to a better understanding of their structure and of the whole process that leads to them. In other words, what we expect to find are the links supposed to exist between the interpretation and some underlying unconscious theories.

All this can be described as the intent to build rational theoretical statements relating the clinical facts of a session to the statements that the interpretation is made of, knowing beforehand that interpretations are, much to our regret, "secondary process infiltrated by primary process" (Anzieu, 1972). I consider this approach to be worth, at least heuristically (see Leuzinger-Bohleber, Dreher, & Canestri, 2003), further exploration which could open up great possibilities, both for psychoanalysis and epistemology. Some of them important and mutually related immediately come to the fore: on one hand the investigation of theoretical production itself in various mental states, with coexisting different and conflicting mental levels of theorisation; on the other the separation between the contexts of discovery, justification, and application of theories, that intertwine in our clinical practice permanently.

As in other sciences, psychoanalysts have devoted themselves for years to the development of new and often opposed theories, but not so much to their own relationship with them. With the passing of time a growing care for their soundness from an epistemological point of view appeared. To this second end one important impulse came and still streams from the intents (at times hostile) to install the idea that psychoanalysis has no right to claim scientific status. For different reasons, some psychoanalysts also share this point of view, the main one being that psychoanalysis belongs to the hermeneutic field. I will not enter into this discussion here or into other related topics such as the linguistic turn or the relativistic, post-modern approach to psychoanalysis. I will assume as a fact the scientific status of psychoanalysis and resort to reason, although admitting its limits, in order to go ahead with my ideas.

In 1910 Freud was the first to introduce the concept of counter-transference, thus calling attention to the importance that the analyst's capacity to perform psychoanalytically in the session has for the outcome of treatments. After an eclipse of almost forty years it reappeared with strength in analytic literature and began to expand steadily, making many researchers enter into the field corresponding to what happens to the analyst's mind at work and how it influences its results.[3] It is in the study of the transference–countertransference relations that we gain access to explicit and implicit theories both of the patient and the analyst, to the way they are built and to their consequences. Infantile sexual theories are present per se because at the same time they are the raw material of the patient's transferential neurosis and of the analyst's theorisation process "on the battle-ground", meaning that he is exposed while working to their emotional impact. When the impact is for him or her to much to deal with in the clinical setting, the possibility of the analyst's acting out instead of interpreting increases.[4]

So, it is the need of a psychoanalytical comprehension of the role played by theories in the human mind and the vicissitudes of their practical use in our own field that led me to advocate for a metapsy-chological approach to theories in general (Zysman, 2009), and to psychoanalytical ones in particular. The idea that I wish to introduce (which may also be called a theory) is to consider them as "objects", both internal and external, employing this term with the meaning and scope it has in the theory of object relations. Such particular "objects" would consist in the theoretical statements they are made of, and they would establish relations among them and with other similar "objects". In turn, and in this condition, they could be included regularly in metapsychological statements, which is precisely what we need to account for their vicissitudes as contents of our minds.

The possibility this idea opens up for us now is to produce mixed statements, including the factual (clinical), the theoretical, and the metapsychological terms, in a way that permits us to explain psycho-analytically the fate of theories in our minds and their use in the clinical setting.

I am aware that this may sound too audacious or far-fetched because we are used to deal with theories *about* objects, and not theories *as* objects. Many related problems arise here which can only be dealt with partially in this chapter. As a first step towards their consideration I will present some of them roughly assembled into the three following paragraphs: mostly clinical, mostly epistemological, and mostly metapsychological, although no definite boundary can be drawn between them and this classification is to be taken simply as an aid for discussion.

Mostly clinical

I will introduce some historical examples to show what the fate of theories may be, first in the mind of those who build and develop them while doing it, and then when applied to practical ends in the psychoanalytical setting. It is generally accepted that the setting includes a number of fixed rules that permit to develop a psycho-analytical situation and a transference–countertransference relationship in our consulting room, which may thus be considered our "psychoanalytic laboratory".[5]

Freud himself is to provide a first example historically related to the discovery of countertransference. In that same year (1910d) he had answered Ferenczi's letter asking him why he had not been repri-manded during their shared trip to Italy, where he had pestered Freud with all kinds of demands and complaints. The answer was: "I am not the psychoanalytic superman you have forged in your imagination and *neither have I overcome the countertransference*. I could not have treated you in such a way, as I neither could with my three sons, because I love them too much and I would be sorry for them" (Freud & Ferenczi, 1993, my italics). Good for Freud, who behaved in a civilised way during their trip, and who was also honest enough to recognise his own obstacles with a problematic patient, those which led him to postulate the study of countertransference as one of the future prospects of psychoanalytical therapy. I want however to point to the nature of his difficulties prior to the trip: Freud had treated Little Hans in 1907 and the paper "On the sexual theories of children" appeared in 1908 (Freud, 1908c). So Freud had enough knowledge of the existence in small boys of homosexual drives towards their fathers, as well as feelings of hatred and frustration, but all his knowledge, his own theories, were practically unavailable to him while in his consulting room and working with this special patient. The questions arising might be: why and/or how? I think the first question may lead us to more history and perhaps to descriptive statements about personal traits in these two great pioneers. The second one lends itself better to metapsychological statements addressing both the infantile sexual theories and the psychoanalytical theories dealing with them as internal and external objects, and I will come back to this.

We could resort to other examples taken from Freud's work, as for instance the case of Little Hans but it may be interesting and fair to have a look at another pioneer's work, Melanie Klein. As we know, Klein treated in Berlin in the 1920s a very disturbed small girl who appears in different places of her writings with the name of Erna. Chapter Three of *The Psychoanalysis of Children* deals in length with her and her obsessional neurosis. In a footnote Klein says: "We have here an interesting analogy to the case described in Freud's 'History of an Infantile Neurosis' (1918)" (Klein, 1975).

I wrote about this supposed analogy elsewhere (see the paragraph on "Erna and the Wolfman" Tabak de Bianchedi, Etchegoyen, Ungar de Moreno, Nemas de Urman, & Zysman, 2003) and I will only touch here what may be relevant to the topic of this paper. The concept of *"Nachträglichkeit"* was introduced in the case study published in 1918, and entered analytic literature with synonyms as "deferred action" and *"après-coup"*. In Freud's account we can find contradictory statements: a) a child aged eighteen months could have woken up to see his parents' genitals and understand what he was witnessing (intercourse) and its meaning; and, b) understanding was deferred until the age of four, to the time of the dream. "It was then that it became possible . . . owing to his development, his sexual excitations, and his sexual researches". And later again: "We shall perhaps find in what follows reason to suppose that it produced certain effects at the time of its perception, that is, from the age of one and a half onwards" (1918b, pp. 44–45). It is important to notice the contradictory views and remember also the stress that lay upon Freud's investigation because of his conflict with Jung, whose opinion was that neuroses entail an escape from present conflicts back into a refuge in infantile phantasies. We may assume that this point of view might have been present in Freud's contradictions. But what can we say about Klein? When reading her case carefully it is easy to see that she attributes to the little girl the capability to observe and understand the primal scene right from the first time, at the age of two and a half years. The whole of her case study is devoted precisely to demonstrate the early presence of sexual phantasies and of some knowledge—although distorted—of sexual facts from a very early age. Also their forming part of the delusional "theories" the girl developed about the sexual relationship between her parents, and, not least, the developmental consequences all this had on her. Actually, the complete *Psychoanalysis of Children* and all her later theoretical developments turn around this assumption.

Briefly, in Klein's account, and from the perspective she was developing, to introduce *"Nachträglichkeit"* as a similarity with Freud's case was contradictory both theoretically and epistemologically. But she did so. Again, why, and how? Might it be that Freud's presence and the wish to tread on the same path at his side weighed much on her, perhaps as much as Jung's opinions did on Freud? In any case this is just one aspect of the whole story showing that we find ourselves in need of metapsychological statements to approach the problem of the unaware coexisting contradictory theories, especially remembering the close relationship, both in Freud and Klein, between theories and actual interpretations in the consulting room. We need as well metapsychological statements referring to the "forgetting" of a whole piece of theory, and with this perspective to consider theories as objects seems acceptable enough to account for their fate in the mind.

Mostly epistemological

The same examples that we have just quickly examined also put under scrutiny the epistemological problem of the contexts of discovery, application, and justification of theories. If we accept the idea that when interpreting, our explicit (public) theories can be more or less modified by coexisting levels of a private theory that owes much to the impact of the countertransference, then we should sustain that in psychoanalysis the contexts are clearly in a relation of continuity, and to separate them can only be understood as a methodological device.

For a long time Popper's ideas—coinciding with Reichenbach in this point—gravitated much on the scientific community, whose members had, and many still have, a great reluctance to enter into any psychological—let alone psychoanalytical—considerations. We have to admit that this is quite understandable, because a theory may be qualified as good or bad, useful or not, but always on the basis of its own structure and its ability to explain better something we are trying to investigate, and from this perspective statements of any other kind may seem irrelevant, irrespective of whether they contain some truth or not.

We, as analysts, also adopt often such a position in regard to our own theories, at least when it comes to judge if they fit with our clinical empirical data and if they are more or less instrumentally useful. However, things are not that easy and this sharp difference has been put to the test by different authors, some of them stressing the idea that the circumstances in which a given theory is produced have much to do with its structure and with the theoretical terms employed.

Popper's pupil Lakatos did not agree with him on this point, and according to Kuhn, historical and sociological factors mark the passing from one stage to another in scientific development until reaching the "normal" one, with its prevailing and organising paradigm. Perhaps in this context psychological factors can be advocated as well, but as we know "psychological" does not mean "psychoanalytical", unless explicitly stated so. Piaget, who was in his time one of the sharpest critics of the separation of contexts, could not advance much more on this point of view (maybe, because in spite of his being a genetic psychologist he felt at a great distance from psychoanalysis).[6]

Let us try to put this problem in such terms as we are more used to. To start with I ask the reader to accept them provisionally and in a very broad sense. We could say that theories have an apparently "independent" life in "reality" since as we all know they belong to the public domain, where they are published, discussed, and taught. We agree to call them "explicit" or "public" theories and they are mainly conscious.[7] This makes them appear in some way as autonomous entities, admitting one or more authors, but removed at that point from the intimate process of their production. As we said, the inner structure of these theories is expected to show a logical coherence, and their validation or refutation should not be based on feelings or on emotionally biased reasoning.[8]

As producers and beneficiaries of theories we are regularly concerned with their applicability and usefulness with regard to that piece of reality that we happen to be interested in. In other words, and deliberately including analysts in the broad spectrum of people in need of theories in their respective fields of labour, we are all dealing with theories as a part of a reality that consists of sets of statements concerning other parts of reality, and we expect a gain in knowledge thanks to them. There are cases where the knowledge we seek is expected to have practical results and therefore we have to deal with "mixed statements", related to empirical facts as well. Such a thing is precisely what happens in psychoanalytical practice, when we have to test the usefulness of some of the theoretical terms as part of the mixed statements (or rules of correspondence) that may help us, or not, to sustain statements related to our actual conduct in the clinical field.

But when we are in the consulting room trying to follow Freud's advice and abandon ourselves to (free) floating attention in order to receive the patients' (free) associations, something happens in the midst of an emotionally complicated mutual involvement. Looking at it from our side I will formulate it provisionally as follows: the so called "public" (or explicit) theories we sustain undergo a selection of those parts that seem to us to fit best in the new and transient theory we have to build on the spot based on the patient's material, and they are supposed to sustain the interpretation we give.

So we can speak of a given theory being public in the sense that it is taught in psychoanalytical Institutes, and at the same time we can refer with the same term to the theories underlying interpretations. But there is simultaneously an unconscious part to this process, during which the "public" theory can suffer changes, and components of other (and sometimes widely different) theories can be intertwined under the influence of the shared emotional involvement. Therefore this whole process is not only about theoretical selection, but also and to some degree, about modification and/or distortion of the theoretical and empirical terms of the public theories, be it of meaning or of use. The result of this again is partly conscious and explicitly present in the interpretation, and partly unconscious ("private" or "implicit") and has to be inferred. Please notice that when I refer to intertwining widely different theories I leave open the possibility that some of them might not belong clearly to the psychoanalytical field. The contact with "reality" in the clinical situation is by definition impaired or may even be grossly absent in the patient, while in the analyst such a situation may appear to a very variable extent depending very much on his or her capacity to stay at the same time emotionally involved and yet producing mostly rational theories about the nature of this involvement. So, finally it is possible to affirm, at least in the case of psychoanalytical practice, where theories are put to use, that the whole process of construction of a theory seems to be inseparably linked to the contents it has to deal with, and furthermore it is essential to the possibility of its practical application.

There is yet another meaning of the word "public" that is necessary to keep in mind when referring to theories, and it has to do with Bion's theory of thinking. In it he introduces the idea that we need an apparatus to cope with (to think) thoughts: such thoughts can be classified according to their developmental history. One outcome of the functioning of this apparatus is to make thoughts available for translation into action. One item involved in this translation is called "publication". This term "is reserved for operations that are necessary to make the awareness that is private to the individual, public. The problems involved can be regarded as technical and emotional" (Bion, 1961).

So, with his perspective, to call a theory "public" means not only to attribute to it a quality that is descriptively true. It especially means to admit the existence of a long and complex series of unconscious mental operations related to the development, awareness, communication, and use for action, of human thought. The possible belonging of whole parts of the theory building process to the dynamic unconscious stays open for further investigation.

I concentrated myself on some epistemological problems posed both by psychoanalytical theories and their practical use, but apparently they can be approached simply as cognitive problems. It is a surprising fact that psychoanalysts have not found yet the proper way to a thorough critical examination of present cognitive research, that habitually does not include the psychoanalytical theory of the unconscious. Psychoanalysis has always included the cognitive side of the phenomena it studied. Let us remember that Freud defined "psychoanalysis is a post-education", and that Melanie Klein started by trying "to explain" sexuality to children, and discovered that it was only through interpretation that the children's obstacles to learn the facts of life could be removed. Her theory of the "positions" entails widely opposed "theories" about the contents of both the inner and outer world, their difference consisting basically in the capacity to recognise all the constitutive aspects of the objects. As Jean Michel Petot holds (1990, 1991), "the unification of the object brought about by the depressive position is a cognitive phenomenon".

The K link introduced by Bion together with L and H, and Money-Kyrle's (1968) idea of the "cognitive component of innate responses, preceding the affective and the conative", and Matte Blanco's idea (1988) of the human mind in a permanent activity of discrimination, classification, and recognition, are all clear signs of the cognitive side in psychoanalytical theories. From a strictly epistemological point of view, Klimovsky (2004) contends that there is a similarity between "theoretical reality" and "psychic reality", since both consist in some sort of description of reality; "the non empirical condition of theoretical terms is similar to the non conscious quality of the phantasied objects of psychic reality". This similarity rests upon the fact that both constitute a "non empirical addition to the knowledge of reality", and these ideas attribute a certain "knowing capacity" to psychic reality. Thus, we can admit some levels of "theoretical" activity to be going on permanently in our minds, and it would be a difficult task to keep trying to solve epistemological (and other related) problems without including them in the general picture.

The metapsychology of theories. Why theories as objects?

We know that in psychoanalysis statements can belong to theories of different levels of abstraction. Any set of (psychoanalytical) theoretical statements about theories will forcibly have to employ theoretical terms taken from one of the existing psychoanalytical theories. To put it clearer, each existing psychoanalytical theory has its own metapsychology, and when using any metapsychology to be applied to theories we run the risk of simply producing statements about other statements. Such a risk can only be worth running if we think it can help us in the end as practicing analysts to face difficulties in our daily work, to the extent that they are linked precisely to these theoretical problems.

As far as I could examine available literature, most contributions to theoretical problems do not approach them from a metapsychological point of view. I would only add that metapsychology is "implicit" in many of its assertions. For instance Hartmann, as one outstanding ego psychologist, seems to have written his papers on the assumption that theories can only come from an autonomous ego and belong to the conflict free area. On the opposite side and curiously symmetrical, for Lacan and his followers it seems that theories worth their name belong naturally to the symbolic order.

Joseph and Anne-Marie Sandler (1983) took up Freud's topographical and structural points of view to address the current facts of psychoanalytic sessions and the theories involved. As said before, they can be either conscious or "descriptively" unconscious, that is, belonging to the system Pcs (preconscious), where,

> the analyst, as he grows more competent, will preconsciously [descriptively speaking, unconsciously] construct a whole variety of theoretical segments which relate directly to his clinical work. They are the products of unconscious thinking, are very much partial theories, models or schemata, which have the quality of being available in reserve, so to speak, to be called upon whenever necessary. *That they may contradict one another is no problem. They coexist happily as long as they are unconscious.* (Sandler & Sandler, 1983, my italics)

The possibility to enter the system Cs. (conscious) would depend here of the "second censorship", the one between Pcs. and Cs.—a concept taken from Freud upon which the Sandlers based their Three Box Model.[9]

The coexistence of contradictory theories needs to be scrutinised because its effects on our performance in daily work, and this situation opens for us the possibility to add other ideas to those based on the topographical and structural models that could help to lessen the impact of such effects. As a matter of fact these models came under a critical examination in recent years. One important contribution is Charles Brenner's paper (2003) where he holds that the theory that the mind is composed of identifiable, separate or separable structures should be revised because "it is not supported by available, relevant data". It is noteworthy that both psychoanalysis and modern neuroscientific research seem to have reached similar views about the functioning of brain and mind in terms of plastic, compatible "learning" systems (see Ansermet & Magistretti, 2006; Damasio, 1999).

It is a known fact that Freud never totally gave up his working models but he rather let them stay included in the following new and enriched formulations. It is also known that since "Mourning and melancholia", *Group Psychology and the Analysis of the Ego*, and *The Ego and the Id* (Freud, 1917e, 1921c, 1923b), the role of objects in relation to the psychic agencies they were supposed to be part of became more and more important.

So, a possible different approach to the mind and its contents would then be that the mind's different ways of functioning depend on the work of structures which can be supposed to contain certain "objects" whose qualities and their "location" in the structures are exposed to permanent change. This characteristic of objects as not belonging permanently to one given structure is inherent in Klein's theory of the continuous processes of introjection and projection as the basic mechanisms that create and modify those structures under the conditions imposed on them by the two schizoid–paranoid and depressive anxieties, and it is consistent also with the fact that the contents of the mind can alternatively be or not be conscious.

So, the Freud and Klein perspectives do not seem to differ enormously when it comes to describing theories in the analyst's mind as being conscious or (descriptively) unconscious. But they do so in regard to the role the dynamic unconscious plays in them, and to the importance of the role of mental contents and their developmental history. This broader view was taken up and expanded mostly in Bion's theory of thinking mentioned above.

In Klein's terms objects are important for themselves and participate actively in building up internal and external reality through the functioning of introjective and projective mechanisms. Other theories of object relations besides Klein's also assign special importance to objects and their participation in mental building up, although they exhibit important differences about the early stages of psychic development (Fairbairn, Winnicott).

From a classical Kleinian point of view unconscious theories contained in the "internal world" (the psychic reality) can be equated to or compatible with the "unconscious phantasies" about objects and the nature of their relationships. The individual can then project into the "external world" all these intricacies, mainly in the guise of "theories" whose shape and value are akin to that of infantile sexual theories. At the same time they can undergo internal processes that account for their complexity, their changes, their greater or lesser adequacy to external reality, their inner contradictions, and the ways they are put to use.

This approach makes it possible to consider theories as complex objects. When trying to explain the vicissitudes of theories whose existence can be inferred from our thoughts and behaviours it becomes evident that to test the possible "ontological status" of theories as "objects" can be psychoanalytically and epistemologically legitimate because it clarifies and provides a broader comprehension of the different roles they play in our minds. They can be introjected and projected—therefore be internal and external; they may be attacked, debased or idealised, and repaired; they may be perceived as hostile, persecutory, or protective; they may be "ours" as an identity sign, or completely alien—in one word they may have the same fate as any other object. Their fates in our mind, as component parts in its structures and functions, can be better understood with the help of Wisdom's (1967) "planetary model" which includes nuclear and orbital introjections. According to this model we can identify with a given theory in different ways: one would be as a nuclear introjection which requires special pre-conditions and opens the way for a "mature" use of theories. In case it were an orbital one our relation with such an object would mainly show persecutory traits, that is, they would be stereotyped and of little or no use from the cognitive point of view. A paranoid relation to it would entail a dogmatic use with no regard to its explanatory power. Along this path we can also consider identity as based on "projective identification into an internal object" which results in "becoming one with the theory", melted so to say, in a grotesque way usually found in our own and in many other professions. A common trait in all such pathological identifications is confusion in different degrees and a lack in the rationality needed to deal with objects and admit, so to speak, their own autonomous life. If the object were a theory, it would be an impossibility to differentiate properly the values of the theory from those of its user.

In conclusion, and in awareness of its faults and of its opening more questions than the answers it provides, I will summarise the successive steps I followed in this paper. First, the strong evidence pointing to the existence of innate cognitive capacities in our minds and the early use of them in common daily life. Second, the relationships with similar capacities present in other species and their overall evolutionary relevance. Third, the different observational data pointing to the existence of a developmental process leading to higher and more sophisticated cognitive levels. Fourth, the inclusion of a "theoretical" production process as a regular part of this development, no matter its being grossly flawed in the early stages. Fifth, that this process can be found both in scientific and not scientific matters as well. The semantic expansion of the noun "theory", if it is accompanied by a process leading to epistemological greater solidity, should not damage the original limits and the prestige of the concept. And finally, something about the role psychoanalysis can play. I see it as twofold: on the inside, a better understanding of our theories, their place in our minds, and their impact on clinical practice. On the outside, a possibility to have a needed and useful word in some ongoing epistemological debates and profit while collaborating with neuroscientific research.

Should there be any merit I would claim for the ideas exposed, it would be for trying to call the attention of my colleagues to the fact that our minds produce theories that we can later employ to understand how our minds can perform such work. The need to respectfully include all theories—the psychoanalytic ones as well—in the big lot of materials to study with psychoanalytic tools is long overdue. Many of the existent psychoanalytical theoretical and metapsychological statements can be used in such endeavour. My aim in this respect is that my proposal to consider theories as objects can clarify and be of help.

Notes

1. For a completely opposite opinion based on research see one of many recent papers: Onishi and Baillargeon (2005), holding that "babies are born with an innate abstract computational system they use to interpret the conduct of others".
2. According to Klimovsky, (1994) a theory consists of a set of hypothesis; an initial one and all those appearing as its consequence; also the laws trying to generalise empirical regularities.
3. In Argentina, first as a result of Racker's papers on countertransference, and later due mainly to the pioneering teachings of Gregorio Klimovsky

on the epistemology of psychoanalysis, many seminal contributions to such subjects have begun to appear since the mid sixties by authors as Liberman, Grinberg, Zac, Etchegoyen, and others.

4. In a previous paper I described three possible levels of involvement along this path which I called "action"; "acting-out"; and "active technique", each one with its own technical and ethical problems (Zysman, 1999).

5. As Michael Rustin (2001) calls it, because of the existence of a set of fixed rules that permits systematic observation, collection, and comparison of data, and advancing of hypothesis.

6. In his words: "In flagrant internal contradiction they looked for no empirical base to sustain their assertions, adopted as dogmas" (Piaget and Garcia, 1982, referring to the strict separation of contexts by the neo-positivists, NA).

7. It was Joseph Sandler (1983) who introduced the adjectives "public" (explicit) and "private"(implicit) to be applied to theories.

8. In the psychoanalytical situation proper, patients are "expected" to sustain emotionally biased theories, while analysts, because of their therapeutic responsibility, could be "suspected" of such a possible error.

9. This is also the basis of the "Mapping" project, put forward by Canestri (2006).

References and Bibliography

Ansermet, F., & Magistretti, P. (2006). *A Cada Cual su Cerebro*. Buenos Aires: Katz Editores.

Anzieu, D. (1972). Dificultad de un estudio psicoanalítico sobre la interpretación. *Revista de Psicoanalisis, XXIX*(2): 255.

Bion, W. R. (1961). *Experiences in Groups*. London: Tavistock.

Bion, W.R. (1977). *Seven Servants*. New York: Aronson.

Bion, W.R. (1988). A theory of thinking. In: *Melanie Klein Today, Vol. 1*. London: Routledge—Institute of Psychoanalysis.

Bleger, J. (1973). Criterios de curacion y objetivos del Psicoanalisis. *Revista de Psicoanalisis, XXX*(2): 317.

Brenner, C. (2003). Is the structural model still useful? *International Journal of Psycho-Analysis, 84–85*: 1093–1103.

Canestri, J. (2006). Implicit understanding beyond theory. In: J. Canestri (Ed.), *Psychoanalysis:Ffrom Practice to Theory*. Chichester: Whurr.

Canestri, J., Bohleber, W., Denis, P., & Fonagy, P. (2006). The map of private (implicit, prconscious) theories in clinical practice. In: Canestri, J. (Ed.), *Psychoanalysis: From Practice to Theory*. Chichester: Whurr.

Damasio, A. (1999). *The Feeling of What Happens*. New York: Harcourt Brace.

Freud, S. (1895a). *A Project for a Scientific Psychology*. S.E., 1: 283–397. London: Hogarth.

Freud, S. (1908c). On the sexual theory of children. S.E., IX: 209–226.

Freud, S. (1910d). *The Future Prospects of Psycho-Analytic Therapy*. S.E., XI: 139–152.

Freud, S. (1917e). Mourning and melancholia. S.E., 14: 237–258. London: Hogarth.

Freud, S. (1918b). *From the History of an Infantile Neurosis*. S.E., 17: 1–122. London: Hogarth.

Freud, S. (1921c). *Group Psychology and the Analysis of the Ego*. S.E., 18: 67–143. London: Hogarth.

Freud, S. (1923b). *The Ego and the Id*. S.E., 19: 12–66. London: Hogarth.

Freud, S., & Ferenczi, S. (1993). *The Correspondence of Sigmund Freud and Sandor Ferenczi, Volume 1, 1908–1914*. E. Brabant, E. Falzeder, & P. Giampieri-Deutsch (Eds.), Letter 171F, 6 October, 1910.

Klein, M. (1975). The psychoanalysis of children. In: *The Writings of Melanie Klein, Vol. 2*. London: Hogarth.

Klimovsky, G. (1994). *Las Desventuras del Conocimiento Cientifico*. Buenos Aires: A-Z Editores.

Klimovsky, G. (2004). *Realidad Psíquica, Algunos Aspectos Epistemológicos*. Buenos Aires: ADEP-Biebel.

Leuzinger-Bohleber, M., Dreher, A. U., & Canestri, J. (Eds.) (2003). *Pluralism and Unity? Methods of Research in Psychoanalysis*. London: Karnac.

Matte-Blanco, I. (1988). *Thinking, Feeling, and Being*. London: Routledge.

Money-Kyrle, R. (1961). *Man's Picture of His World*. Aylesbury: Duckworth.

Money-Kyrle, R. (1968). Cognitive development. In: *The Collected Papers of Roger Money-Kyrle*. Pertshire: Clunie Press, (1978).

Onishi, K. H., & Baillargeon, R. (2005). Do 15-month-old infants understand false beliefs? *Science*, 308(5719): 255–258.

Petot, J.-M. (1990). *Melanie Klein: Volume I*. Madison, CT: International University Press.

Petot, J.-M. (1991). *Melanie Klein: Volume II*. Madison, CT: International University Press.

Piaget, J. & Garcia, R. (1982). *Psicogenesis e Historia de la Ciencia*. Mexico: Siglo XXI.

Popper, K. R. (1973). *La Logica de la Investigacion Científica*. Madrid: Tecnos.

Rustin, M. (2001). "Give me a consulting room". The generation of psychoanalytic knowledge. In: *Reason and Unreason*. London: Continuum.

Sandler, J. (1983). Reflections on some relations between psychoanalytic concepts and psychoanalytic practice. *International Journal of Psycho-Analysis, 64*: 34–45.

Sandler, J., & Sandler, A. M. (1983). The 'Second Censorship', the 'Three Box Model' and some technical implications. *International Journal of Psycho-Analysis, 64*: 413–425.

Tabak de Bianchedi, E., Etchegoyen, R. H., Ungar de Moreno, V., Nemas de Urman, C., & Zysman, S. (2003). Erna and Melanie Klein. *International Journal of Psycho-Analysis, 84*: 1587–1603.

Tuckett, D. (2008). *Psychoanalysis, Comparable & Incomparable*. London: Routledge.

Wisdom, J. O. (1967). Un acercamiento metodológico al problema de la histeria. *Revista de Psicoanalisis, XXIV*(3): 485–527.

Zysman, S. (1998). *La Psychiatrie de l'enfant, XLI*: 2.

Zysman, S. (1999). Consideraciones sobre la acción en psicoanálisis. In: *Teoría de la Acción, Perspectivas Filosóficas y Psicoanalíticas*. Buenos Aires: ADEP.

Zysman, S. (2006). Infantile sexual theories and cognitive development, psychoanalysis and theoretical production. In: J. Canestri (Ed.), *Psychoanalysis: From Practice to Theory*. London: Wiley.

Zysman, S. (2009). The metapsychology of theories. Presented at the Panel with the same name, 46th. IPAC, Chicago.

Zysman, S., Villa Segura, A., Bordone de Semeniuk, L., & Pieczanski, A. (2009). Las teorías en la mente del analista durante su trabajo. *Psicoanalisis, XXXI*: 1.

CHAPTER EIGHT

Conclusions

Jorge Canestri

Ten years after beginning our research it is now perhaps possible to outline the various observations we have made as well as what we have learned from them. In this chapter I will also try to suggest how this work could be continued and I will mention some of the problems that still remain unsolved.

Initial questions

First of all, I think we should ask ourselves whether the initial questions that we formulated ten years ago have been answered.

Perhaps the first question in order of importance—and that provides the title for one of the chapters of this book as well as for our participation in the ApsaA Congress, "Do analysts do what they say they do?"—can easily be answered. No, as Joseph Sandler said in his work (Sandler & Sandler, 1983) on which our research is based, analysts do not do what they say (and believe) they do. In a chapter of the previous book, *Psychoanalysis: From Practice to Theory* (Canestri, 2006a) Peter Fonagy summarised in one sentence what we had hypothesised following Sandler's ideas, and that would subsequently become the result of our research: "Psychoanalytic clinical practice is not logically deducible from currently available theory" (p. 72). To the extent that we can demonstrate it—and this has been one of the results of our work, that in clinical practice an analyst certainly uses "official" theories not only according to how he has assimilated them but also interposed with his own theoretical segments, patterns, and models—Fonagy's words prove to be true. Clinical practice is not logically deducible from currently available theory because the psychoanalyst, in his clinical practice, does not work with "currently available theories" but with a combination of "official" theories and implicit theories or models. Therefore, the definition of theory that we have proposed, in a broad sense, is: theory = public theory based thinking + private theoretical thinking + interaction of private and explicit thinking (implicit use of explicit theory).

Our project has been developed as a qualitative and empirical research preceded and accompanied by a conceptual research, and has been carried out on an extensive population of analysts who presented hundreds of hours of clinical material. In order to analyse this material we used an instrument created ad hoc, so as to be able to categorise the observed and analysed reality. As we have already pointed out in the previous book, an analysis such as this is only possible with the collaboration and feedback of the analysts who presented the material; and from them have come the innovations, adjustments, and changes that we have progressively made to the instrument: the map of private (implicit, preconscious) theories in clinical practice. Every research instrument conforms to a defined methodology. In our case the working method consists of an analyst voluntarily presenting clinical material, usually from several sessions, to a group of analysts who have asked to participate. After the presentation of the material, the coordinator/discussant analyses it by using the map. Since it is composed of vectors (seven) that are able to explore various aspects of the analyst's implicit theories, the coordinator/discussant has the task of helping the participants to bring them to light as they examine the material. The group actively participates in the work, while the analyst who presented the clinical material abstains from replying to the commentaries until the end of the process, at which time he offers his feedback. The work then continues until the end of the agreed time. A reporter takes note of the group's work.

The central nucleus of the Working Party on Theoretical Issues composed, as we have said, of a Chair and three consultants, then reviews the presentation and the work of the group. This has allowed for integrations and modifications to be made to the programme and to the original instrument.

What all this work has revealed increasingly clearly is the accuracy of our initial hypothesis set out in the definition of theory proposed above. The theory used by the analyst in his clinical work is always a complex configuration involving theoretical fragments, concepts, and patterns of different derivation belonging not only to recognisable theories but also created ad hoc in a preconscious manner.

The use of the word "configuration" is intentional because it will help us to decide whether, at the end of our discourse, we are able to single out more frequently used "typologies" that will then give us an idea of theories that are not official or "pure", but are more similar to those we effectively work with in clinical practice. I think this is one of the most interesting issues in our contemporary theoretical discussion and I will return to it later in more detail.

Experience. Applications in different contexts

The experience that we have gained shows us, on the one hand, what we already know: that is, that it is usually very difficult to share a clinical experience without a tendency on the part of the participants to suggest a reformulation of the case or to supervise the analyst's work. As I have already said, in our work the methodological regulation obliges us to deal with the analyst's inferential processes and with his comprehension of psychoanalytical understanding, and consequently to consciously avoid drifting towards a supervision. On the other hand, the experience has been welcomed with great interest and participation because, through the same regulation, we have been able to collectively explore the mind of the analyst at work, to investigate the theories used, and to gain a better understanding of the configurations created in order to meet the requirements of psychoanalytical clinical work. Moreover, and without being persecutory, it is easy to show the analyst at work how he may often think that he is using a "classical" and "pure" psychoanalytical theory when in fact in most cases he, like most of us, is using "inter- or trans-theoretical" compositions.

For all these reasons a project and an experience that began essentially as a research undertaking has proved to be very useful in facilitating the sharing of clinical experience and the fruitful discussions arising from it. Hundreds of analysts have participated in the various congresses held in the three regions of the International Psychoanalytical Association as well as in the Component Societies; this has meant that a larger number of analysts than in any other previous undertaking have been able to exchange opinions and observe working methods that are different from their own or from those with which they are more familiar.

Psychoanalytic training. The transmission of psychoanalysis

Perhaps it has been even more surprising to discover how useful this methodology is in the teaching of psychoanalysis. In institutes of psychoanalysis, theory and psychoanalytic technique are taught at seminars, and candidates' clinical cases are for the most part supervised individually or, in some institutes, (e.g., in France, the SPP) also through collective supervisions.

We have tried the experience of organising seminars in psychoanalytical institutes using the same rules as for the working groups formed for our research at congresses or in societies. A candidate presents various sessions of a patient in analysis to a group of peers coordinated by a teacher. This is followed by an analysis of the material presented and a discussion. The coordinator has the same functions as those described above. Due to the difference in expertise between the candidates and the teacher, in this case his more decisive work will be in identifying the elements that make up the candidate's theoretical configuration; the comparison between what he thinks he is doing and what he actually does.

Normally, in the seminars in psychoanalytic institutes, theory and technique are always taught separately from clinical work, while with this type of teaching, theory, technique, and clinical work are all taught as one. As I said before, this is helpful in showing the candidate not only the different configurations that his work assumes, but also in teaching or deepening the ideas of those authors who he is using, whether consciously or not; it is also helpful in exploring the relationship between the theories he has studied and says he in fact applies, and his own his clinical practice and clinical practice in general. If Fonagy's statement quoted on p. 158 is true—"Psychoanalytic clinical practice is not logically deducible from currently available theory"— then we think that the candidate must often find himself in considerable difficulty as he wonders how to deal with certain contradictions. We believe that this type of teaching can be of great help. In the same way as psychoanalysis bases most of its therapeutic power on confronting the patient with the truth, so the teaching of psychoanalysis should have a similar quality of showing the candidate in training how things really stand in the relationship between theory and clinical work.

A theory is an instrument; it is not an idol nor must it be treated as such. Even psychoanalytic theory/theories can be idolised As Green points out in his "L'idéal: mesure et démesure" (1983), the ideal ego never disappears (p. 282), and, as Freud says, the values it contains undergo a reversal inasmuch as the renunciation of satisfaction is carried out in the name of a superior well-being and in favour of an over-valued object. This "great and disincarnate" object, adds the author, "can become a great idea, for example psychoanalysis itself" (p. 287) (Canestri, 2008). In *Psychoanalysis: From Practice to Theory*, we wrote: "The way in which the internalization of theories is produced depends on both strictly personal factors and on others linked to the teaching in the institutes and to relationships of 'affiliation' " (p. 40) (Canestri, 2006a). We also said that it was important to try to clarify the type of relationship that we have with our own theories and with those of others; and how, by applying the theory of attachment as an instrument of analysis, we could hypothesise different types of relationships which, according to one's greater or less confidence in the relationship with one's own theory, would allow for a calm and interested exploration of other people's theories.

In the training of analysts, institutes cannot modify the strictly personal factors for these are entrusted to the candidate's personal analysis; but they can certainly intervene on the elements connected to teaching and to affiliation.

Supervision

Supervision is an essential instrument in analytic training. One chapter of the book is dedicated to it and on this occasion I should only like to emphasise some of the ideas presented.

In this chapter I asked myself what was the object of the supervision, "what" was being supervised. Basically, the reply took into consideration the "change in outlook that has progressively moved the analyst's focus from the life events and pathology of the patient to an analysis of the situation, the relationship and the analytic process" (p. 109).

I also suggested that "Supervision can be seen as a field of variable dimensions. The configuration of this field ensues from the vertex of observation chosen by the supervisor, and it derives directly from the theory that informs the supervision and from its pre-established goals" (p. 114). This allows the supervisor to choose a goal, an objective, that in the supervision would enable him to orient the work towards identifying the candidate's implicit theories. In this way the supervisor can help the candidate describe the theoretical configurations that he uses in his clinical practice, where the "official" theories that he has studied fit in with his implicit theories deriving from various sources.

The main objective of this type of supervision is not that of ascertaining the greater or less pertinence of the candidate's interpretations, or how well he understands the clinical material. Basically, the objective is to make the candidate aware of the nature of the inferential processes that he has used in his clinical work. We are in the habit of theorising, teaching, and using the countertransference as an inevitable component of the experience of the session, and we are particularly attentive to the sensitivity and awareness that the analyst shows in its regard. I believe we must be equally attentive to studying what happens in the mind of the analyst relative to the inferences that lead him to understand the material and subsequently to interpret it.

This is why I have said that:

> ... supervision appears as a privileged place in which to link theory and practice: to methodically explain what theoretical hypotheses can be drawn from the clinical material; to show how the theoretic choice informs the reading of the material and conditions it; to emphasise the aspects of the clinical reality in which the chosen theory proves to be insufficient or contradictory; to discover the use that is made of ad hoc hypotheses in order not to abandon a theory; to investigate the presence of implicit or personal theories; to accustom the candidate to consider every interpretation as a work hypothesis derived from a certain theoretic model. (p. 126)

Although the "supervision could be the preferred place to deepen, investigate, and work on translating theory into practice and practice into theory" (p. 127), it is necessary to carefully select how to outline or "cut" the field so that it best suits the pre-fixed goal. Carrying out the type of task necessary for identifying the implicit theories of the analyst at work is better done in group supervisions in the form of clinical–theoretical workshops. On the contrary, managing the countertransference problems of the analyst is easier in individual supervision than in a group.

The variety of theoretical configurations

We have always insisted that in clinical practice analysts do not work with "pure" official theories but with a combination that we have defined as the sum of *public theory based thinking + private theoretical thinking + interaction of private and explicit thinking (implicit use of explicit theory)*. A careful observation of the actual reality of clinical work could convince us that the factors involved in this calculation are even more numerous. In fact, an analyst does not resort to one official theory alone, but he generally uses a combination of concepts taken from different theories or models that he integrates with a greater or lesser degree of skill and coherence.

We are currently faced with problems caused by the integration of concepts deriving from different theories and in contradiction with each another. One of the frequent exercises in the teaching at seminars is, in fact, to find out the provenance of the concepts used and whether they are reciprocally compatible. While from the point of view of theoretical work contradiction between incompatible concepts is quite rightly not well tolerated, Sandler points out how, in clinical practice, the analyst has no problem in accepting the simultaneous existence of contrasting theoretical fragments that contradict each other. This is possible as long as they are preconscious (unconscious from a descriptive viewpoint).

By taking examples from a reflection on the clinical work of some well-known analysts (e.g., Bion and Ferenczi), we have underlined the creative quality demonstrated by the analyst's implicit theories; sometimes these theories become public and assume a definite theoretical value. A well-known example is Bion's concept of "alpha function";

in his book *Cogitations* (Bion, 1992) it is possible to follow the thought process that leads to its formulation.

Certainly, not all implicit theories become "official" theories, nor do they all necessarily prove to be useful or positive. Bohleber (in Chapter One) has emphasiaed that these theoretical fragments and implicit theories that the analyst constructs in clinical practice, are not always useful and do not always lead to a better understanding of clinical phenomena. In some cases the opposite is true: the emerging implicit theory proves to be "regressive", and rather than increasing our understanding of the clinical phenomenon, it diminishes it, even to the point of cancelling any insight that we may previously have gained about these phenomena. Bohleber goes on to analyse some aspects of the Freudian theory of transference which he considers have been lost or forgotten due to subsequent theoretical integrations.

However, having said this, we must not overlook the essential heuristic role of clinical experience in psychoanalysis, systematically investigating and analysing with an appropriate instrument all that occurs in the relation between practice and theory from the viewpoint of the creation of new theoretical segments in clinical work. "Grasping psychoanalyst's practice in its own merits" are the words that Juan Pablo Jiménez uses to express this concept (Jiménez, 2008).

In the Introduction to *Psychoanalysis: From Practice to Theory* (Canestri, 2006a) we discussed the proliferation of theories in post-Freudian psychoanalysis, the preoccupation that this provoked in many theorists of the discipline, and the attempts made by some of them to find a "common ground" in the hope of preserving the uniqueness of psychoanalytic theory.

We cannot deny that the exploration, individuation, and consideration of the implicit theories of the analyst at work inevitably lead towards an increase in theoretical pluralism. If we consider this phenomenon of "proliferation" in our work and research in the field of implicit theories in clinical practice, besides observing the increase of theoretical pluralism already hypothesised, we find ourselves facing another interesting and less obvious phenomenon.

Returning to our original definition of theory as the sum of *public theory based thinking + private theoretical thinking + interaction of private and explicit thinking (implicit use of explicit theory)*, it becomes self-evident that there is a possible increase in theoretical variety on account of the construction (pointed out by Sandler and subsequently studied in our research) of theoretical fragments according to the requirements of clinical work and the creative capacities of the analyst.

What is less self-evident is the fact that in the theoretical variety that emerges from the analysis of the clinical material presented, there are certain regularities, tendencies, and convergences. These are "configurations" that diverge from official theories; they are produced by the sum described above in our definition and may take the form of new theoretical structures. Intuitively, one would think that their variety could be very great, and would not allow for "categories" to be identified or a theoretical "map" to be drawn. Experience proves this expectation to be wrong because a careful observation reveals regularities and convergences that, despite a presumably inexhaustible variety of possible configurations, and taking into due account the potentially infinite number of combinations, could represent a limited set of "neo-theories".

The impression obtained is that these "functional neo-theories", closer to everyday clinical experience, may apparently and paradoxically offer a way out from an excessive theoretical pluralism which some people (e.g., Fonagy) define as "theoretical fragmentation". Already in Chapter Five of *Psychoanalysis: From Practice to Theory*, Fonagy suggested that the use and study of the analyst's implicit theories in his clinical work could be considered as the main way out of a theoretical entropy, and that an "action oriented" use of theory could allow psychoanalysts to be more in line with post-empirical views of science (Canestri, 2006a, pp. 70–71). After all, every form of knowledge is based on forms of action.

As well as the pragmatic aspects of these considerations (that is, which "functional neo-theories" are outlined in our research, how are these neo-formations identified, what are their characteristics, how do they diverge from or converge with our accepted "official" theories, etc.), it is certain that the previous statements present epistemological problems that we must at least mention.

These pragmatic problems, that is, the characterisation of the "functional neo-theories", are among the problems that remain unsolved about which I will talk later and that could be the object of a new research project. Now I will deal briefly with the epistemological problems.

Some epistemological considerations

From an epistemological point of view, our starting point ten years ago was the adoption of a post-empirical epistemological stance, definitely discarding the classical distinction—introduced by Hans Reichenbach and reformulated by Karl Popper—between context (or logic) of discovery and context (or logic) of justification (see Canestri, 2006a, Chapter One) in the sense of systematically investigating and analysing with an appropriate instrument everything that occurs in the relation between practice and theory from the viewpoint of the creation of new theoretical segments in clinical work.

This rejection was necessary not only because of the logic of "real" research (see the comment by Lakatos (1976) on the short-sightedness of Popper's approach to this issue), but also because of the specificity of our research. Our intention was to explore the inferential processes of the mind of the analyst during his clinical practice—those mental processes that led him to the implicit formulation of theoretical segments that would help him to understand what his clinical experience demanded of him. It would have been contradictory to radically separate the context of discovery from that of justification; it would have left us with our hands tied. This was clearly understood by mathematicians as they dealt with mathematical invention, and it has been effectively conceptualised by Poincaré, Hadamard, Einstein, Chandrasekhar, to name but a few. All these authors point out that every creative activity and every inferential process has its roots in the researcher's unconscious and preconscious: Lakatos spoke of "surreptitious activity", Polanyi of "tacit activity", Einstein of "combinatory plan", but the essence is the same.

To this we should add that we were aware of the well-known fact that the "observative terms" are "observative" in a Pickwickian sense and that there is neither "pure observation" nor a neutral observative language. The meaning of the observative terms is a function of "conceptual patterns", and these conceptual patterns or implicit theories are constantly at work in clinical practice.

As well as pointing out Popper's short-sightedness concerning the separation between context of discovery and context of justification when dealing with the logic of scientific research, Lakatos (1976) also rejects a clear-cut demarcation between the history of a discipline and the discipline itself. He says that in order to understand a theory, one must understand the problems it originally intended to solve and verify which problems it de facto succeeds in resolving. To understand this, it is necessary to reconstruct the situation in which these problems were originally formulated and the modalities by which they were progressively transformed.

Let us take an example from the history of psychoanalysis. Freud had originally confronted problems connected with neurotic pathologies. The "topical" theory seemed sufficient for resolving these problems, even though part of the pathology described in Freudian clinical work by then lay beyond neurosis. Gradually the insufficiency of the topical theory and the gravity of the pathology being treated—Ferenczi's clinical work is an example—induced Freud to formulate the so-called structural theory. Towards the end of his life it became increasingly evident that the problems that the psychoanalysis of the early years had intended to solve had changed. The situations and the corresponding problems continue to change and the solutions must inevitably adapt to them. The Lakatosian saying of "improving by demonstrating" is based on the idea that not only is an accepted demonstration relevant, but that every attempt to demonstrate a conjecture is relevant.

All that we have said so far is an attempt to emphasise the heuristic role of clinical experience in psychoanalysis, and this heuristic characterisation is accompanied by a heuristic course of theory.

Some preliminary remarks are necessary in order to define the meaning of a heuristic course of theory (Motterlini, 1994):

a)   Popper's *background knowledge* is to be interpreted as the group of facts used in the construction of theory: *background-knowledge-of-a-theory*.

b)   We must presuppose a three-way relationship between evidence, theory and heuristic progress: i.e. *theory-arrived-at-in-a-certain-way* (*theory together with its heuristic*). (p. 329, my italics)

Motterlini concludes that "if the way in which the theory was constructed becomes decisive for the evaluation of its scientific merits, then—against Popper's ideas—the empirical support is heuristic-dependent . . ." (p. 330).

In the light of these considerations we can say that in order to emphasise the heuristic role of clinical experience in psychoanalysis we have had to equip ourselves with an epistemology that is congruent with our objective, a methodology appropriate to the aim, and an instrument (the map) suitable for a qualitative research on the clinical material.

At this point, if the above described process has led to the enunciation of a theory or partial outline that from implicit has become explicit, we are confronted with the question of how to transform a speculative hypothesis into a controllable theory. Contrary to the tendency of some colleagues to believe that psychoanalysis does not need to find a proof, a post-empirical heuristic-dependent epistemology does not exempt us from the task of verification or falsification of theories according to the epistemological orientation that we want to adopt.

The proof, that is, the support provided by the facts and the capacity of the theory to account for them, is essential in order to decree its own scientificity; in the same way that being more capable of obtaining confirmation of the facts than a rival theory, makes it easier to judge it. Comparison between the quality of rival theories (psychoanalytical in our case) is one of the problems that we frequently avoid. Entering into the question of the reasons why, and of the possible procedures for "testing" the rival theories within a discipline such as ours, goes way beyond the possibilities of these conclusions and was not part of the objectives of our research. However, it is something that we must take into serious consideration and that deserves to be mentioned.

Our presentation of the heuristic role of clinical experience can be enriched by a contribution by Juan Pablo Jiménez. He emphasises an aspect that has not been sufficiently taken into consideration in the map (and that subsequently led us to introduce a seventh vector): the manner in which the different vectors described in the map interact in the mind of the analyst and the analytic situation, that is, the "movement" or the dynamics of the partial theories, the models, or the implicit patterns. Jiménez suggests that this dynamic

> is determined by the patient in his interaction with the analyst. It is an interpersonal and intersubjective heuristic inasmuch as it is the link between two minds working together. By this I suggest that in the mind of the analyst a continuous process of decision-making is produced which, against the background of the "implicit use of

explicit theories", is permanently influenced by the actions and reactions of the patient. (Jiménez, 2008)

This is an aspect that is part of the process—and the reason why Jiménez then speaks about the dynamics of implicit theories—and therefore it is difficult to describe it in a static vector in the map. The analytic process is a function of the dynamic interaction created between analysand–analyst-implicit and official theories in situation. From my point of view, it is therefore necessary to put to work temporal models "in situation" that are able to evolve dynamically and that possess an important heuristic potential (Canestri, 2004, 2006b).

Let us now briefly discuss the issue of the proof.

Testing the theory

Even though the modality with which a theory was constructed becomes decisive for the evaluation of its scientific merits, this alone is not sufficient for deciding about its merits. And even though, as W. J. McGuire—a real champion in the study of the hypothesis generation—states many times (McGuire, 1997): "a science is a process of creativity and discovery and not just a hypothesis testing and falsification", this does not mean that we do not have to take into account the usefulness of testing. According to which orientation and for which purpose? The same author (McGuire, 1999) suggests that "all knowledge representations are imperfect but differ in type and degree of imperfection. Which is the least imperfect depends on the use to which the knowledge is put" (p. 400). McGuire's "perspectivism" is concerned with determining, above all, how and when a theory is true rather than deciding on the truth of a theory in the abstract sense.

In the series of epistemological considerations outlined so far we have stated that: a) there is neither "pure observation" nor a neutral observative language. The meaning of the observative terms is a function of "conceptual patterns" (implicit theories); b) we must consider the *background-knowledge-of-a-specific-theory*; c) the theory we are speaking about is a *theory-that-has-been-reached-in-a-certain-way* (*theory together with its heuristics*); d) the empirical support is *heuristic-dependent*; and e) it is necessary to ascertain the merits of a theory through the use of methods of "control", whether of verification or of falsification.

However, at this point it would be useful to take a step backwards and try to investigate the quality of the inferential processes of the analyst from an epistemological point of view. In Chapter Eight of the previous book, Jorge Ahumada developed a convincing version of the analytic mind at work, suggesting that "This peculiar scientific endeavour, clinical psychoanalysis, *amounts to a huge observational, counterinductive extension of everyday practical logic*" (Ahumada, 2006, p. 144).

Charles Sanders Peirce, (Pierce, 1931–1958), brilliant logician and inventor of semiotics, described three different "ways of reasoning", that is, three types of inference: induction, deduction, and retroduction, this latter being later named abduction, according to Aristotle. "Abduction" is of Latin etymology and means "to conduct" (*ducere*) "away from" (*ab*), moving away.

In Peirce's version, abduction is an inference to the best explanation. The reasoning goes more or less like this: "It is a fact that A. If things are like this and this, then this would explain A. Therefore, perhaps things are like this and this." The word "perhaps" should be emphasised in this context. The term "abduction" (in Greek *apagōghé*) was used for the first time by Aristotle who differentiated it from induction as well as from deduction (cfr. *Analitici primi, II,* 25 sgg.). Abduction has a less demonstrative value inasmuch as in the syllogism that represents it, the greater premise is certain while the minor premise is doubtful; the conclusion is therefore characterised by probability—a probability equal to that of the minor premise. Or, as Aristotle says: it is obvious that the first term is pertinent to the middle term, while it is not obvious that the middle term pertains to the third term, although this could be possible.

In Collected Paper (CP) Five Peirce says that: "Abduction consists in the study of the facts and in the conception of a theory to explain them" (p. 145). According to the American logician this is the only logical operation capable of introducing a new idea, since the induction determines a value and the deduction serves to produce the inevitable consequences of a pure hypothesis. In CP Five, (p. 171) he states, in fact, that abduction creates a hypothesis, the deduction verifies it, and induction applies it. His reasoning derives from ascertaining that an explanation is needed when the facts, for example, contradict our expectations or remain outside what we are able to explain immediately. At this stage "a hypothesis must be adopted that is in itself probable and that renders the facts probable. The stage of adopting a hypothesis inasmuch as it is suggested by the facts, is what I call abduction" (CP Seven, p. 121).

Umberto Eco (1990) points out that in CP Two, (p. 623), Peirce "says that, while induction is the inference of a rule from a case and a result, a hypothesis is the inference of the case from a rule and a result". What is relevant, from the point of view of the Italian semiologist, is the middle term, "the keystone of the entire inferential movement . . . The invention of a good middle term, this is the stroke of genius" (p. 234).

From Eco's viewpoint, hypothesis and abduction—sometimes differentiated by Peirce and sometimes treated as synonyms—are in essence what we know as *conjectures*. In his opinion this means that scientific discoveries, medical reasonings, criminal investigations (e.g., Sherlock Holmes), philological interpretations of texts, etc., are "all cases of conjectural thinking" (p. 236). Obviously, from what has been said, we can hypothesise that the inferences of the psychoanalyst at work belong to the type of inference developed by Peirce also: abduction (or conjectural thinking).

Not all abductions are the same. Peirce, as mentioned above, sometimes distinguished a hypothesis (a case was associated to the already codified rule by inference) from abduction (adoption of an explicative inference that needs an experimental verification and to find the rule).

Following other authors including Thagard, Eco (pp. 237–238) distinguishes four types of abduction:

1) *Hypothesis or hypercodified abduction*: the law in this case is provided automatically or semi-automatically according to the obviousness of the case in question.

2) *Hypocodified abduction*: "The rule must be selected from a series of equally probable rules put at our disposal by our current knowledge of the world . . . In this sense we undoubtedly have inference to a rule, that Thagard calls "abduction" *strictu senso*.

3) *Creative abduction*: "the law has to be invented *ex novo* . . . In any case this type of invention obliges . . . to carry out a meta-abduction". Eco recalls those "revolutionary" discoveries that change an established paradigm, following the ideas of Kuhn.

4) *Meta-abduction*: "consists in deciding whether the possible universe delineated by our abductions at the first level is the same as

the universe of our experience". In the previous cases the laws we use are known and "controlled"; in this case of "creative" abduction it is not so.

Without entering into a detailed analysis of the cases and of the possible examples—something that would lie way beyond the possibilities and intentions of these conclusive pages—I would suggest that the reader think about how these various abductions could be actualised within his own clinical experience.

Peirce considers that the beginning of this inferential process is to make all the necessary observations and to find the *fil rouge* that will tie them together. Peirce calls this passage *colligation*. Then follow the steps described above that lead to abduction or *conjectural process*. All these passages are definitely present in analytical work, and we have devoted a great deal of our research to a better specific knowledge about their identification or in creating the rule to link to the cases.

If abduction means reasoning about the best possible explanation that stems retroactively from the effects to the cause, then we must keep in mind that, to a greater or lesser extent and according to whether one is closer to the first or the fourth type of abduction in Eco's typology, the explanations are only probable.

After this brief foray into the universe of "abductive" inferences in the mind of the analyst in his daily clinical work, let us return to the problem of testing the theories that we work with and the respective merits of each one of them.

The problems regarding the "confirmation" of scientific hypotheses are too well known for it to be necessary or useful to go into details. I think it is only worth mentioning the well-known divergence between Popper and his falsification methodology and the methodology of Carnap and others intent on constructing a solid theory of inductive inference. To avoid misunderstandings, it must be said that Peirce's theory of abduction, although with its own particular characteristics, forms part of the theories of inductive inference.

We know that Popper objects to the fact that theories are the product of inferences stemming from a growing (and potentially infinite) accumulation of observations; rather, from his point of view (and, as we have seen before, also from Peirce's point of view), they are "conjectures". The *criteria of demarcation*, therefore, will not be the verifiability of a system, but its *falsifiability*. Infallibilism, with the corresponding concepts of truth and of certainty, is replaced by a falli-bilistic concept of scientific knowledge. The philosophy of science acknowledges the concept of likelihood in the place of truth, and of probability in the place of certainty.

The discussions that have mobilised the psychoanalytical field on the subject of the two rival positions concerning the scientificity of psychoanalysis (verifiability *vs.* falsifiability) are well known and of little weight. But perhaps it would be interesting to examine an aspect of the novelty represented by the development, in the field of induc-tive inference, of the theory of probability.

In our case, probability is to be understood exclusively as an epis-temic (or inductive) probability, to be distinguished from objective physical probability. Carnap (1950) made a special effort to study and defend the usefulness of these concepts.

When I say that in our case we are interested essentially in the concept of epistemic probability, it is because it can tell us something about the inferential processes in the mind of the analyst. Further-more, it offers an interesting perspective on the problem of testing and of the comparison and competition between theories.

In "Induzione, probabilità e verisimilitudine" R. Festa (Giorelloo, 1994) develops the idea according to which in a probabilistic concep-tion it is only possible to reach non-absolute degrees of certitude. If we were to attempt to solve the problem of developing a theory of likeli-hood, we should have to provide an answer to two essential prob-lems—one logical and the other epistemic: a) what does it mean that a theory is nearer to truth than other theory? and b) how can we ratio-nally conjecture, on the basis of an empirical evidence, that a theory is nearer than another to truth? (As mentioned earlier, in this case truth has the meaning of likelihood).

Festa suggests that the problem could be treated using a Bayesian approach to the inductive inference. This is a probabilistic fallibilism in the style of Carnap.

But what is the so-called Bayes theorem and how do we collect consistent or inconsistent evidence for a hypothesis?

The mathematician, Reverend Thomas Bayes, who lived in the eigh-teenth century, gave his name to a theorem that tries to make a numer-ical estimate of the researcher's degree of belief in a hypothesis before evidence has been observed, and calculates a numerical estimate of the degree of belief in the hypothesis after evidence has been obtained.

If we call P (E/H) *conditional probability* of seeing the evidence E if the hypothesis H happens to be true (also called likelihood function or plausibility), and P(E) is called *marginal probability* of E (a priori probability of witnessing the new evidence), we call P(H) *prior probability* of H that is inferred before new evidence E, and then we call P(H/E) the *posterior or final probability* of H given E, the formula of Bayes' theorem that allows us to calculate the final probability will be:

$$P(H/E) = \frac{P(E/H)P(H)}{P(E)}$$

The final probability (P(H/E)) of a hypothesis (H) is directly proportional to its initial probability P(H) and to its plausibility P(E/H), and inversely proportional to the initial probability P(E) of the evidence E.

By applying the theorem we could say that a hypothesis is confirmed when the final probability is greater than the initial probability and disconfirmed when the final probability is minor than the initial probability.

From the point of view of my argument, it would be useless to enter into the algebraic complications of Bayesian probabalistic calculus. What seems to me to be interesting from our viewpoint is the possibility offered by the epistemic or inductive Bayesian probability conception to estimate degrees of a researcher's belief, a subjectivist account of evidence.

For each hypothesis H on which the researcher has a firm belief or conviction, the theorem tries to evaluate the level of confidence or belief in H's truth.

It is reasonable to think that the choice of the initial probability (conditional probability) will be essential, since it will contribute to the determination of the final probability. An important subjective variability in the choice of the initial probability will produce a strong subjective variablity in the attribution of the final probability. This means that the same evidence can be used to make different evaluations of the final probability of hypothesis H.

The way that leads to obtaining a greater likelihood of the hypothesis is also the way that leads to modifying and updating the level of confidence in a hypothesis.

Is the Bayesian approach an inductive inference? It is a statistical inference, but it is different from the conventional frequentist inference inasmuch as probability is used to quantify *uncertainty*.

The question we must ask ourselves at this stage is whether the Bayesian inference can be used to discriminate between conflicting hypotheses. Those who deny this possibility object that this method could be biased due to the initial beliefs that one holds before any evidence is ever collected. However, besides the fact that the Bayesian inference tries to estimate the degree of belief in a hypothesis before and after the collection of evidence, and can protect itself from possible distortion through an accurate control of the conditional probability, to us analysts the consideration of the degree of belief in a hypothesis before evidence has been collected seems to be extremely important. The degree of belief is also significantly connected to the implicit, private, and preconscious theories of the analyst at work.

The importance and the role of the preconscious in inferential processes

In the first chapter ("Implicit understanding of clinical material beyond theory") of the book *Psychoanalysis: From Practice to Theory*, one section was dedicated to the concept of preconscious. I had on that occasion matched the Freudian concept of preconscious with the concept of "zone of proximal development" by Vygotskij (1934). In Vygotski's thought, the zone of proximal development represents the area of what the child can do with the collaboration of the adult in the process of learning. The Russian thought that in infantile cognitive development, the interaction between the spontaneous concepts of the child and the non-spontaneous, learned ones is relevant.

In the theorisation of Sandler and Sandler (1983), followers of Freud, the preconscious elaborates the derivatives of the unconscious. The preconscious fantasies (and we could add implicit theories) sink their roots in the dynamic unconscious, even if they obey the rules of the secondary process. Sandler underlines the great tolerance of contradictions of the preconscious system, a system that is oriented towards the present in its search for adaptive solutions and is defined as the creative centre of fantasies and thoughts. This latter characteristic is fundamental to our research and our ideas on implicit theories; it is equally essential, from our point of view, for whatever conception one may have on the analyst's inferential processes during clinical work.

Freud, Vygotskij and Sandler agree, in synthesis, on recognising in the preconscious system a creative factory of phantasies and spontaneous ideas, tolerant of contradictions, and fuelled by the dynamic unconscious as well as by the secondary process and the word representations.

In her excellent article on "The role of the preconscious in psychoanalysis" Kantrowitz (1999) adds to the above description the function of what she calls "the interdigitation of the intrapsychic structures of both patient and analyst". I quote a brief paragraph from the abstract:

> The analytic process inevitably involves the interdigitation of the intrapsychic structures of both patient and analyst. This interplay is expressed in transference-countertransference interactions. Drawing a dichotomy between intrapsychic and interpersonal factors as central agents of psychic change is a faulty construction. Affective, behavioral interchanges between patient and analyst reflect their individual intrapsychic organizations and their interplay, which influence the form and nature of psychological change. The safer both patient and analyst feel in relation to each other, the more freely will they relax their customary cognitive controls and permit the emergence of preconscious responses. Preconscious resonance between patient and analyst is likely to facilitate the lifting of repressive barriers and the emergence of unconscious material in both participants.

In a subsequent work, "The analysis of preconscious phenomena and its communication", (Kantrowitz, 2001), she analyses the role of preconscious phenomena in the communication between patient and analyst.

To those analysts who considered it possible to substitute the topographical with the structural theory, Sandler and Sandler, in the work mentioned above (1983), argue that this is not possible without a considerable loss:

> The transition from the topographical to the structural theory of the mind has left us with theoretical problems which Freud was unable to solve and with which a number of psychoanalytic authors have subsequently grappled. For some a solution has been to discard the topographical model in its entirety (e.g. Arlow & Brenner, 1964). Others (e.g. Kris, 1950); (Eissler, 1962) have been acutely aware that the topographical theory cannot simply be replaced by the structural, and that the two cannot readily be dovetailed into each other. Ernst Kris has

commented that "The introduction of these new [structural] concepts has never been fully integrated with the broad set of propositions developed earlier" (1950). It is clear that terms and concepts from the topographical theory are still important for many analysts (see Abrams, 1971), and it is equally clear that such concepts must have a significant function to fulfil in psychoanalytic thinking. (p. 413)

Kantrowitz, Sandler, Rapaport and others are in agreement in quoting Ernest Kris' pioneering considerations on this issue.

Let me now consider the important and pioneer role of Ernest Kris in the investigation of the relation between practice and theory, and the participation in it of the preconscious mental processes.

I refer to two of Kris' papers: "On preconscious mental processes", 1950 and "Ego psychology and interpretation in psychoanalytic therapy", 1951, both published in *The Psychoanalytic Quarterly*. In the first paper Kris points outs out how in the psychoanalysis of his times, preconscious mental processes are rarely mentioned. He adds, however:

> This would not be remarkable or invite comment were it not that, in the area of ego psychology, certain aspects of preconscious mental activity have been studied with greater care and by a larger number of investigators than ever before in the history of psychoanalysis: to quote Freud's last formulation on the subject, ". . . the inside of the ego which comprises above all the intellectual processes has the quality of being preconscious" (1939, p. 42). (p. 539)

I could say that they have not been very much discussed subsequently either, until J. Sandler reconsidered them. Both authors refer to the difficulty of integrating the topographical with the structural concepts. Kris emphasises the difference between the Freudian elaborations during the years 1915–1917 when Freud analysed the functions of the Pcs system that he subsequently attributed to the ego, and the later considerations (1932 and 1939) in which the preconscious is described above all in terms of a "mental quality" (Kris, 1950, p. 541). Kris is concerned with the theoretical assumptions that must serve to differentiate the conscious from the preconscious mental processes, and he points out the danger of considering as a prerequisite the connection with a verbal mnestic trace (Freud, 1940a[1938]). He privileges the energetic explanation, in terms of free or bound energy and of the two types of discharge that characterise the primary or secondary processes. Kris mentions three types of problems: a) not all preconscious processes reach consciousness with the same facility, b) "preconscious mental processes are extremely different from each other both in content and in the kind of thought processes used; they cover continua ranging from purposeful reflection to fantasy, and from logical formulation to dreamlike imagery", and c) when this material emerges in consciousness the reaction is extremely variable.

By considering free or bound energy and the types of discharge in the primary and secondary processes, Kris is able to hypothesise a continuum (transition between extremes) that proves extremely useful and reliable when examining the analyst's inferential procedures linked with interpretation. The hypothesis of cathexes and counter-cathexes allows material to sink into the unconscious or alternatively to emerge in the preconscious and subsequently in the conscious with relative ease. Independently of the fact that one may prefer one theoretical explanation to another to account for this phenomenon, it is the existence of the phenomenon itself in the mind of the analyst at work that we are interested in on this occasion.

Under the sub-heading "Discharge and regression" Kris, in reviewing Varendonck's book on daydreaming and based on observations on clinical material of his own, underlines the variety in preconscious thinking. The "stream of preconscious" has highly varied expressions of highly varied contents (Kris, 1950, p. 548). In this the author finds confirmation of his introductory remarks "on the existence of two continua, one reaching from solving problems to dreamlike fantasy and one reaching from logical cohesive verbal statements to dreamlike imagery".

On this occasion I want to focus on what the author considers an indicator of the regression of the ego, a regression in which, obviously, "the id intrudes upon the ego functions". It is here that Kris announces the thesis that I am most interested in, on the nature and the functions of the preconscious system. I quote the entire paragraph:

> Topographically, ego regression (primitivization of ego functions) occurs not only when the ego is weak—in sleep, in falling asleep, in fantasy, in intoxication, and in the psychoses—*but also during many types of creative processes (my italics)*. This suggested to me years ago that

the ego may use the primary process and not be only overwhelmed by it (Kris, 1936b, 'The Psychology of Caricature. *International Journal of Psycho-Analysis*. XVII, p. 44). This idea was rooted in Freud's explanation of wit (1905) according to which a preconscious thought "is entrusted for a moment to unconscious elaboration", and seemed to account for a variety of creative or other inventive processes.

However, the problem of ego regression during creative processes represents only a special problem in a more general area. . . . The clinical observation of creators and the study of introspective reports of experience during creative activity tend to show that we are faced with a shift in the cathexis of certain ego functions. Thus a frequent distinction is made between an inspirational and an 'elaborational' phase in creation. The inspirational phase is characterized by the facility with which id impulses, or their closer derivatives, are received. One might say that countercathectic energies to some extent are withdrawn, and added to the speed, force, or intensity with which the preconscious thoughts are formed. During the "elaborational" phase, the countercathectic barrier may be reinforced, work proceeds slowly, cathexis is directed to other ego functions such as reality testing, formulation, or general purposes of communication. . . . Briefly, we suggest that the hypercathexis of preconscious mental activity with some quantity of energy withdrawn from the object world to the ego—from the system Pcpt to preconscious thinking—accounts for some of the extraordinary achievements of mentation" (Kris, 1950, pp. 551–552).

Later Kris suggests that there is a "gain in pleasure", what Freud called a *Lustgewin* in the solution of problems and in all the areas of creativity. The study of the processes of "thought formation" and problem solution particularly interest Kris, who suggests the history of science as appropriate material for the study of these phenomena. But it is Freud's work *Aus des Anfängen der Psychoanalyse* (at the time only recently published) that he feels is the most indicative for studying these problems "in relation to psychoanalysis itself" (Kris, 1950, p. 555). I myself recommend the reading of such texts as Ferenczi's *Clinical Diary* or *Cogitations* by Bion for the same reason.

In his work of the following year called *Ego Psychology and Interpretation in Psychoanalytic Therapy* (Kris, 1951), in the section "Planning and Intuition", Kris underlines how not only the controversy between Theodor Reik and Wilhelm Reich, but the problem itself it attempted to clarify is spurious. It is merely to be determined at what point preconscious thought processes *in the analyst* (my highlight) "take over" and determine his reaction, a question which touches upon every analyst's personal experience. . . . Once we assume that the optimal distance from full awareness is part of the "personal equation" of the analyst, the contribution of preconscious processes gains considerable importance. . . . Whenever we speak of the intuition of the analyst, we are touching upon a problem which tends to be treated in the psychoanalytic literature under various headings. We refer to the psychic equilibrium or the state of mind of the analyst. One part of this problem, however, is directly linked to the process of interpretation. Many times a brief glance in the direction of self-analysis is part and parcel of the analyst's intervention. The interconnection between attention, intuition, and self-analysis in the process of interpretation has been masterfully described by Ferenczi (1927, *Der Elastizität der psychoanalytischen Technik)"* (Kris, 1951, pp. 27–28)

At this point Kris took the step that connected what has been said above about preconscious processes to the mind of the analyst at work, and in thus doing he characterises his inferential processes. All this is at the base of our hypotheses on the role and the importance of implicit, private, preconscious theories in clinical work; moreover, it opens up the way to a research that attempts to identify and evaluate them. The fact that Kris was a careful observer of the creative processes facilitated his task of discovering the heuristic value of preconscious processes.

The continuation of a line of research

I should like to end this final chapter by briefly mentioning some possible lines of research that still remain open. Many have always existed and have been the object of reflection (and controversy) on the part of analysts from different schools. Others are more directly related to our own research that has brought them to light.

Let us begin with these last ones, specifically with what I mentioned above on the variety of theoretical configurations emerging from our experience. As we said earlier, these configurations go beyond our definition of theory as being the sum of *public theory based thinking + private theoretical thinking + interaction of private and explicit thinking (implicit use of explicit theory).* To the presumable proliferation of theories following in the wake of this definition, can be added the appearance of regularities and confluences that indicate a *limited* variety of "functional-neo-theories" closer to everyday clinical experience. They are certainly connected to Fonagy's concept of "action-oriented use of theories". These "functional-neo-theories" confront the researcher and the clinician with a great variety of queries of an epistemological, theoretical and clincial nature. We do not need to develop this argument now, but to keep it in mind as being extremely fertile ground for the future and, from a certain point of view, potentially revolutionary as far as our theoretical habits are concerned.

Another line of research which takes into serious consideration the fact that the thoughts and phantasies that appear at a preconscious level have their roots in the descriptive and also in the dynamic unconscious, is represented by the ideas of Zysman who began the diffusion of this project and the corresponding research within the psychoanlaytical field of Latin America. The idea that Zysman introduces is that of considering theories as "objects", internal and external, using the term in the sense that it assumes in the theory of object relations. I think this line of thought and of research has excellent possibilities in the future for producing interesting results that will add to those that the author and his group write about in this book.

Bohleber extends some of his reflections set out in the chapter in the work that he, Fonagy, Jiménez, Scarfone, Varvin, and Zysman carried out in the "Conceptual Integration Project Committee" of the International Psychoanalytical Association. The problem of conceptual integration—not to be confused with the fantasy of constructing a unique or "true" psychoanalytical theory, or with the intention of imposing a particular theory—in my opinion definitely seems relevant at the present time, taking into due account our work and our research. In a certain way, the attempt to seriously study the possibility of (and the need for) conceptual integration is an extension of everything we have acheived until now. This author likes to consider contemporary theoretical pluralism in the light of what Bion proposed by prolonging the thinking that characterised the integration of non-Euclide geometries at the end of the nineteenth century; that is, seeing the different psychoanalytical theories as being part of a "group of transformations". Clearly this is not the only possible approach to this issue; there are others that can and ought to be explored.

If, instead, I look at the first group of problems, those that have always been and still are the object of reflection and controversy among analysts, I would isolate as the central theme that of testing the theories, of the need for devising procedures for testing rival theories, and the importance of being able to discriminate which theory succeeds in accounting for (and how) the clinical facts that it is called upon to interpret. We think that through the use of instruments and orientations that are of necessity different, psychoanalysis should not shirk the task—and indeed has the duty—of seriously confronting and providing an answer to the problem of the proof.

References

Ahumada, J. (2006). The analytic mind at work: counterinductive knowledge and the blunders of so-called "theory of science". In: J. Canestri (Ed.) *Psychoanalysis From Practice to Theory*. West Sussex: Wiley.

Arlow, J. A., & Brenner, C. (1964). *Psychoanalytic Concepts and the Structural Theory*. Madison, CT: International Universities Press.

Bion, W.R. (1992). *Cogitations*. London: Karnac.

Canestri, J. (2004). Le concept de processus analytique et le travail de transformation, *Revue Français de Psychanalyse*, 5: 1495–1541.

Canestri, J. (2006a). *Psychoanalysis: From Practice to Theory*. West Sussex, UK: Whurr.

Canestri, J. (2006b). Harmoniser à l'affiloir du ciel. Le travail de transformation dans le processus psychanalytique. In: *Le voies nouvelles de la thérapeutique psychanalytique. Le dedans et le dehors*. Sous la direction de André Green. Paris: Presses Universitaires de France.

Canestri, J. (2008). Ideology, Ideals and Idols in psychoanalysis. Read at the Delphi Conference.

Carnap, R. (1950). *The Logical Foundations of Probability*. Chicago: University of Chicago Press.

Eco, U. (1990). *I limiti dell'interpretazione*. Milano: Bompiani.

Freud, S. (1940a[1938]). An outline of psychoanalysis. *S.E., XXIII*.

Giorello, G. (1994). *Introduzione alla filosofia della scienza*. (Ch. V). Milano: Bompiani.

Green A. (1990). *La Folie Privée, chap. VII, L'Idéal: mesure et démesure*. Paris: Gallimard.

Jiménez, J. P. (2008). Theoretical plurality and pluralism in psychoanalytic practice. *International Journal of Psycho-Analysis, 89*: 579–599.

Kantrowitz, J. L. (2001). The analysis of preconscious phenomena and its communication. *Psychoanalytic Inquiry, 21*: 24–39.

Kantrowitz, J. L. (1999). The role of preconscious in psychoanalysis. *Journal of American Psychoanalytical Association, 47*: 65–89.

Kris, E. (1950). On preconscious mental processes. *Psychoanalytic Quarterly, 19*: 540–560.

Kris, E. (1951). Ego psychology and interpretation in psychoanalytic therapy. *Psychoanalytic Quarterly, 20*: 15–30.

Lakatos, I. (1976). *Proofs and Refutations: The Logic of Mathematical Discovery.* Cambridge: Cambridge University Press.

McGuire, W. J. (1997). Creative hypothesis generating in psychology: some useful heuristics. *Annual Review of Psychology, 48*: 1–30.

McGuire, W. J. (1999). *Constructing Social Psychology: Creative and Critical Processes.* New York: Cambridge University Press.

Motterlini, M. (1994). La metodologia dei programmi di ricerca scientifici: una revisione. In: Giulio Giorello (Ed.), *Introduzione alla filosofia della scienza.* Milano: Bompiani.

Peirce, C. S. (1931–1958). *Collected Papers.* Cambridge, MA: Harvard University Press.

Sandler, J., & Sandler, A.-M. (1983). The "Second Censorship", the "Three Box Model" and some technical implications. *International Journal of Psycho-Analysis, 64*: 413–425.

Vygotskij, L. S. (1934). *Myšlenie I reč*, Moskva-Leningrad. [Italian translation L. Mecacci. *Pensiero e Linguaggio*. Roma-Bari, Laterza, 1990.]

Appendix

*Theory = public theory based thinking + private theoretical thinking
+ interaction of private and explicit thinking (implicit use of
public theory)*

Vectors

1. Topographical vector (three box model)
   a. *Conscious but not public*
   b. *Preconscious theories and theorisation*
   c. *Unconscious influences upon the use of theories*

2. Conceptual vector
   a. *Worldview or cosmology*
   b. *Clinical concepts*
   c. *Clinical generalisations*
   d. *Psychoanalytic process*
   e *Theories of change*

3. Action vector
   a. *Listening*

   b. *Formulating*
   c. *Wording or interpretation*
   d. *Behaving*

4. Object relations of knowledge vector
   a. *History of knowledge*
   b. *Transgenerational influences*
   c. *Sociology of knowledge*
   d. *Internalisation of theory*
   e   *Attachment theory*

5. Coherence versus contradiction vector
   a. *Public where coherence is expected*
   b   *Using metaphors or polymorphous concepts*
   c   *Creative solutions*

6. Developmental vector

7. Intersubjective heuristics vector

INDEX

For Product Safety Concerns and Information please contact our EU
representative GPSR@taylorandfrancis.com
Taylor & Francis Verlag GmbH, Kaufingerstraße 24, 80331 München, Germany